GREGORY THE GREAT

Gregory's life culminated in his holding the office of pope (590–604). He is generally regarded as one of the outstanding figures in the long line of popes, and by the late ninth century had come to be known as 'the Great'. He played a critical role in the history of his time, and is regarded as one of the four great fathers of the Western Church, alongside Ambrose, Jerome and Augustine.

This volume provides an introduction to Gregory the Great's life and works and to the most fascinating areas of his thinking. It includes English translations of his influential writings on such topics as the interpretation of the Bible and human personality types. These works show Gregory communicating what seem to be abstruse ideas to ordinary people, and they remain highly current today.

John Moorhead teaches late antiquity and medieval history at the University of Queensland, Australia, where he is McCaughey Professor of History. His publications include *Theoderic in Italy* (1992), *Ambrose of Milan* (1999) and *The Roman Empire Divided* (2001).

THE EARLY CHURCH FATHERS
Edited by Carol Harrison
University of Durham

The Greek and Latin Fathers of the Church are central to the creation of Christian doctrine, yet often unapproachable because of the sheer volume of their writings and the relative paucity of accessible translations. This series makes available translations of key selected texts by the major Fathers to all students of the Early Church.

CYRIL OF JERUSALEM
Edward Yarnold, S. J.

EARLY CHRISTIAN LATIN POETS
Carolinne White

CYRIL OF ALEXANDRIA
Norman Russell

MAXIMUS THE CONFESSOR
Andrew Louth

IRENAEUS OF LYONS
Robert M. Grant

AMBROSE
Boniface Ramsey, O. P.

ORIGEN
Joseph W. Trigg

GREGORY OF NYSSA
Anthony Meredith, S. J.

JOHN CHRYSOSTOM
Wendy Mayer and Pauline Allen

JEROME
Stefan Rebenich

TERTULLIAN
Geoffrey Dunn

ATHANASIUS
Khaled Anatolios

SEVERUS OF ANTIOCH
Pauline Allen and
C.T.R. Hayward

GREGORY THE GREAT
John Moorhead

GREGORY THE GREAT

John Moorhead

Routledge
Taylor & Francis Group

LONDON AND NEW YORK

First published 2005
by Routledge
2 Park Square, Milton Park, Abingdon, Oxon OX14 4RN

Simultaneously published in the USA and Canada
by Routledge
270 Madison Ave, New York, NY 10016

Routledge is an imprint of the Taylor & Francis Group

© 2005 John Moorhead

Typeset in Garamond by
Keystroke, Jacaranda Lodge, Wolverhampton
Printed and bound in Great Britain by
TJ International Ltd, Padstow, Cornwall

British Library Cataloguing in Publication Data
A catalogue record for this book is available from the British Library

Library of Congress Cataloging-in-Publication Data
Moorhead, John, 1948–
Gregory the Great / John Moorhead.
p. cm. – (The early church fathers)
Includes bibliographical references and index.
1. Gregory I, Pope, ca. 540–604. 2. Theology. I. Gregory I, Pope,
ca. 540–604. Selections. English. 2005. II. Title. III. Series.
BR65.G56M66 2005
270.2'092–dc22   2004017572

ISBN 0–415–23389–5 (hbk)
ISBN 0–415–23390–9 (pbk)

CONTENTS

ABBREVIATIONS

CCSL	*Corpus Christianorum Series Latina*
Dial.	*Dialogorum libri iv*
Ep ad Leand.	(Letter to bishop Leander introducing *Moralia*)
Hev.	*Homiliae xl in Evangelia*
Hez.	*Homiliae in Hiezechihelem*
In CC	*Expositio in Canticum Canticorum*
MGH Ep.	*Monumenta Germaniae Historica Epistolae*
Mor.	*Moralia sive Expositio in Iob*
PG	*Patrologia Graeca*
PL	*Patrologia Latina*
Reg.	*Registrum Epistolarum*
Reg. past.	*Regula pastoralis*

1

INTRODUCTION

The voice of Gregory the Great is a strange one, which speaks in accents alien to the modern West. Yet his works reveal great intellectual ambition, his *Moralia in Iob* being among the longest books to have been written in Latin at the time of its composition; the response to them was extraordinarily immediate, widespread and enthusiastic; and the sustained interest taken in them during the centuries which followed Gregory's life has made him one of the most influential authors ever to have written in the West. Moreover, his books were not the products of an idle mind but written during the exercise of very demanding duties. Such considerations suggest that it may be worthwhile coming to terms with his achievement. Even in his strangeness, Gregory may speak to modern readers.

Life and deeds

Gregory's life culminated in his holding the office of pope (590–604). He is generally regarded as one of the outstanding figures in the long line of popes, and by the late ninth century had come to be known as 'the Great', a title which is still applied to him. Yet he was unusual among the popes of late antiquity. These tended to be men of no great social standing who acceded to papal office on the basis of seniority among the clergy of Rome. Gregory, however, came from an established and wealthy family, and became heir to a large home on the Clivus Scauri, just opposite the Circus Maximus, which can still be seen in Rome.[1] The family had strong church connections. Gregory was a great-great-grandson of an earlier pope, Felix III (483–92), and may have been related to another holder of that office, Agapetus I (535–36). His father, Gordianus, was an employee of the Roman church, three of whose sisters became nuns, although one later scandalized her nephew by marrying.[2] We do not know the year of Gregory's birth, but in about 573 he was holding public office, perhaps the important post of prefect of the city of Rome. However, following the death of his father, he turned the family home into a monastery, and established six monasteries in Sicily on the family estates. The gesture was a common one in the period: we know of monasteries founded in various parts of Italy not long before by two other men who had been administrators, Cassiodorus and Liberius, as well as the general Belisarius. But Gregory went one step further than many founders of religious houses by becoming a monk himself. He entered the monastery at Rome and devoted himself to monastic life with the utmost seriousness. He was in contact with some of the disciples of St Benedict, who some decades earlier had written what was to be the most important Rule in western monasticism. His followers had fled to Rome following the destruction of their monastery at Monte Casino by Lombards in about 585. Gregory's dealings with them were to be of great importance in the fame of St Benedict, and his enthusiasm for the earlier monk suggests the importance of such ideals in his own life. In years to come, after he had been forced to abandon monastic life, he looked back with nostalgia on life in his monastery.

His family origins, secular career and monastic state make Gregory stand apart from most popes of the period. Yet he became marked for preferment in the Roman church. He was made deacon, that is a member of the clergy holding the rank from which popes were generally selected, and pope Pelagius II (579–90) used his talents in attempting a rapprochement with a group in Italy who had broken away from communion with Rome over what were called the Three Chapters, a body of texts which had been condemned, wrongly according to the schismatics, at the Council of Constantinople in 553. In about 579/580 Pelagius pulled Gregory out of his monastery and sent him to Constantinople, seat of the emperor, as papal ambassador, or apocrisiarius. While in the city, in many ways more central than Rome in the Christian world of the time, he developed a network of friends and acquaintances, although he did not learn Greek. This failure is a little hard to account for, particularly in a diplomat, but for much of the sixth century Constantinople was the most important city for Latin letters, and it may have been quite possible to discharge his duties without the need to learn the language which had come to predominate in the city.[3] A few decades later this would have been much more difficult. His diplomatic activities are unknown to us, but it is reasonable to suppose that Gregory exerted himself to try to gain military aid for Italy, then suffering from a group of Germanic new-comers, the Lombards, but the resources of the empire were stretched, and any attempts were not successful. On returning to Rome in about 586 he re-entered his monastery. But no-one can have been surprised when, following the death of pope Pelagius in February 590, he was elected pope. Approval was obtained from the emperor Maurice in Constantinople, and Gregory was consecrated as his successor on 3 September 590.

Gregory therefore brought a number of qualities to papal office: the self-assurance which came from belonging to a wealthy and established family; a genuine concern with the spiritual life; and a track record of practical administration, both secular and ecclesiastical. But when he was elected he asserted vehemently that he did not wish to assume the office of pope. Before long it was being said in Gaul that he had written to the emperor declining the job.[4] In a series of letters written during the month after he became pope, Gregory used metaphors to express his position. He told the patrician Narses that in advancing outwardly he had fallen from his lofty quiet and, while he may have looked like a lion, he was really an ape the (*Reg.* 1.6); the emperor had ordered that an ape become a lion, 1.5fin). But another metaphor came more readily to him. He told John, the patriarch of Constantinople, that he had received an old ship which the waves were washing into, its rotten timbers sounding shipwreck (*Reg.* 1.4). To the emperor's sister he complained that, having become a bishop, he found himself having to deal with more business than he remembered having to transact when he was a layman, so that his outward rise involved an inner fall. He was being thrown about by the waves of business and sunk by storms (*Reg.* 1.5). To a former bishop of Antioch he wrote:

> I am being smashed by many waves of affairs and afflicted by the storms of a life of tumults, so that I may rightly say: *I am come into deep waters where the floods overflow me* [Ps. 69:2]. And so, you who stand on the shore of virtues, stretch out the hand of your prayer to me in my danger (*Reg.* 1.7).

It would be possible to interpret Gregory's reluctance, so vehemently expressed, in a negative way, for unwillingness to accept the office of bishop could, paradoxically, be seen as a sign that one was well suited to it. Such protestations of unworthiness, particularly coming from someone who must have been generally seen as *papabile* for some time, could therefore have been hypocritical manoeuvres designed to display his worthiness of the office. But as we shall see, such sentiments fit well with the general structures of Gregory's thought. And beyond this, the situation of Italy at that time was parlous. It was a bad time to come to the exercise of authority.

At the beginning of the sixth century, Italy had enjoyed peace and a degree of prosperity under the long rule of Theoderic, king of the Germanic Ostrogoths (493–526). But in 535 it was invaded by an army sent by the emperor Justinian to bring it back under the control of the Roman Empire, the capital of which was now Constantinople. The war between the Ostrogoths and the Empire lasted for some twenty years, devastating the countryside and disrupting social organization. Rome suffered from repeated sieges, and during 546 the city lay uninhabited for forty days. The final victory of the imperial forces left Italy dangerously open to the attentions of another Germanic group, the Lombards. In 568, under their king Alboin, they made their way into Italy, and by force of arms steadily established themselves over most of the peninsula. Their advent and settlement, marked as it was by continuing military conflict, widespread expropriations of land, and a degree of religious persecution, the Lombards being sometimes of an anti-catholic disposition, were much more violent than that of the Ostrogoths had been.[5] In the opinion of Gregory, the race of the Lombards was simply 'most unspeakable'.[6]

Yet he had to deal with them. During late antiquity, bishops had come to shoulder heavy burdens of leadership in secular affairs; just a few decades earlier, for example, bishop Paulinus of Aquileia is said to have responded to a Lombard threat by the dramatic step of leading his people to a more secure settlement.[7] Moreover, it took something like a month for a message to pass from Rome to Constantinople, and the Empire was involved in intermittent warfare with its old enemy Persia and pressing military difficulties of a new kind in the Balkans, so that Italy, which had so enticed Justinian, suddenly became a secondary concern. The official responsible for Italy, the exarch, did his best with few resources from his base in Ravenna, a town due north of Rome on the Adriatic coast, but his priorities were not always those of the bishop of Rome; what seemed like judicious compromise to a pope could look like treason to a servant of the emperor. And it had become clear during the sixth century that emperors looked on papal office in a way very different from the way the popes themselves did. In 537 pope Silverius had been deposed by the imperial authorities; his successor, Vigilius, who owed his appointment to the patronage of the empress, was later arrested and taken to Constantinople, which he was not to leave for ten years, while the following pope, Pelagius I, was an imperial nominee. The omens for relations between Gregory and Maurice were not good.

As it happened, Gregory became pope at a time of new leadership among the Lombards. Just two months after his consecration, Agilulf became their king, ruling from the northern town of Pavia, while the following year saw duke Ariulf installed at Spoleto, a town dangerously placed some 100 km to the north of Rome from which he was able to control traffic along the Via Flaminia, the traditional route between Ravenna and Rome, and another new duke at Benevento in the south of Italy. Before long, Gregory had to cope with attacks from Ariulf. In a way which must have been utterly uncongenial to someone who had already lamented the need to become involved in secular affairs, he now found himself organizing supplies and overseeing the movements of troops. In July 592 he concluded a peace with the duke of Spoleto, and in 593, when king Agilulf besieged Rome, Gregory was said to have met him on the steps of S Peter's and prevailed upon him to leave. In 595 he chose to pick a quarrel over the assumption by the bishop of Constantinople of the title 'universal patriarch'. To the emperor's claim that Gregory was a fool he replied, thinking of one of his heroes from the Bible, that in this respect he was like Job (*Reg.* 5.36), and in a passage of wonderful hyperbole he expressed himself on the secular and ecclesiastical situations:

> Behold, all things in the regions of Europe have been handed over to barbarians, cities have been destroyed, fortifications overthrown, provinces depopulated, no cultivators occupy the land, idol worshippers rage and lord it over the faithful every day to the point of killing them; and nevertheless priests, who should be throwing themselves onto the ground weeping with ashes, seek for themselves empty titles and take glory in new and profane words (*Reg.* 5.37).

Gregory was furious at the assumption of the title, although by this time it was scarcely 'new', seeing it as diabolical arrogance and a sign of the coming of the Antichrist, but the sustained campaign he waged against its use by the patriarch, like a number of his operations, could make no headway; such failures are a reminder of the weakness of papal authority in the period. The vehemence of his response suggests it touched something very deep, and later we shall note the importance of pride in Gregory's thinking.

However, in important respects the situation in Italy improved as Gregory's pontificate continued. Towards the end of 598 peace was concluded between the Empire and the Lombards, although trouble would rumble on. He was able to cultivate a Bavarian catholic,

Theodelinda, who, being successively the wife of kings Authari and Agilulf, turned out to be an influential queen of the Lombards, sending her a copy of one of his books. He rejoiced when Adaloald, the heir to the Lombard throne, was baptized a catholic in 603.[8] In 602 Phocas, an unsavoury soldier, overthrew the emperor Maurice, with whom Gregory's relations had often been cool, and acceded to the throne, a development at which the pope professed hearty satisfaction. By the time of his death in March 604, Gregory could look with a degree of satisfaction on the affairs of Italy and the Empire.

As the bishop of the city, Gregory had particular oversight over Rome, which was by no means immune from the difficulties which faced Italy.[9] Preaching at a particularly difficult time, Gregory wondered whether there was anything in the world which could give pleasure. Everywhere there were things to grieve at and groans to be heard. Cities had been destroyed, fortifications overthrown, fields depopulated, and the land turned into a wilderness.[10] There was now no senate in Rome and its people were perishing; the few people who were left had to endure greater sufferings every day. In its old age, the eagle, formerly the symbol of Roman power, had become bald.[11] The misery of the times prompted Gregory to speculate concerning the end of the world. He discussed the signs expected to precede this at the start of a homily preached to the people of Rome a few months after he became pope, which was placed at the beginning of his collection of homilies on the Gospels. Grimly, Gregory worked his way through a list given by Jesus: nation was rising up against nation and there was distress of nations on the earth more than in the past; earthquakes were destroying countless cities in other parts of the world; there were incessant plagues; although signs in the sun and moon and stars were not yet clearly to be seen, a change in the air showed that they were not far off; and while as yet there was no roaring of the sea and waves, the accomplishment of many of these signs left no doubt that the few which remained would follow (*Hev.* 1.1). At the end the Judge would come, to punish evil people and reward the good, and Gregory asked his congregation to consider the terror, confused embarrassment and dread with which people would be afflicted on that day (*Hev.* 12.4). When the deacon Peter asked why many things about souls which had previously been hidden had recently become clear, Gregory replied that, as the present world approaches its end, the future world comes close to touching it (*Dial.* 4.43.1f). And while no-one knew when the last hour would come, complacency was out of the question; the best plan was to prepare for the Judge by weeping and lamenting every day (*Hev.* 13.6). Gregory's sharp concern with the end of the world stands out against the mainstream of preceding post-biblical Christian thought, although it is paralleled by the earliest suras of the Qur'an, revealed just a few years later, and a sense of the imminence of the end also occurs in some Christian works of the later seventh century.

It would be fatally easy to gain, on the basis of a number of power-fully worded passages such as those we have been considering, an overwhelmingly negative picture of Gregory and his times. We must resist the temptation to do this. Gregory found it possible to put a positive spin on temporal losses: they were the means through which one could return to eternal joys, so the whole aim of the Bible could be seen as providing a hope of abiding joy which would strengthen us in the midst of passing hardships (*Mor.* 26.16.26). And, quite apart from consolations of this kind, in some ways the Rome of his day was a congenial place. The forum remained a centre. A person going there or to the baths could invite someone with time on their hands to keep them company (*Hev.* 6.6). A story known in England has Gregory, before becoming pope, joining a crowd of people looking for things to buy there,[12] and a few years after Gregory died the last monument known to have been erected in the forum, a statue in honour of the emperor Phocas, was placed atop an older column. Gregory was also tireless in finding ways to make life more tolerable. In the ninth century a big book could still be seen in the Lateran palace, the headquarters of the bishop of Rome, which showed the names, ages and professions of all those, in Rome and elsewhere, who received largesse from him.[13] When he heard of a priest from out of town who was able to work miracles, Gregory summoned him and placed him in a hospital: 'If he had the power of healing, it would quickly be proved there!' Before long the priest had laid his hands on a sick person, prayed over him and cured him (*Dial.* 3.35). We know of 3,000 nuns resident in Rome who received a large sum annually, but Gregory considered the money well spent, believing that it was because of their tears and abstinence that Rome had been able to hold out for many years against the swords of the Lombards (*Reg.* 7.23).

Gregory also proved remarkably energetic in other areas.[14] In some parts of Italy churches had been devastated by the coming of the Lombards; elsewhere there were clergy of appallingly low calibre. A letter to the bishop of Cagliari in Sardinia mentions a whole raft of issues: the archdeacon had defied the bishop's direction to cease living with women; peasants who were not Christians were living on estates owned by the church; clergy were falling into sins of the flesh, so that it was imperative that only men capable of continence were ordained;

and some people were scandalized by Gregory's prohibiting priests to touch people who were to be baptized with chrism (*Reg.* 4.29). But the bishop of Cagliari may not have been the best man to deal with abuses, for word later came to Gregory that he had ploughed under someone's harvest before mass one Sunday, and returned afterwards to pull up that person's boundary markers (*Reg.* 9.1). There were all too many bishops whose conduct left much to be desired, and it is clear from Gregory's correspondence that, no less than in other spheres of his activity, compromises continually had to be made in this area as well. Not surprisingly, where he was free to act, Gregory devoted considerable care to the appointment of men likely to be good bishops.

He also acted vigorously in distant areas. His greatest success was in Britain, whither in 596 he dispatched a team of forty monks to convert the English, who lived in a part of the world of which Gregory knew very little.[15] He was able to report to the bishop of Alexandria that more than ten thousand people 'placed in a corner of the world' had been baptized at Christmas 597,[16] and in centuries to come the English fondly remembered Gregory as 'our apostle'. This was a stunning coup, and while the mission was soon to experience serious difficulties its consequences, which Gregory cannot have foreseen, made it of major significance in the history of the church. In Gaul, where he had little power to intervene directly, Gregory encouraged kings and queens to overcome problems in church affairs, but found the going hard. In Africa he turned his attention to problems created by people he referred to as Donatists, but to no avail. He was also involved in the daily grind of dealing with issues that arose in the massive estates owned by the Roman church. The creation of wealth on the land and its expenditure by people in towns had been a familiar pattern around the Mediterranean for centuries, and their income from the widely dispersed estates of the church of Rome allowed popes to take costly initiatives. The patrimony, as it was called, was concentrated in Sicily and southern Italy, areas which escaped the worst of the impact of recent warfare, but estates were also to be found in other parts of Italy, Gaul and north Africa. His correspondence suggests that Gregory took enormous care in the administration of these estates. An author of the ninth century was able to name twenty-three rectors of estates who Gregory had appointed in various regions of Italy and adjacent lands.

Gregory, then, emerges as a remarkable administrator. He had been born at a time when the senate was still important in Rome, the civil service of the state remained a respected calling, and the land-owning aristocracy retained much of its wealth; but he came to exercise authority in a new world in which power had come to reside with military commanders and ecclesiastics to a degree which would have been unthinkable a few decades earlier. He had a formidable appetite for work; were he employed in a modern university he would have been an active dean who attracted a heavy burden of committee work and looked back with regret at the life of a teacher and scholar he used to lead. Yet Gregory found it possible to maintain relationships with all kinds of people who looked to him for guidance. It will be worth our while investigating a group of letters bearing on the affairs of one family.[17]

The activities of the patrician Venantius exasperated Gregory. He abandoned life as a monk, a step which the pope warned him in no uncertain terms laid him open to the judgment of God, and suspected that he had been led to take it by people who loved his goods rather than himself. Some years later, Gregory received word that his wife, Italica, was oppressing poor peasants. Then a complaint came that armed men in the service of Venantius had entered the palace of bishop John of Syracuse and made trouble, because of a quarrel between him and the bishop. But some years later, having heard that Venantius was in poor health, he sent him a warm letter of advice, which concluded by asking him to pass on his greetings to his daughters, Barbara and Antonina. In the following month he wrote to the young women, assuring them that he would see to their interests when their father died, and to bishop John, asking him to encourage his old antagonist to resume the monastic habit and to consider what could be done for his daughters. Several months later, after Venantius had died, Gregory replied to a letter which his 'sweetest daughters' Barbara and Antonina had written to him. They had told him that they planned to visit S Peter's in Rome, and Gregory responded that he longed to see them there, married to good husbands. He thanked them for some pieces of woven fabric they had sent him as a gift, while professing to believe that they had tried to deceive him by passing off the work of others as their own. The women clearly believed that they had a claim on Gregory's goodwill, and there is a tone of warm if bemused affection in his last letter to them.

In the midst of a life filled with such activities and concerns, Gregory wrote books which attracted immediate attention far from Rome and have nurtured generations of readers. To these we shall now turn.

Works

Some authors toil away in obscure garrets or studies, to emerge from years of solitude with polished works. Gregory, on the other hand, even more than others among the fathers of the church, was a bishop pressed for time, whose books often began life as oral presentations. We can imagine him sitting in a chair like the one, allegedly his, still to be seen in the church of San Gregorio Magno in Rome, a book containing part of the Bible open on his lap, expounding the text to an audience. His experience was that of many good teachers, who find that the act of trying to explain things to others enables them to understand them better themselves:

> [B]y the generous gift of God it happens that, when I am teaching in your presence what I am learning on your behalf, my understanding becomes greater and pride smaller, because, to tell the truth, I am hearing with you many of the things which I say (*Hez.* 2.2.1).

Despite the abstruse nature of some of his concerns, Gregory's works reveal the no-nonsense style of a practised teacher.[18] Phrases which recur across the corpus of his writings have an air of the classroom: concepts are introduced by the phrase 'we need to know' (*sciendum est*), while the expression 'a question arises' (*quaestio oritur*) signals a change in the flow of material. He made a practice of classifying material, and often used phrases like 'there are two kinds of . . .' (*duo sunt genera*); hence the observation that there were two kinds of temptations, those which come suddenly and those which come gradually (*Mor.* 12.18.22). There were also two vices, those of the spirit and those of the flesh (*Mor.* 33.3.9), but the human race was particularly suscep- tible to three temptations, those of loose-living, malice and pride (*Mor.* 33.15.30f.). Another vice was gluttony, which tempted in five ways (*Mor.* 30.18.60). The old enemy, as Gregory called the Devil, had three ways at his disposal to make our good deeds of no avail (*Mor.* 1.36.51). There were four ways in which pride was demonstrated (*Mor.* 23.6.13), just as the soul of the just man could be turned to grief in four ways (*Mor.* 23.21.41). This impulse to schematize, of which the examples given here provide a tiny indication, cannot have always been effective in oral discourse. But Gregory, who felt that the hearts of hearers were often moved by examples rather than words (*Reg. past.* 3.6.18ff.) also had the knack of using memorable stories to back up specific points. These are often drawn from the Bible, in his expositions of which he frequently darts from one incident to another, but anecdotes occur at the end of a good number of his sermons to the people, while the whole of the *Dialogues* is devoted to telling stories.

Gregory's greatest work is his commentary on the book of Job, the *Moralia in Iob*. It was based on talks which he gave to the group of monks who accompanied him from Rome when he was dispatched to Constantinople as papal ambassador, in which he aimed to disclose the mysteries which he felt lay deeply hidden in this book of the Bible. In a letter introducing the work, Gregory explains that the monks asked him not only to consider the words of the history in an allegorical manner, but also to direct the allegories towards the practice of morality, and this was the principle which governed his approach to the text. Notes were taken of the addresses Gregory gave on the first part of the book, and he later dictated his commentary on the remainder of it; subsequently, he revised the entire work. This turned into a long process. In 591, shortly after becoming pope, he promised to send bishop Leander of Seville, whom he had met in Constantinople,[19] a copy, but as late as 595 was able to send him only the second of its four parts.[20] The work was directed towards people who had dedicated themselves to the religious life. When Gregory heard that the bishop of Ravenna was having it read out publicly at services, he reacted badly, explaining that it was not a popular work and could harm rather than assist ignorant hearers (*Reg.* 12.6).

Gregory begins his exposition by commenting on the opening portion of Job in three ways, these being what he describes as the history, the secrets of allegory, and the proper way to live, but before long he gave up the attempt at threefold analysis, and as the work proceeds it has little to say about the 'history', or the literal meaning of the text. Such a movement within a work away from an expressed intent towards a preponderantly allegorical and moral interpretation can be found among other patristic writers, for example Ambrose. Gregory did not examine all parts of the book of Job in the same detail. He skates lightly over chapters 12 to 24 of Job in books 11–16 of his commentary, but this was because of a request of his monastic brethren not to revise this portion, and he was aware that the brevity of this section allowed more lengthy treatment of parts he felt were more obscure (*Mor.* 16.69.83; cf. 11.1.1), and the discussion which follows is indeed more leisurely. Later he signals his intention to run quickly through some words of Job which were not particularly obscure (*Mor.* 20.18.44fin). Gregory feels that the things which Elihu, the fourth of

Job's interlocutors, says in his pride needed to be touched on rather than expounded attentively (*Mor.* 23.5.12), which leaves him free to deal with his massive speech (Job 32–7) relatively quickly, whereas the mighty words of God which follow them and bring the discussion to a complete close (Job 38–41) are examined in far greater detail: they take up nearly 400 pages in a modern edition, whereas only about 250 were needed to deal with Elihu's speech. But the concluding chapter, Job 42, was easy, and could be run over more loosely (*Mor.* 35.1.1). Gregory thus regarded the book he was expounding as having varied textures.

In his preface, Gregory explains what the characters in the book signify: Job, a name which he takes to mean suffering, stands for the suffering Lord or his suffering body the church; his wife represents the life of fleshly people; the three friends who tried to comfort him with words that seemed to be good but in fact were evil were heretics, and Elihu stood for an arrogant person who falsely appeared to be faithful. Gregory may have identified with the central figure: he thought that God's providence may have brought it about that he, a person who had been smitten, should expound on the smitten Job, and that he who was being scourged would be more sensitive to the mind of someone who had been scourged. The spiritual teaching Gregory offers in the book is certainly not for the faint hearted, as when he asserts that the bitterness of the present life should be welcomed: a mind which is turned towards God considers whatever is bitter in this life as sweet, thinks of its afflictions as rest, and seeks to pass through death so as to obtain fuller life (*Mor.* 7.15.18). But his identifying Job with Christ allowed Gregory to take a more positive view of his sufferings than most readers of this book, and his reading of it can be placed beside those provided by other commentators, among them, recently, René Girard; both he and Gregory interpret the central character in the light of Christ. The book Gregory ended up writing is extraordinarily long; when he rebukes Elihu for the 'immense loquacity' which makes him, as soon as he has finished speaking of some things, immediately go on to other topics (*Mor.* 26.9.14, with reference to Job 35.1), one immediately thinks of its author. And unlike some long books written by the church fathers, for example Augustine's *City of God*, the material is not laid out to constitute a sustained line of argument; Gregory's forte was not in developing systems, but in the application of a set of principles to a text in a systematic way. So it is that his longest book is made up of discursive comments, often lengthy ones, on a text which he follows like a teacher, line by line, and while its conclusion is highly effective it gives no sense of summarizing an argument. The satisfaction the *Moralia* gives its readers is that which comes from the different ways in which themes appear and are later restated, often in a way which reinforces them, so that major statements emerge as it were by a series of overlays.

In the months immediately following his becoming pope, Gregory wrote a work on a topic highly relevant to his new situation, which is generally referred to as the *Pastoral Rule* (*Regula pastoralis*). Dedicated to another bishop, John of Ravenna, it was presumably written in the expectation of being primarily useful to those holding episcopal office. Part of it was included in a letter Gregory sent to the eastern patriarchs when he became pope, and copies of it were often given to newly appointed bishops in later centuries, although its intended readership could not be established with certainty from the work itself. It is divided into four books, which treat issues which must have suddenly come to weigh heavily on Gregory: how one should come to government, the life of a pastor, how a ruler ought to teach and admonish his subordinates, and how, finally, a preacher ought to return to himself, lest his life or teaching make him proud.[21] Much of the material in this book also occurs in the *Moralia*, and the simplest way to account for such recycling is to think of Gregory, writing in haste shortly after he had acquired heavy new responsibilities, reusing material which already lay to hand in the draft for the longer work. Not surprisingly in a work on such a topic, the book of the Bible most often referred to is Proverbs. His purpose was to write a practical handbook, perhaps the book he wished someone had placed in his hands when he became pope.

A little later Gregory delivered a series of lectures on another part of the Hebrew Bible, or the Old Testament as it is commonly known, the book of Ezekiel, the *Homiliae in Hiezechihelem*. One of these was almost certainly given towards the end of 593, and it is likely that the whole sequence was delivered at about this time. Eight years later, Gregory worked some notes which had been taken while he was giving the lectures into a form which, while it bore traces of its original delivery, he felt could be published. The work comprised two books, the first expounding the text of Ezekiel as far as the beginning of the fourth chapter and the second examining the vision of the temple described in the fortieth chapter. Gregory considered this vision the most obscure received by the prophet; it simply made no sense on the literal level, and so cried out for allegorical interpretation. So, with Ezekiel as with Job, it was the most obscure parts that attracted the most detailed commentary. From the homilies we can build up a picture of their audience. They were people of scholarly inclinations capable of completing a quotation from the Bible for themselves (*Hez.* 1.9.29), who could be expected to be interested in differences between the text of the Septuagint and the Hebrew versions of the Old Testament (*Hez.* 2.1.10). They would also be interested in the characteristics of a good preacher (*Hez.* 1.10.9], and could be relied upon to sympathize with the frustration of a preacher whose words are despised (*Hez.* 1.10.23ff.; the mentality of preachers; their grief and consolation, was a concern for Gregory, cf. *Mor.* 35.14.27). We may take it, then, that Gregory was speaking to people he may have regarded as fellow professionals, presumably parish clergy as well as the monks he addressed in the *Moralia*. Of all his works, this was composed in the worst times. Gregory planned to stop at the end of the first book, but allowed himself to be persuaded by his hearers to comment on the vision of the temple. News had come when he began what turned into the second book that the Lombard king Agilulf had crossed the Po on his way to besiege Rome, but Gregory persevered: the work he and his hearers would be considering was indeed very obscure, but he invited them to see themselves as making a journey by night (*Hez.* 2 *praef.*). The exposition stopped a little before the end of the fortieth chapter, with Gregory asking not to be rebuked for concluding where he did: surrounded by swords, and in peril of death, he was in a state of despair (*Hez.* 2.10.19). Nevertheless, the subtlety and depth of this work, perhaps in particular its evaluation of how the Bible is to be understood, has made it a favourite of many of Gregory's readers.

The most widely read of Gregory's works, his four books of *Dialogues*, offer very different subject matter.[22] They were written at about the same time as the Homilies on Ezekiel, for Gregory was still gathering material for the *Dialogues* from various contacts in July 593, but a person mentioned in the work as being alive died in November 594; not surprisingly in a work composed in this period, the *Dialogues* are very negative towards the Lombards. Gregory describes the work as having developed from a discussion with his deacon Peter, who had been unaware that there were still people in Italy working miracles. As we know that Gregory wrote to informants gathering material for such a book, we cannot accept that it is a literal record of discussions he had with Peter, but its fictitious setting and the role played by his interlocutor, who seems to develop as a character as the book proceeds, add to its charm. The book Gregory ended up writing overflows with stories of holy men working miracles, some 200 in number. Its content gives the work a popular, folksy feeling, but for Gregory the occurrence of astonishing events which seemed to contravene the natural order was not the real point about miracles. For him they were signs, that is, things which pointed to a reality beyond themselves, whether the holiness of the person who worked them or the will of God. Perhaps it would not be too far off the mark to think of the role of miracles in Gregory's mind as corresponding in some way to the role of the miracles of Jesus reported in St John's Gospel, rather than to the role they play in the synoptic Gospels. It was necessary, in Gregory's view, to go beyond a simple exposition of what happened when considering the miraculous; as we shall see, he followed the same principle when explaining scriptural texts. Various indications suggest that, despite its apparently popular nature, the work was, like the others we have considered so far, directed towards an elite public. The second book is entirely devoted to St Benedict; most scholars place Gregory's account of his life next to Benedict's Rule for Monks, as constituting our two primary sources for Benedict.

Another product of Gregory's early years as pope was a collection of forty homilies he preached to the people of Rome in 590–2 on passages of the Gospels read during the liturgy, the *Homiliae xl in Evangelia*. Gregory, who did not enjoy good health, dictated the first twenty homilies to a secretary who read them out; then, he says, yielding to the wishes of the people, he delivered the latter twenty himself, and notes were taken as he spoke; perhaps surprisingly, the sermons in the second group turned out to be longer than those in the first. In these homilies Gregory, as usual, was concerned with the allegorical meaning of the texts and the moral reform of his hearers; in respect of their content his homilies can be contrasted with those of another pope of late antiquity, Leo the great, which are solidly doctrinal. But, uniquely among Gregory's works, the homilies were directed to a wide audience, and he seems to have found some difficulty in pitching his message at a level appropriate to a congregation of ordinary Christians. They are considerably longer than the homilies preached by his predecessor Leo, and Gregory seems to have felt that his congregation appreciated long sermons, for at the beginning of one exceptionally long address he told them that, with the passing of the summer heat, he was able to address them at the length they liked (*Hev.* 34.1). Perhaps there is a hint here that Gregory lacked sympathy for secular people; on one occasion he told the congregation that anyone who did not rejoice as the end of the world drew near was a friend of the world and an enemy of God (*Hev.* 1.3). His hearers must sometimes have been astounded at what they heard. Preaching on the text 'And when she has found it, she called her friends and neighbours together, saying Rejoice with me, for I have found the piece which I had lost' [Luke 15:9], Gregory asserted that the friends and neighbours of the woman who had lost a coin were the powers of heaven, and launched into a long discussion of the nine ranks of angels, at the end of which he lamely gathered himself together: 'But lo, while exploring the secrets of the citizens of heaven, we have strayed far from the sequence of our exposition.'[23] But he did make some concessions to his popular audience. In accordance with the principle that preachers should use abstract teachings with the learned, but examples for the unlearned [*Reg. past.* 3.6), many of the sermons conclude with a story.

One other work discusses a portion of the Bible, the two homilies on the Song of Songs (*Expositio in Canticum Canticorum*), which, in the form it has come down to us, discusses the text until chapter 1 verse 9 (verse 8, Vulg.) Gregory is known to have given talks on a number of books in the Old Testament which an abbot, Claudius, wrote up from notes he had taken. Nevertheless, he was displeased with Claudius' version, and in 602, after the abbot died, he asked that all his material be delivered to Rome (*Reg.* 12.6), although oddly enough two years earlier an Irish monk Columbanus, then living in Gaul, asked Gregory for a copy of this work.[24] The version of the exposition which we possess is almost certainly that for which Claudius was responsible, and it is easy to see why Gregory was unhappy with it. It is written in a jerky and awkward style, and contains a number of sentences which cannot be construed. Nevertheless, it allows us to see how Gregory approached a book of the Bible with very erotic content. He took this in his stride, holding that its words about unclean love were able to excite the soul to a higher love. Hence, its opening words, 'Let him kiss me with the kisses of his mouth', could be seen as having been uttered by the whole human race, or more precisely the whole church, seeking not angels, patriarchs and prophets, but the presence of Christ, the one she was going to marry. Gregory felt that this interpretation was supported by a reference to Jesus opening his mouth (Matt. 5:2; *In CC* 3, 12).

A large number of letters written in the name of Gregory have come down to us, having been preserved in the archives of the Roman church in fourteen papyrus books, one for each year of his pontificate. Some 850 of these letters survive, approximately as many as the surviving letters of all preceding popes combined, but many of theirs, and many of Gregory's, have disappeared. We cannot tell how many letters he dispatched while pope, but, given that 240 letters survive from just one twelve-month period, we may assume that Gregory was responsible for some thousands of letters. His correspondence gives an impression of boundless energy and a capacity to involve himself resolutely in apparently humdrum matters, but Gregory was not the author of all the letters which went out in his name. While some of his correspondence, such as his letters to close friends, must have been dictated, although not physically written, by Gregory himself, most of the letters were presumably written on his behalf by his staff, who sometimes followed standard forms, as in the case of letters written appointing a bishop as visitor to a church after the death of its own bishop.[25] Not only do the letters form a unique source for the history of the period, but they also later became crucial in the formation of canon law.[26]

Gregory has also been credited with an exposition of the biblical book of 1 Kings. The authenticity of this work has been widely debated, but it seems likely that, while there is Gregorian material within it, it was written in the twelfth century, at least in the form it has come down to us, so we will not be concerned with it here.[27]

These works, despite their varying content, have a remarkable degree of coherence. This may partly reflect the short period within which most were written, for we have nothing from the period before Gregory became pope, although the *Moralia* are based on material from an earlier time, and it may be that his accession to the office of bishop, which was seen as involving a responsibility to teach, stimulated Gregory to write; preaching, as we shall see, stood at the centre of his view of the church. But if this were so, is noteworthy that the bulk of his writings date from the early years of his pontificate. Perhaps he came to office with a cache of material which he was able to exploit for some years (there are numerous textual parallels between the *Moralia* and both the homilies and the *Pastoral Rule*); perhaps, experiencing the toils of office more keenly as time passed, he came to have less energy to spare for writing; perhaps his health, never robust, declined. Yet it is hard to believe that works from different periods would reveal Gregory developing as a thinker. The unity of themes found right across the spectrum of his works, and their tight coherence, suggest that Gregory, quite possibly at an early age, had developed a body of ideas and a style of thinking from which he would not move. One of Gregory's finest readers, the Venerable Bede, noted a similarity between works of his which one would have thought likely to be very different. Comparing the works in which Gregory expounded the Bible and the *Dialogues*, he observed: 'Just as he taught in his books of exposition what virtues we exert ourselves to obtain, in the same way he revealed, describing the miracles of holy people, the brightness of those same virtues.'[28] But it is worth noting that the great bulk of Gregory's output as a writer, no less than that of Bede, took the form of expositions of parts of the Bible. This book lay at the very centre of Gregory's life, and he approached it with awe.

The Bible

Gregory can easily seem a very 'medieval' figure. But he began his career holding an old Roman office, apparently that of prefect of the city of Rome, the traditional responsibilities of which had included presiding over the senate, and the epitaph on his tomb credited him with having been 'God's consul'.[29] He largely worked with ideas passed down from the classical world. His protestations of unhappiness at having to abandon a quiet life to undertake administrative work, while apparently sincere, reflect a commonplace familiar among the Romans, that of a longing for leisured freedom (*otium*) and a disdain for business (*negotium*, the reverse of *otium*).[30] But Gregory did not merely use the concepts of the ancient world to express his situation; his intellectual practices and concerns were often very traditional. The writing of exegetical commentaries on important texts had been a feature of intellectual life for centuries; indeed, medieval Scholasticism can be seen as 'the logical continuation of the ancient exegetical tradition.'[31] Moreover, the emphases in his expositions of texts were standard. Allegorical approaches to the texts of authors such as Homer and Vergil had become common in the literary criticism of late antiquity, while the overwhelming interest in morality shown by Gregory, and others of his time, can be interpreted as part of a 'pendulum swing' in philosophical thought which saw a move back towards the concerns of earlier periods.[32] More specifically, in some of his teaching Gregory presented a kind of 'Christianized stoicism.'[33] The concern of intellectuals of the ancient world for self-knowledge, summed up by the injunction over the entrance to the oracle of Apollo at Delphi, 'Know thyself', finds resonance in Gregory's response to words which occurred in the translation of the Song of Songs he read, 'if you do not know yourself': 'every soul should know itself, for the one that knows itself, realises that it is made in the image of God.'[34] He expressed himself in a Latin which is correct and often elegant, and, to judge from his sermons to the people, he expected ordinary inhabitants of Rome to have no difficulty in following what he said, although his adherence to classical practice in his style of writing may not have been reflected in his pronunciation.[35] But against these things which, in different ways, allow Gregory to be identified as a participant in the concerns, practices and speech of classical antiquity, stands one massive change. For some centuries prior to the time of Gregory secularity had been draining out of the intellectual landscape, so that the life of the mind had come to be constrained within the forms of Christian discourse, in 'a self-limitation to one of the constituents of what had once been a richer variety', from which followed 'an exuberant development of thought within this newly-defined world of discourse.'[36] Not surprisingly, the Qur'an, whose earliest revelations occurred within a decade of Gregory's death, persistently refers to Jews and Christians as 'people of the Book'. Energies which in earlier times had been scattered in trying to come to terms with many texts were now concentrated, as the case of Gregory makes very clear, on just one book, which had come to enjoy centrality of a kind hitherto unthinkable in western intellectual life.

Gregory thought of the Bible (a word unknown to him; he refers to it by expressions such as holy scripture or the divine utterances) as a letter sent by God to humankind, which people able to do so should not neglect to read passionately. They should meditate every day on the words of their creator (the unremarked passage from reading to meditation is significant).[37] His conviction that it had been written by God made Gregory impatient with the question, which he felt had all too frequently been raised, of the authorship of the book of Job. The question was 'utterly redundant' (*valde supervacue*), since its author was the Holy Spirit, who used the human writer as nothing more than a pen.[38] To be sure, the Bible was a difficult book, yet in Gregory's eyes its very obscurity was a source of pleasure; as we have seen, he chose to linger over the hard parts of Job and Ezekiel. What happiness there was in turning towards it and penetrating its secrets! It was like entering a dark, cool forest in which it was possible to shelter from the heat of this world (*Hez.* 1.5.1). Sometimes, however, its readers would welcome a change from its more difficult parts: after the dark woods of its difficult beginning, people working through the book of Ezekiel came with joy to the open plains of what followed (*Hez.* 1.9.1). Such imagery haunted Gregory. When the prophet Habbakuk said, 'God will come from Lebanon, and the holy one from a shady and thickly covered mountain' [*Hab.* 3:3 Vulg.], Gregory believed a promise had been made: God would come through the pages of his testament, which had been appropriately described as a shady and thickly covered mountain, because it is made dark by the dense obscurities of allegories (*Mor.* 33.1.2). The apparently recherché quality of much of what Gregory says concerning the Bible may have been connected with the circumstance that almost all of his writings were directed to elite groups; it is possible that they stimulated him to look for out-of-the-way meanings, and perhaps even to seek to impress them. Nevertheless, Gregory never tired of enquiring into the mysteries of this book, the depths of which could never be plumbed. His commentary on Job is about fifty times longer than the text he was commenting on, and Gregory was well aware that he had not said all that he could have.

The Bible was not uniformly informative. This was partly because, as it made clear itself, knowledge became more complete as time passed. Abraham spoke with God, yet the Lord later said to Moses, 'I am the God of Abraham and the God of Isaac and the God of Jacob, and I did not tell them my name, Adonai' [Exod. 3:6, 6:3]. Later, the psalmist, who says, 'How have I loved your law, Lord! It is my meditation the whole day' (Ps. 119:97; Gregory understood by the 'law' that given to Moses), went on to say, 'I have understanding above all my teachers, because your testimonies are my meditation' [Ps. 119:99], and again, 'I have understood more than the ancients' [Ps. 119:100]. But the apostles were taught more than the prophets, for Truth says, 'Many kings and prophets wished to see what you see, and did not see it, and wished to hear what you hear, and did not hear it.'[39] Yet, despite God's increasingly rich revelation of himself, the Bible could also be said to teach the same things all the way through. The Old and New Testaments were like the two angels who sat where Jesus had been buried, one at his head and the other at his feet, for they told of the incarnation, death and resurrection of the Lord in the same way; the first told what would take place, and the second shouted out what had happened (*Hev*. 25.3 on John 20:10, as well as Exod. 25:20). Such a claim made the Old Testament's statements, more obscure than the shouts of the New Testament, an object of limitless fascination; it is not accidental that Gregory, among others of the fathers of the church, had more to say about it than the New.

People enjoy works of art in which they can continually see new things, and go to concerts to hear pieces of music they know well in the expectation that a new performance will provide a different interpretation of something with which they are already familiar. One of the characteristics of the greatest pieces of art and music is that there is no final and definitive way of understanding them, whereas some other expressions of art and music, while they may yield intense passing pleasure, do not repay being revisited. Similarly, the deepest books are those which are most open to different readings and, in a sense, allow themselves to be perpetually remade as people read them in various ways. Far from standing firm, particularly rich texts may be potentially the most unstable. With the important caveat that God, the ultimate reality, stood behind the Bible as guarantor of its truth, it could be seen as unstable. All kinds of lessons could be drawn from it, just as necklaces, rings and bracelets could all be made from the one piece of gold (*Reg.* 3.62). The words of God are like substances being ground in a pestle: the more they are ground, the more their power is increased in the bowl (*Mor.* 29.8.19). The Bible positively invites different kinds of interpretation, for it has a kind of flexibility which enables it to adjust itself to the capacities of its readers and grow with them (*Mor.* 20.1.1). Hence, when one of the saints makes progress in holy scripture, holy scripture itself makes progress with him, so that the Bible grows with those who read it. Gregory therefore saw scripture and its readers as having a complex relationship: you find in the Bible a degree of progress which is related to the progress you have been making in it, so that different people could derive different forms of nourishment from the same passage (*Hez.* 1.7.8,10). So Gregory sees the Bible as operating in different ways with different readers: 'Have you made progress in the active life? It walks with you. Have you made progress to an unchanging, constant spirit? It stands with you. Have you arrived, through the grace of God, at a life of contemplation? It flies with you.'[40] In a famous image, Gregory explains that the Bible is like a river in which a lamb can walk and an elephant swim.[41] This adaptive power of the Bible meant that it could never be definitively understood. The multiplicity of possible readings imposed humility on exegetes, who were engaged in a shared enterprise in which they toiled on behalf of each other: Gregory believed that whatever someone had understood better than he had, in fact, been given to himself as well.[42]

Central to Gregory's project was allegory, the notion that behind the surface meaning of a text could lie hidden something more important. He saw it as having the power to lead souls far from God from the unknown to the known; when we receive the outward words we come to inward understanding, so that, for example, the erotic language of the Song of Songs could teach us how passionately we should be fervent for the love of God (*In CC* 3; so too 5). The circumstance that the prophet Ezekiel was presented with the roll of a book which was written on the inside and the outside meant that the Bible was, on the one hand, written allegorically and according to a spiritual understanding, promised invisible things, gave assurance of heavenly things and spoke of heavenly secrets, and on the other hand, in a simple literal sense suited to the weak, laying down right conduct by its precepts in a visible fashion, teaching how earthly things are to be despised, whether they were used or avoided, and ordering how people were to behave outwardly (*Hez.* 1.9.30, on Ezek. 2:9f.). Needless to say, there were some things in the Bible which did not lend themselves to allegorical treatment, such as its teachings on the person and work of Jesus. What could be read in the Gospels on such matters was only to be taken literally. But Gregory felt that much of the Old Testament was really about these very things, and that when it was understood to be referring to them in an allegorical manner its apparent obscurities vanished. This approach, however, was one which the Jewish people failed to adopt. This people could be characterized by a failure to read its own scriptures correctly: it accepted the words of God only according to the letter, which kills, whereas the gentiles penetrated into them by means of the Spirit, which gives life. Adopting such an attitude towards the Bible meant that Gregory set his face against what he took to be the Jews' understanding of the part of it which they held in common with Christians.[43] But it would be a long jump from the alleged failure of the Jews to comprehend the message of the Bible to the racially based anti-Semitism familiar from later periods of European history. Any connection Gregory made between the Jews of biblical times and those whose inadequate reading of Scripture he condemned, and the Jews of contemporary Italy, need not have been close. Indeed, even to think of Gregory as dealing with a category of people such as 'the Jews' in day-to-day life may conceal the different ways in which he responded to different kinds of Jewish people.[44]

The need to interpret the Bible allegorically, and the possibility that something could have more than one meaning, allowed Gregory to see words as being unstable in what they signified. Depending on its context, the word 'waters' could mean one of six things in the Bible: the Holy Spirit, sacred knowledge, evil knowledge, tribulation, the passage of peoples, and the minds of those who followed the faith (*Mor.* 19.6.9). The word 'mountain' had five meanings, those of the incarnate Lord, the holy church, the testament of God, the apostate angel, or a heretic of some kind. If this range were not broad enough, the plural 'mountains' could refer to the apostles and angels in their height, or the swelling of secular powers (*Mor.* 33.1.2; it is worth noting that in both cases the significances of a word could be positive or negative). If modern scholars were to offer such interpretations of words in the Bible, we would immediately think they had looked the words up in a concordance, but Gregory lived centuries before such an aid was possible, the familiar division of the Bible into chapters and verses having taken place long after his time, and we may assume that he summoned up such comprehensive lists from his memory. Gregory therefore possessed both an extraordinary familiarity with the words of the biblical text, which must have arisen from his being exposed to it by hearing it as well as reading, and an interpretative technique which allowed him remarkable freedom in decoding its meaning.

While he was fascinated by words and their possible meanings, Gregory also looked beyond them. Hence he thought of Job as having prophesied not only in his words but also in his suffering (*Mor.* 23.1.2), and of Christ as sometimes speaking in his words and sometimes in his deeds, so that his parable about the fig tree and action in healing a woman who was bent over were to be taken together.[45] The principle that other things could do the job of words allowed Gregory to defend the practice of placing pictures on the walls of churches, for these could function as books for those unable to read (*Reg.* 9.209; cf. 11.10). In a parallel manner, Gregory instructed a bishop to reveal himself through what he did in such a way that people who neglected read or were unable to be influenced by reading would be able to have him as a scripture (*Reg.* 3.13). The life of good people could be a 'living reading' (*Mor.* 24.8.16). His world was one rich in meaning, in which events as well as words could point beyond themselves.

Gregory believed that the 'old fathers', by whom he meant people mentioned in the biblical narratives, could be understood of as being like fruit-bearing trees which were not only beautiful to look at but also, in the abundance of their fruits, useful. So the lives of these people could be thought of in such as way that, when we marvel at their greenness according to history, we also discover how much fruitful richness was to be found in the allegory; while the leaves of a tree are pleasant, the taste of the fruit is sweet (*Mor.* 23.1.2). But this principle held true of other people, and it will be worth our while considering a graphic story Gregory told of his hero St Benedict in the *Dialogues*. He describes the holy man, at the beginning of his monastic career, experiencing a violent temptation of the flesh when there came before the eye of his mind a woman he had once seen. So vehement was the fire which the recollection of her appearance kindled that he was on the point of abandoning the wilderness. But suddenly, in a very Gregorian movement, Benedict 'returned to himself'. The phrase is a standard one, but the action which accompanied it was remarkably violent. Catching sight of some nearby nettles and thick thorn bushes, Benedict took off his clothes and plunged naked into the stinging thorns and burning nettles. There he rolled about for some time, with the result that the wounds of the skin took a wound of the mind away from his body, and fire of a different kind enabled him to overcome the sin. He was not to experience a temptation of this kind again.[46] It is a powerful story, suggesting as it does aversion therapy of a most drastic kind, but we need not take it literally. Thorns and nettles are mentioned together in a passage in the Bible [Isa. 34:13], and Gregory discussed what significance they might have had there in his *Moralia*:

> What are we to take by nettles if not itchy thoughts, and what by thorns if not the stings of vices? . . . Nettles and thorns spring up because in the confused mind of someone who is lost there arise desires and thoughts which irritate them, and sinful works which sting them (*Mor.* 33.4.10).

While Benedict was not yet 'lost', the concepts which the thorns and nettles suggested to Gregory were very relevant to the particular temptation which assailed him. The transfer of the image to the monk does not quite work, for in his case the nettles and thorns are not so much the manifestation of the problem of sexual desire as the way in which the problem was overcome, and the slippage in meaning raises questions about Gregory's use of material we shall have to consider later; his integration of the image into his narrative without proper consideration for the way it functioned raises the possibility that he was inclined to force other people's ideas into the structures of his own thinking in violent ways. Be this as it may, it was the significance of the plants rather than the plants themselves that was important, and, whatever literal truth may lie behind the story about Benedict, the literal details were subordinate to its meaning.

In such ways Gregory's approach to the Bible can give the appearance of almost wilfully denying the plain force of the words of the text. Sometimes, even when he is concerned with the literal meaning of the words, one has the feeling of an intelligent person asking questions which, if they are not wrong, are at the very least unexpected. For example, observing that when Paul came to Malta he healed a man suffering from dysentery and fever by praying, yet when his helper Timothy was ill he told him to take a little wine for his stomach's sake, Gregory is puzzled why Paul cured an unbeliever by prayer yet dealt with his assistant in the way a doctor would have, by prescribing foods.[47] But his allegorizing way of approaching Scripture is one followed by the apostles themselves, to judge from their earliest sermons reported in the Acts of the Apostles, and indeed by the authors of the Gospels. It meant that Gregory, unlike some modern Christian scholars of the Bible, would never find it difficult to read a text he had come to know well in a spirit of devotion; for him, there were always new riches to discover. It is also one for which contemporary readers are coming to have increasing sympathy. It will be enough to mention the Ancient Christian Commentary on Scripture currently being published under evangelical auspices, which is based on the works of writers of the first seven centuries of the Christian era, among whom Gregory has an honourable place. And despite its infinite complexity, Gregory had no doubt as to the central message of the Bible. Even if someone understood some of its words in a sense contrary to that intended by the agent through whom they were pronounced, it did not matter, as long as that person sought to build up love, for 'throughout holy scripture God speaks to us with one purpose only, to draw us to love of himself and our neighbour' (*Hez.* 1.10.14).

As a thinker

Gregory expressed disdain for worldly knowledge. He praised St Benedict, a dropout from school, as being 'ignorant yet knowledge-able, wise yet uninstructed'.[48] Thinking of another holy man, Gregory compared his 'instructed ignorance' with his own 'poorly instructed knowledge'.[49] A sentence in the prophet Isaiah, 'Ah, land of whirling wings which is beyond the rivers of Ethiopia; which sends ambassadors by the Nile, in vessels of papyrus upon the waters!' [Isa. 18:1f.], prompted Gregory to assert that, whereas the incarnate Truth had chosen as preachers people who were poor, uneducated and guileless, at the end of the world the enemy would send forth people who were clever, duplicitous and possessed the learning of this world (*Mor.* 13.10.13). Gregory advised those with oversight of the wise of this world to tell them to let go knowing what they knew (*Reg. past.* 3.6). It may be that such sentiments reflect a break with the world of antiquity which occurred at the time,[50] and that, rather than being the products of a mind disquieted by the threat posed by secular learning, as would have been possible in Italy as late as the Ostrogothic period, they proceed from a view that such learning was finished and was not worth worrying about. We may conjecture that its apparently anti-intellectual nature may have been part of the appeal of the book of Job for Gregory. Unlike some modern readers of Job, Gregory did not find the arguments by which his friends and Elihu sought to make sense of the situation of the afflicted man and reconcile him to it particularly interesting; the worldly wisdom which they stood for could be seen to have been completely trumped late in the book by the decisive speech of God, who did not bother to respond to their arguments or argue a case but simply pointed to his power and the extraordinary nature of what he had created. It could therefore be said:

'Our knowledge is ignorance in comparison with God. For we are intelligent from participation in God, not in comparison with him' (*Mor.* 16.1.1).

Unlike Ambrose and Augustine, Gregory wrote no work specifically on a theological topic, and in the history of Christian theology his place is secondary. But this may have reflected the time in which he lived more than anything else. It has been a recurrent pattern in Christian thinking that major statements of doctrine have often been made when beliefs have been seen to be under attack, so that developments in theology have largely been a series of reactions against positions felt to be deviant. Augustine, seeking to refute the views of heretics and non-Christians, was moved to write numerous books with titles beginning 'Contra', whereas Gregory's period was a quiet one from the point of view of theological debate, and the one issue he is known to have engaged in could be considered somewhat marginal when placed beside the subjects of earlier controversies. While in Constantinople he became involved in a fiery debate with Eutychius, the patriarch of the city, over the nature of bodies at the time of the resurrection. Eutychius held that they would not be able to be touched, whereas Gregory argued that they would be. The controversy was concluded only when the emperor ruled in favour of Gregory's view, and ordered that the writings of his antagonist were to be burned; we may note in passing that the manner by which the issue was resolved exposed Gregory to an aspect of life in the Christian East which he may not have found congenial. Both men emerged from the controversy in ill-health, and Eutychius soon died.[51] Otherwise, Gregory found little need to argue for his convictions.

Gregory's relative lack of interest in doctrine is shown by the role St Paul plays in his works. He certainly admired the Apostle, apparently being unable to think of anyone more sublime in this life than he (*Dial.* 2.33.1), and very frequently quoted his description of Christ as 'the mediator between God and humanity' [1 Tim. 2:5]. Yet, with the possible exception of his teaching on grace, there is little sense of him wrestling with Paul's ideas. When something in St Paul drew his attention it was usually the Apostle's spiritual experience, his teaching about diversity of gifts, or instructions about the organization of the church. The figure of Paul is particularly prominent in the *Pastoral Rule*, in which Gregory draws on his letters more than he does the Gospels, but his interest is in the model of leadership he provides. Elsewhere, we learn that Paul's letters show how to present arguments (*Hez.* 1.11.15, 18–20), that he was a loving father to his spiritual children and a veritable rhinoceros in his good qualities (*Mor.*

31.12.17; 31.16.30) and that, in the midst of his difficulties, he cared for others (*Mor.* 30.9.31, 31.40.80; each of these passages in the *Moralia* quote a number of passages from the epistles or Acts). Paul is an important person for Gregory, but he cuts a very different figure in the writings of Augustine. And, unlike Augustine, Gregory does not seem to have been particularly interested in exploring doctrine in a systematic way. We can see him appropriating the ideas of earlier writers, and nuancing various positions, but he neither staked out important new ground nor repackaged traditional teachings in novel ways. For it was not only in its relationship with the thought-world of antiquity that a new day had dawned.

Gregory had to deal with a very different situation from the church fathers of earlier centuries. He certainly did not live in the heroic days of the early church, when St Paul's dictum that it was a good thing to wish to be a bishop reflected the reality that the leaders of the people would be the first to be led to the torments of martyrdom (*Reg. past.* 1.8; cf. 1 Tim. 3:1). But neither was he a member of one of the generations which lived immediately after the conversion of Constantine, in an environment in which orthodox Christianity still had to deal with serious enemies. Its leaders of that time looked with sorrow on three groups who appeared to have turned down God's invitation to his banquet, the adherents of Greco-Roman polytheism, often unhelpfully called, by their Christian enemies and modern scholars, by the all-embracing term 'pagans', Jews, and heretics, who held dissident positions within Christianity. True, such people still had the power to irritate. Non-catholic Lombards caused problems in Italy, but polytheism was something which had chiefly to be confronted in distant places, such as Britain, to which missionaries were dispatched in the expectation that they would preach and attract people to faith by performing miracles in the presence of the unbelievers,[52] and the backwoods of Italy, where the steps Gregory felt could be used to encourage conversions among non-believers were less spectacular.[53] Jews had been successfully marginalized, and while occasions such as Easter could still see violence break out between them and Christians, in towns they could be dealt with by applying the laws issued by Christian emperors.[54] The Three Chapters schism proved intractable in Italy, and the persistent identification of Job's comforters with heretics indicates that Gregory found heresy a problem, perhaps a greater one than we may have thought likely.[55] But, to judge from his letters, the stories in the *Dialogues* and the content of his homilies, he did not see the traditional enemies of catholic Christianity as posing a major threat. Now, the chief dangers came from within.

Two hundred years before the time of Gregory, Augustine, while aware of the ability of pagans, heretics, schismatics and Jews to lead new converts astray, had already thought that the 'chaff' they would encounter within the church would be more dangerous.[56] The great success of the church turned out to have come at the price of hypocrisy. When wicked people who in earlier times would have been blatant non-believers saw earthly rulers humbling themselves before God, they practised deception, so that the church had to deal no longer with overt enemies but false brothers, and was engaged in warfare even in a time of peace (*Mor.* 31.7.10; cf. 13.8.10f). At a time when secular authority bowed with reverence towards religion, many leaders within the church sought high positions and a place above others (*Reg. past.* 1.1). And, as Gregory remarked in a homily to the people, there were many nominal Christians, who did no more than follow the belief of their faithful parents. Such people were like the box tree in the desert, which was low and fruitless despite being green (*Hev.* 20.13). Gregory's concern recalled the polemic of Augustine against the Donatists, a schismatic group in Africa who, recoiling at what they saw as the laxness of the catholic church, claimed to be the true church. Against them, Augustine had held that the visible church held in its bosom both the redeemed and the damned, and that only at the end of time would the identities of the saved and the lost become clear. This emphasis was taken over by Gregory, who repeatedly stressed the mixed character of the church, within which good and bad people were jumbled together. Many who entered the church would be excluded from the kingdom of heaven, for as the church grew many reprobates had been gathered into it (*Mor.* 25.8.21). Gregory knew of some who, wishing to gain the goodwill of a powerful person, did not hesitate to lie about a neighbour, and others who, when they saw something wrong being committed, did not criticize it for fear of losing the favour of the powerful. Such people were to be found within the church, appearing to be what they were not, but at the coming of the Judge their true identity would become clear (*Mor.* 29.7.16f.). And this was without taking into account the ways in which people could change: every day Gregory saw many shining with the light of justice who would end in darkness, and many covered in the darkness of sins who would end in light. It was also the case that there were many who held onto the way of justice until they died, but very many who, having begun to commit sins, kept piling them up until they died (*Mor.* 29.18.32). Often people, impelled by remorse for their evil ways and terror, arrived at the highest virtues, but in their pride they were caught in the trap of empty glory and went back to their old lethargy (*Mor.* 29.30.59). Yet, in the face of such worrisome people, Gregory felt that God's love extended to very average Christians. Towards the end of his exposition of Job, he mentioned those who were unable to attain to the things they wished to, but nevertheless avoided evils to the extent that they were able; these people, he felt, the church clasped to her kindly bosom (*Mor.* 35.18.45). While Gregory's preaching summoned its hearers to transcend the ordinary, he could not forget the people who were destined to remain there.

So it is that when he preached doctrine, Gregory took care to pitch his message at an appropriate level, in the belief that, when holy preachers saw that hearers were unable to receive the word of Christ's divinity, they should descend to the words of his incarnation alone. Contemplation of his divinity is food, but because hearers cannot perceive the hidden things concerning it, they are sated with the blood of the crucified Lord (*Mor.* 31.53.103f.). He writes with power about central themes in Christian theology, such as the person and work of Christ (*Mor.* 22.17.44), and can be intriguing on such topics as Christ rising in his human nature: before his resurrection he was greater than the angels in his divinity but less than they in his humanity, which made him subject to death, but after he trampled down death by rising again, his human nature was placed above the majesty of the angels (*Hez.* 8.23). Nevertheless, in the situation Gregory found himself in, the task of the preacher was not so much to preach doctrine, for the battle to get people to believe had been largely won,[57] as to get them to do better.

But how could this be done? Gregory was well aware of people whose eyes were wide open in believing, but who held them shut when it came to acting, and who needed to be persuaded to reform their lives (*Mor.* 25.10.25). But he was realistic. One of the phrases of Job on which he meditated at great length was the enigmatic 'I would give him an account of all my steps' [Job 20:22]. He believed that the steps were merits, and that it was not a question of coming to the highest one all at once; rather, the mind was led to the heights of virtue through steps (*Mor.* 22.20.46–51). Similarly, when expounding Ezekiel he lingered on a passing reference to a man going up the steps of the Temple. The steps, he thought, could only be the merits of virtues, which we climb as we pass from small things to great (*Hez.* 2.3.3–6, on Ezek. 40:6). The prophet's description of seven steps which led to the north gate of the Temple brought to Gregory's mind the sevenfold grace of the Holy Spirit, and, having made this connection, he was able to interpret the gifts of the Spirit as a ladder which one could climb in ascending from virtue to virtue.[58] These principles, asserted by Gregory in expositions directed towards monks in the case of Job and towards a spiritually alert audience in the case of Ezekiel, can be placed beside two classical monastic texts of the period. In the seventh chapter of his Rule, St Benedict worked his way through twelve rungs (gradus) on a ladder of humility, the first being the need to have the fear of God always before one's eyes and the last, neatly circling back to the first, the stage at which a monk came to the love which casts out fear.[59] A little later, a monk of Mt Sinai, St John of the Ladder (John Climakos) wrote his Ladder of Divine Ascent, in which he envisaged a ladder with thirty steps, each one representing a virtue or a vice which a monk would gain or overcome as he progressed.[60] The ladder was an old motif for making progress, already used by Plato in his *Symposium*,[61] and Boethius wrote of a design on the clothes of Philosophy which showed a ladder ascending from one Greek letter, Pi, to another, Theta, presumably standing for practice and theory respectively,[62] while the motif of a ladder was also used by a number of eastern Christian authors. The image of a ladder recalls the biblical story of Jacob's ladder [Gen. 28:12], although Gregory does not seem to use this ladder to represent ascent in virtues. And while Gregory's expositions of Job and Ezekiel were directed to specialists in the religious life, everyone could understand the importance of moving forward in the Christian life in steps, as two of Gregory's aunts had done, growing by daily increments in the love of their Creator, and increments of goodness could be obtained by the simple means of feeding the poor (*Hev.* 38.15, 40.10; cf. 43.11 on increments in virtues). Perhaps Gregory's life as a monk placed him in a position from which he felt called to diffuse a kind of monastic ascesis among laypeople, at a time when moral reform seemed to have become more important than the preaching of doctrine.

Such concerns may suggest that Gregory saw the Christian religion as being a matter of performing good works, but this was not the case. He certainly makes much of the concept of merit, and believes that the giving of alms can compensate for sins. Discussing a text he found in Job, 'by any price he is redeemed' [Job 15:13 Vulg.], he observes that we pay the price for our bad deeds whenever we give alms after doing something wrong, which was why it could be said of someone who failed to do this, 'For he will not give God his propitiation, or the price of the redemption of his soul' [cf. Ps. 49:8 Vulg.]. Nevertheless, almsgiving does not function to redeem people in a mechanical way, for it only frees us when we are sorry for what we have done and stop doing it (*Mor.* 12.51.57; cf. *Reg. past.* 3.20.89ff.), and Gregory explicitly states that the price of the redemption of sinners is the blood of the Redeemer (*Mor.* 13.23.26). In one of his homilies, Gregory asserts that, while we keep on weeping and repenting, we have a Priest in heaven who intercedes for us. While he is just, and our cause unjust, if we accuse ourselves the Judge will defend us: 'Let us put our trust not in tears, nor in our deeds, but in the pleading of our Advocate' (*Hez.* 1.7.24). Towards the end of the *Dialogues*, Gregory tells a number of stories about sufferings undergone by people who had died, and the efficacy of the mass in bringing their torments to an end.

His adherence to a theme in the works of Augustine also pointed Gregory away from a theology based on works. In a controversy which broke out in the early fifth century between him and the British thinker Pelagius and his supporters, Augustine had argued strongly for the primacy of God's grace over human works in salvation, and Gregory was insistent in maintaining this position. Basing himself to an uncharacteristic extent on St Paul [1 Cor. 15.20], he argues that people cannot be saved by the cleanness of their own hands, for it is God who first acts within us, and he does so independently of us, with our free will following behind.[63] Commenting on Job 25:3, 'upon whom does his light not arise?', Gregory explained that the 'light' is prevenient grace. If it failed to rise in our hearts, our minds would remain obscured by the darkness of their sins (*Mor.* 17.14.20). From this followed a need for baptism, which raised difficulties. How could one make sense of the case when two children were born, one being baptized and the other dying without baptism? It could be argued that God knew that the latter would have gone on to do bad things had he been baptized, and so there would have been no point in his coming to baptism. But it would follow from this that sins were sometimes punished before they were committed, which could not be true, as God sometimes freed people after they had committed sins. In the face of such hidden judgments one could only be humble (*Mor.* 27.4.7). Indeed, the judgments of God were beyond understanding, and Gregory could only advise against speculating why one person was a member of the elect, and another rejected (*Mor.* 29.30.57).

Our suggestion that Gregory sometimes followed Augustine raises the general question of his appropriation of the works of his predecessors. Unfortunately, this is maddeningly difficult to establish, in a way that it is not, for example, in the case of Ambrose, whose unacknowledged quotations and paraphrases from the works of earlier authors can be blatant. When Gregory wrote approvingly of a bishop constantly drinking from the deep and clear waters of Ambrose and Augustine (*Hez. praef.*, to the bishop of Ravenna) he certainly implied that this was a good thing for bishops to do, but it is hard to catch him in the act of doing it. What are we to make of Gregory's assertion, made to another bishop, that the book of Job was hitherto undiscussed (*Mor. praef.*, to Leander of Seville), and his similar claim that the book of Ezekiel had been hitherto untouched (*Hez.* 2.2.1)? Neither statement was true, for Ambrose had written a work on the complaints of David and Job and Augustine a series of comments on difficult passages in Job, while there was a tradition of commentating on Ezekiel.[64] Was Gregory unaware of earlier work, or was he using a tactic authors have been known to employ to suggest the novelty of his own work? We cannot be sure, and Gregory can be difficult to place in the context of preceding Christian thought. For example, it has been strongly argued that he was influenced by eastern theology in such matters as his understanding of the atonement, but explicit borrowings cannot be established.[65] Perhaps we should not be surprised at this, for Gregory's resolutely synthesizing mind may have been able to turn whatever he read to his own purposes; just as he sometimes gives the impression of making portions of the Bible mean what he wants them to mean, he may well have used the writings of earlier authorities as launching pads for his own thoughts, rather than as bodies of ideas to be engaged with. And, if the case of Benedict's thorns and nettles is anything to go by, his appropriation of things he read may have been sloppy. Moreover, the bulk of his works are the fruits of orally delivered teaching in which he would have been relying on what he remembered of his reading, and he may not have been concerned to go back later and check his recollections against texts.

If we seek precise quotations from earlier authors in the writings of Gregory, it would be reasonable to look for them in his letters, written with access to the archives of the Roman church. One of these, sent to an administrative official leaving for Spain, quotes a number of passages from the laws of Justinian (*Reg.* 13.49), while another quotes Hilary, in a slightly wayward way, and Augustine (*Reg.* 1.41). In a third letter, which dealt with the problem of bishops sharing a house with women, the example of Augustine is instanced: 'For it is read that the blessed Augustine would not agree to live with his sister, saying: "The women who are with my sister are not my sisters."' (*Reg.* 9.111). The words reflect Augustine's sentiments as reported by his biographer Possidius, but they certainly do not reproduce what he said, as the direct speech of the apparent quotation implies they do.[66] We are on awkward ground here, for as we have seen Gregory was not responsible for many of the letters written in his name. But part of the difficulty in catching Gregory using the work of others may be a lack of precision in such borrowings as he made.

Let us turn to two topics widely discussed in the contemporary world, and see what Gregory says concerning them. He has a good deal to say about the body.[67] It would be easy to accumulate evidence suggesting that he was hostile towards it. Take, for example, the pleasure he took in the increasing importance of chastity as time passed. Evidence for this was to be found in the three cases of people known to have been taken into heaven: Enoch was born through intercourse and had children; Elijah was born in the same way but had no children; and the Lord was neither the fruit of intercourse nor a parent (*Hev.* 29.6). And he persistently disparaged the flesh, although for Gregory, as for Paul, this was something distinct from the body. Indeed, for Gregory, the action which counted took place inwardly. 'What is the function of the body but to be the instrument of the heart?'[68] The human race could be said to have been born during the day but conceived at night because it never takes delight in sinning without having first been weakened by a voluntary darkness of the mind (*Mor.* 4.13.25). Behind pollution of the body lay pride of mind (*Mor.* 26.17.29), so that, for example, it was not food but greed for food that was the problem: 'the old enemy understands that it is not food but the desire for food which causes damnation; he brought the first man under his power not with meat but an apple, and tempted the second not with meat but bread' (*Mor.* 30.28.60, referring to Adam and Christ respectively). Sin was therefore committed interiorly; while chastity was displayed physically, it very often happened that the inward state of pride was the seedbed of loose living (*Mor.* 26.17.27) and, as happened when Benedict tumbled in the bushes, something physical could remove a wound of the mind from the body. Hence, while Gregory is loathe to see the human body in the positive light many would wish to today, the notion of its being unclean, which has sometimes occurred in Christian thought, is similarly alien to him. Moreover, the abdication of responsibility from the body to the mind requires Gregory to devote considerable attention to inward states, a topic we shall consider later.

Similarly, Gregory's attitude to gender would not commend him to most people nowadays. It would be easy to pile up examples of thinking which seem sexist. Some of what he says about marriage, while it doubtless reflects a lack of experience, is scarcely encouraging: Gregory believed that a man begins by making his betrothed feel good as he caresses her sweetly; then, when they are married, he puts her to the test with bitter complaints; and finally he possesses her, secure in his thoughts. But these comments were not offered as part of a marriage guidance course, but in a discourse to a group of monks, and given that the three stages were intended to illustrate the stages of God's dealings with the people of Israel and with people who were converted, the 'man' involved was God (*Mor.* 24.11.28). And he could be more positive, for one of his letters contains the touching remark that married people are invited to weddings so that people who have gone ahead on the path of marriage may share in the joy of a later union.[69] It need hardly be said that Gregory lived in a world in which notions of gender equality were unthinkable, and that he necessarily reflected the views prevalent in his society. Hence, when, in the third book of his *Pastoral Rule*, Gregory dealt with the different ways in which contrasting types of people were to be admonished, men and women constituted the first pair, and his advice was simple: heavy and lighter things were to be imposed upon them respectively, so that great things would exercise the former, and moderate things convert the latter (*Reg. past.* 3.2). Yet it is remarkable how often Gregory avoids distinguishing the genders in a black and white way, as though one contained everything that was good. He felt that someone with rulership should exhibit the kindness of a mother and the strictness of a father to those under him (*Reg. past.* 2.6, lines 182–4). Similarly, referring to the words 'Canst thou mark when the hinds do calve?' (Job 39:1), he noted that true teachers, while they are fathers with respect to the strength of the discipline they impose, recognise that they are mothers in the depth of their kindness; indeed, they conceive and give birth in great pain (*Mor.* 30.10.43). Doubtless this does not imply the highest view of womanhood, but Gregory's correspondence includes many letters to women in which he often adopts a tone, if not of flirtatiousness, at least of gentle banter. An English historian memorably referred to his 'subtle wooing of queens',[70] and we may take it that this represents the lightness Gregory recommended to others in their dealings with women. It is not the kind of equal treatment we would expect now, but it could have been less positive.

Aspects of Gregory's thinking which may be of less relevance to modern culture also have the power to cause surprise. The church, within which there were teachers who presided as though they were kings, was marked by hierarchy (*Mor.* 20.5.12). As usual, Gregory expressed his understanding of the standing of various people within the church by means of images. The church could be seen as an army made of up three detachments, those of preachers who toiled to collect souls, of people living in continence or a state of retirement who were at the ready to fight evil spirits, and married people living together in the love of God who, while not neglecting to pay the debt of the flesh, never forgot the good works they owed to God (*Hez.* 1.8.10). Or it was like a city, comprised of married people who lived in a virtuous way, of people who had done away with the things of the world and devoted themselves to contemplation, and of another group, the highest, who, while they too were involved in contemplation, held a position of command, preaching and ministering to the needs of souls and bodies (*Hez.* 2.1.7). Noah, Daniel and Job could be seen as standing for the groups respectively, in the second sequence, as could three groups mentioned by Jesus, comprising those in a field, those in a bed, and those milling.[71] Some words of Moses could be used against those who set themselves against the authority which God had placed above them: 'Your murmuring is not against us, but against the Lord' (*Reg. past.* 3.4 ad fin, quoting Ezek. 16:8). It is clear that Gregory felt that rulers were to be obeyed.

We may be uncomfortable with this firmly enunciated view, although in various ways Gregory softens it. He emphasizes that power should be exercised in the interests of others; hence, people should take pleasure not in command but in the progress of those under them,[72] and the great glory of priests was the uprightness of those under them (*Mor.* 11.14.22f.). Moreover, the job of ruling was a risky one. Gregory held that those who ruled over the motions of the members of their bodies were rightly called rulers. But he comments that, when such rulers were touched by elation of mind at their continence, God permitted them to fall into unclean works, and destroyed their belt of chastity (*Mor.* 11.13.21). Analogously, when a priest did not do the good things which he preached about, even his speech was taken away from him (*Mor.* 11.15.23). And the grace of contemplation was often given to both great and small; most often it came to those living in retirement, but sometimes it did to married people as well, so that no rank among the faithful was excluded from it (*Hez.* 2.5.19). One cannot help noting that Job, who stood for the rulers or preachers in one of Gregory's schemata, was married. But perhaps little could be expected from married people; in the *Dialogues* holiness is virtually a monopoly of the professionally religious, whether members of the clergy or monastics.[73]

The period in which Gregory lived was one in which power within western Christianity tended to move away from the charismatic figures of unordained monks and nuns, and to some extent the laity in general, towards the ordained clergy,[74] and his emphasis on 'rulers' as being above both married and continent people sits well with this process. However, the authority which accrued to priests was largely based on their sacramental functions, and it is noteworthy that, while the emphasis Gregory places on offering the sacrifice of the mass on behalf of the dead towards the end of the *Dialogues* was to play a major role in this development,[75] across his works he emphasizes the office of preaching far more than the sacraments. He therefore stands at an odd angle to developments during his period.

Gregory's meditations on Job provided plenty of opportunity for discussion of the Devil, the 'old enemy' as he often called him. Not surprisingly, given Gregory's views, his chief characteristic was his pride (cf. p. 40); despising the social joy of the legions of angels, he had chosen to go it alone (*Reg.* 5.39). He was a 'proud king', Gregory observes, perhaps with a nod to a traditional Roman concept (*Mor.* 4.23.42), and a most subtle tempter. In some ways he resembled God, and Gregory makes much of sinful people being members of the Devil or of the body of Antichrist, apparently in parallel to Christians, who formed the body of Christ.[76] But his interventions in the life of St Benedict are not impressive. Gregory describes him as creating a fuss when the man of God built a chapel within a temple of Apollo, preventing a large stone from being moved, and tricking a devout layman into eating.[77] And his cause was lost. Not only is he tending towards non-being by a daily process of diminution (*Mor.* 14.18.22), but, despite himself, the old enemy serves the hidden dispositions of God, who does not allow him to rage more than is useful; whatever degree of savagery he permits God twists back to the advantage of his elect (*Mor.* 33.18.34). It was generally true that God knew how to use the evil of those who were lost to the benefit of the elect (*Mor.* 34.16.30), and when God allowed the Devil to rage as he desired, in a wonderful way his will was being fulfilled (*Mor.* 33.14.28).

What are we to make of such teaching? Some scholars recoil with disgust from Gregory's views. One authority writes:

> A more motley farrago of Augustinian formulas and crude work-religion (ergismus) could hardly be conceived. Gregory has nowhere uttered an original thought; he has rather at all points preserved, while emasculating, the traditional system of doctrine, reduced the spiritual to a coarsely material intelligence, changed dogmatic, so far as it suited, into technical directions for the clergy, and associated it with popular religion of the second rank . . . [A]n almost naïf monastic soul . . . ever adopting what was calculated by turns to disquiet and soothe . . . Gregory created the vulgar type of mediaeval Catholicism.[78]

Yet many passages in the writings of Gregory can be set against this judgment, among them the conclusion to the *Dialogues*. Towards the end of the fourth book, Gregory tells a series of stories about the efficacious offering of the sacrifice of the Eucharist on behalf of the dead, and he clearly believes that this is a useful thing to do (*Dial.* 4.57–59). This may seem to exemplify some of the features of Gregory's religion referred to negatively in the preceding quotation, but Gregory proceeds to change tack in a way which seems to ground from under what he has been saying. We will not need the saving victim to be offered for us if we turn ourselves into victims. At the very end of the book Gregory proclaims that the saving victim will benefit only dead people who lived in such a way to deserve being helped, and that the best thing was to do oneself, while still alive, what one hoped others would do on one's behalf when one had died. The *Dialogues* conclude with the words: 'I confidently say that we shall not need the saving victim after we have died if we are ourselves a victim for God before we die.'[79] It is as if Gregory, having moved some distance towards what a hostile critic could call 'the vulgar type of medieval Catholicism', immediately distances himself from this in order to emphasize a costly religion of the heart.

Gregory's concerns may seem remote, yet he remains a thinker worth engaging with. Often it is the opinions he throws out in passing rather than the structures of his thinking that catch the eye. Any serious reader of Gregory will be struck by his knack of tersely uttering thought-provoking and often challenging ideas. A friend, he tells us, is the guardian of the heart.[80] Gregory's way of thinking, as well as a tendency towards pessimism, sometimes suggest Pascal: hence the observation that human weakness should not despair of itself; it should consider the blood of the only-begotten, and deduce from what was paid for it how great something that was worth so much is.[81] He often expresses himself by way of antithesis, relishing the kind of paradoxical statement sometimes found in Byzantine hymns, as in his daunting teaching on charity. 'All the earthly things we lose by keeping can be kept by giving them away' (*Mor.* 18.18.28, largely repeated at *Hev.* 4.5). It is a bad giver who gives what is his to God and himself to the Devil (*Reg. past.* 3.20.98f.). 'There is this difference between an earthly and a heavenly building: an earthly building is constructed by gathering together what you have; a heavenly building by scattering what you have' (*Hev.* 37.6). Gregory could contrast those who made use of the things of this world in the manner of a steward, so that they might enjoy God, with those who wished to make use of God in a cursory manner, so that they might enjoy this world (*Mor.* 2.9.15). In a sustained comparison, he observes that bodily pleasures please one's appetites, but when they are experienced they fail to satisfy;

the desire for spiritual pleasures is small, but when they are experienced they satisfy. In the former case one passes from appetite to satiety to aversion; in the latter, from appetite to satiety to further appetite (*Hev.* 36.1). Such expressions reveal more here than the ability to produce well-turned phrases. For Gregory's ability to enter into the minds and hearts of other people was uncanny.

The human mind

One of the key structures in Gregory's thought is the distinction between the inward and the outward, and his invariable tendency to see the former as being the more important. This is reflected, for example, in his privileging of an allegorical rather than a literal approach to the Bible, and of the mind over the body.[82] God's being concerned with inward dispositions allows Gregory to explain an apparent injustice, his punishing for eternity sins which were committed within time. God acts in this way because he weighs hearts, not deeds; had the wicked been able to, they would have wished to go on sinning for ever (*Mor.* 34.19.26). Gregory's interest in inner states found expression in a subtle understanding of sin, which drew on terminology already used by Augustine. He saw it as coming about in three stages. The first was when evil was suggested, which was morally neutral; the second occurred when the person took pleasure in the possibility of committing it, in which case there was an element of sin; and the third stage, definitely sinful, took place when consent was given.[83] The whole process could be seen in the stages by which Adam and Eve yielded. In this case, a being who is variously described as the enemy, the plotter or the serpent began the process by suggesting something which was wrong; Eve, who could be seen as the flesh, then gave herself over to delight; and finally Adam, who could be seen as the spirit, was defeated and gave his consent (cf. *Mor.* 27.26.50, 32.19.33). In Gregory's hands, this way of understanding falling into sin went far beyond what could have been a crude schematization. Discussing some words of Job, 'If I have hidden as a man my sin, and concealed in my breast my iniquity' [Job 31:33], his mind turned to the encounter between Adam and Eve and God after the humans had eaten the fruit of the forbidden tree. He holds that God rebuked them so as to give them a chance to wipe away their sin by confessing; that is why he did not rebuke the serpent at the beginning. But rather than confessing, they chose to defend themselves. Adam blamed Eve and Eve blamed the serpent, and so, in an oblique way, each blamed God, for it was he who had made the woman and placed the serpent in

Paradise. Having come this far, Gregory is able to make an astonishing manoeuvre: those who had heard the serpent say 'You shall be like gods' now tried to make God like themselves, in having made a mistake.[84]

Gregory's insight into the workings of the human mind allowed him to describe psychological conditions we can still identify, such as paranoia. There are no people more happy than those without guile, he asserts, because people who are innocent in their behaviour towards others have no fear of other people doing anything bad to them. The minds of wicked people, on the other hand, are always in turmoil, because they are either planning to do bad things or are afraid that other people will do bad things to them; they dread others plotting to do to them the very things they are plotting to carry out themselves![85] Elsewhere, he makes the point more fully. Almighty God does not merely hold back the punishments of wrongdoers for the future, but he punishes them here and now where they do wrong, so that they harm themselves through the very thing wherein they sin: always restless and uneasy, they fear that they will suffer from others the wrongs which they recall having done to others. And so a wicked mind is always busy, either working to bring harm on other people or fearing that this harm may be brought upon itself by them, for whatever a wicked mind plots against its neighbours, it dreads as being plotted by its neighbours against it. People who always act with deceit cannot imagine that others will act towards themselves in a straightforward way (*Mor.* 12.38.43–39.44).

Not surprisingly, Gregory was more able than most people to place himself in the situations of others. That different people can interpret the same thing in different ways explains why God can be said to appear both tranquil and wrathful at the last judgment, because this is how he will appear to people with good and bad consciences, respectively; in a similar way, when a guilty person appears before an earthly judge, he thinks that the judge is hostile to him, not because of the behaviour of the judge but because he remembers his guilt, whereas an innocent person is confident (*Mor.* 32.7.9). Knowing that people tend to judge their own sins differently from those committed by others, he thought that people needed to look upon themselves as though they were other people (*Hez.* 1.4.9, a rich passage). Sometimes he put himself in the shoes of people in the Bible, interpreting apparently inexplicable things they did in the light of particular purposes they had in mind. Hence, when Moses asked Hobab to help the people of Israel in the wilderness, it was not because he did not know the way, for he was guided by God, but he was using a ploy to overcome the pride of a person he was hoping to be able to lead to life (*Reg. past.* 3.17.73ff.).

Why did Paul give different advice to Timothy and Titus? This was because he saw that one was gentle and the other impulsive.[86] One has the feeling of Gregory attributing to biblical characters insight of a kind which he enjoyed himself in large measure.

What can we tell of Gregory himself? The subtlety of his thought suggests that he was a person with a rich inner life, and indeed he was, although we may find some of its forms disconcerting.

At various points in his writings Gregory accuses himself of failings. Some of these were surely minor, such as a love of chatting, although someone who found so much to say on Job may be suspected of having been garrulous (*Hez.* 1.11.3–6). But, on the principle that preachers often attack most vehemently those faults which they see in themselves, it is surely significant that there was one human failing of overwhelming concern to Gregory, that of pride. One of the passages in the Bible to which he returns most often is that which gives the proud boast of Lucifer: 'I will ascend to heaven; above the stars of God I will set my throne on high; I will sit on the mount of assembly in the far north; I will ascend above the heights of the clouds, I will make myself like the most high' [Isa. 14:13f.]. Every phrase in this passage pointed to the Devil and his pride. But the world seemed to be full of people prone to the same vice. Often, their pride took the form of seeking a good reputation. Gregory knew of those who, having received the gift of teaching, swelled up in the wish to appear great before others (*Mor.* 11.2.4); those who took great care to act in a way which would please human eyes (*Mor.* 12.53.60); and hypocrites who refused corporeal gifts so as to gain praise (*Mor.* 12.54.62). The case which gave him most concern was that of the pleasure which someone who had done something good would experience when praised, for it was often the case that, after some good deed was praised, the mind of the person who did it was altered and came to take pleasure which it had not sought. This was a particular danger for those who taught within the church. Elihu, who addressed Job after his three comforters had spoken, could be seen as representing the lovers of empty glory. There were people within the holy church who preached the truth, but their purpose was not the glory of God but for themselves to be praised, which meant that God could approve what had been said while failing to acknowledge the person who said it (*Mor.* 23.1.7). Not merely are these issues frequently addressed by Gregory, but two of his works, the *Moralia* and the *Pastoral Rule*, end with discussions of the need for a speaker or pastor to return to himself and investigate his own heart. The joy someone could take in his performance was a constant concern for Gregory.

We have seen that Gregory placed great authority in the hands of those who wielded power (see p. 34f). His emphasis on the inner life went some way towards mitigating the dangers inherent in this stance. Gregory meditated extensively on power, both in the *Pastoral Rule* and elsewhere (e.g. *Mor.* 26.25.44–8). He was remarkably self-conscious in the exercise of authority, regarding the eschewing of glory while holding an exalted position and being unaware that one has power while holding it as being the most subtle art of living (*Mor.* 26.26.48). Perhaps power was like sex, something which it was hard to engage in without sin.[87] But power may have been more closely connected with the great sin of pride, and it was on this basis that Gregory objected to use of the title 'ecumenical patriarch' by the patriarch of Constantinople. He sometimes styled himself 'servant of the servants of God' (*servus servorum Dei*),[88] perhaps modelling himself on St Paul, whom he saw as fleeing honour and proclaiming himself the 'servant of the disciples' (*Mor.* 19.22.37; a meditation on humility follows). Against the vice of pride, which Gregory often considered in terms of people being 'lifted up', as was the case with Lucifer, he set the virtue of humility, literally 'lowliness'. God displayed this in the incarnation, when he appeared as a man among men in his humility, opposed to the Devil in his pride (*Mor.* 31.1.1). Humility was 'the teacher and mother of all the virtues' (*Mor.* 23.13.24; elsewhere, charity is the mother of virtues: *Reg. past.* 3.9, 3.23). Two clear signs that a mind was filled with the Holy Spirit were the ability to work miracles and humility (*Dial.* 1.1.6), and humility was most important in the working of miracles. (*Dial.* 1.2.7). But the position of the miracle worker was dangerous, for success in this area could lead to a loss of humility. It was most necessary that the mind of someone working outward miracles was not harmed by temptation inwardly (*Dial.* 1.5.3–6). Hence, when news came from Britain that the missionary Augustine was working miracles, Gregory told him that, while it was appropriate to feel joy that the souls of the English were being brought by outward miracles to inward grace, he should nevertheless be in the greatest dread, in case his soul was lifted up in presumption and, through lifted up in honour outwardly, fell down inwardly through empty glory. He was to recall his wrongdoings in what he had said and done as a way of dealing with the stirrings of pride, and bear in mind that even the damned could work miracles (*Reg.* 11.36).

We have no reason to believe that Gregory had reason to be exercised by this particular problem in his own life, but it was linked with another issue which was of personal significance. As early as the fourth century, the biographer of the Egyptian monk Antony presented his life as alternating between being a hermit and helping others in their lives in the world. This sense of being pulled in two directions, each good, would be a lasting area of difficulty in the Christian tradition. When Gregory came to a verse in the Bible, 'who has let the wild ass go free? And who has loosed its bonds?', he was in no doubt as to whom it referred: the wild ass which dwelt by itself signified the life of those who were remote from throngs of people, and it was free because of the affairs of the world entail great slavery (*Mor.* 30.15.50 on Job 39:5). But it was an unfortunate reality that their love of the brethren compelled preachers to withdraw from the contemplation of high things (*Mor.* 27.24.44). Indeed, holy men who went forth from private contemplation to do something in the interests of everyone were like flashes of lightning. They often went outside themselves in the ministry of active life, but continually ran back to the holy zeal of contemplation; after they receive the grace of contemplation God places them in the service of active life, but nevertheless he always calls them back from exterior goods to height of contemplation within (*Mor.* 30.2.8). The need to look in two directions made the task of the pastor a difficult one. Like many readers of the Bible, Gregory found it to be full of passages which seemed to illustrate the way he was feeling. One of them was in the Song of Songs, 'They made me the keeper of the vineyards; but mine own vineyard I have not kept' [S. of S. 1:6]. He felt that the vineyards were worldly activities, in the care of which the speaker had fallen away from custody of his own soul, and so felt able to provide a paraphrase: 'While devoting myself to watchfulness on the outside, through activities in the world, I have ceased to have proper care for watchfulness on the inside' (*In CC* 40). The differences between the life of contemplation and activity were to be seen in two sisters mentioned in the Old Testament, Rachel and Leah: the former was beautiful but sterile, the latter bleary eyed but fecund, so that the one with better vision produced fewer children. A similar distinction could be made between two sisters known from the New Testament, Martha and Mary: the former sat at the feet of the Redeemer while the latter busied herself with bodily services. Gregory felt that, while the merits of the active life were great, those of the contemplative life were preferable (*Mor.* 6.37.61; the two sets of sisters are also discussed in this way at *Hez.* 2.2.9f.). Moses provided a good role model in this regard, for he kept on going into the tabernacle and then leaving it: inside it he was taken up by contemplation, outside it he was oppressed by the affairs of the weak; inside he meditated on the hidden things of God, outside he bore the burdens of fleshly people

(*Reg. past.* 2.5). But above Moses stood the figure of the Redeemer, who performed miracles in the city yet prayed throughout the night on a mountain, showing the faithful that in their zeal for contemplation they were not to neglect caring for their neighbours, while an immoderate involvement in caring for their neighbours was not to lead them to abandon contemplation (*Mor.* 28.13.33).

This was a source of tension in Gregory's life. At the beginning of the *Dialogues*, he represented himself as having been so weighed down by the tumults of the secular people whose affairs he was forced to deal with that he sought a lonely place where, sitting in miserable silence, he brought to mind everything in his activities which gave him cause for grief. When a friend approached and asked why he was so unhappy, Gregory recalled his life in the monastery, when all passing things were beneath him. But now the obligation to provide pastoral care meant that he had to endure the affairs of worldly people (*Dial.* 1 prol. 5). A sympathetic commentator who knew Gregory's works well, the English author Bede, queried Gregory's self-evaluation. He felt that, rather than losing his monastic perfection through exercising pastoral care, Gregory made his labours for the conversion of many people the occasion of greater progress than he would have made in living a quiet life.[89] But Bede, who had entered a monastery as a boy, wrote as someone with no experience of the trials of public life. It is noteworthy that Gregory often expressed his unease at his situation in letters addressed to other holders of high office (cf. p. 3), whom he may have found more sympathetic to his concerns than Bede was.

Let us now turn to another area of Gregory's inner life. The degree of insight into the motions of the human mind he enjoyed may have been connected with the degree of 'psychological integration' which he attained,[90] and a modern scholar, while noting the importance of dichotomies in Gregory's thought, denies the use of polarities in interpreting him; rather, she helpfully suggests that he lived in an in-between space.[91] But whatever degree of richness there was in Gregory's inner life, whether seen in terms of integration or a lack of black and white, anyone who reads him at length becomes aware that he has an uncomfortable amount to say about people being whipped, an experience which he believes often turns out to be beneficial. This was the case with Job, who was whipped not to extinguish his offences but to increase his merits (*Mor.* 32.4.5). When people being persecuted cry out to God he can disregard their voices, to increase their merits (*Mor.* 20.31.61), for whips could be seen as operating to increase merit, not punish wrongdoing (*Mor.* 26.26.67). Doubtless Job had to suffer more than most people, but Gregory saw his own position as being similar. Writing to bishop Leander, a man from Spain with whom he had become friends when they met in Constantinople, he reminded him of a serious illness he had suffered, and, quoting the biblical text 'Every son who is received by God he whips' [Heb. 12:6], observed: 'And perhaps this was the plan of divine providence, that I, having been struck, might expound the stricken Job, and that, having been whipped, I might better understand the mind of someone who was whipped' (*Ep ad Leand.* 5). Gregory was therefore not surprised when people who were being praised were later insulted; rather, this was a sign of God's wonderful management. The situation of such people would be like that of a tree which was nearly uprooted by a wind blowing from one direction, but was then lifted up by a wind blowing from the opposite direction (*Mor.* 22.7.17). It should be emphasized that there is no reason to believe that Gregory took pleasure from harming his body, by whipping or any other means. But this emphasis is sustained in his thinking, and it may not be coincidental that Gregory was also exercised by something else which most people would not anticipate with pleasure, the last judgment. For not only did he expect that the world would shortly end with the return to it of Jesus Christ, but also he was all too aware of the judgment which would follow. He was ever mindful of the coming of the 'strict Judge', and the person he refers to by this expression is Jesus.[92] Not all the fathers of the church thought in such terms; according to a celebrated aphorism of Ambrose, for example, death could be approached with confidence, because of the kindness of the Lord.[93] The cast of Gregory's thinking can be uncomfortably gloomy.

Yet this was not the deepest part of Gregory's religion. At its centre stood what he referred to as 'desiderium', a kind of yearning or 'the unsatisfied longing of the human heart'. The notion was so central to his thinking that one historian of monastic spiritual life has described him as the 'doctor of desire'.[94] As we have seen, Gregory felt that when people experienced spiritual pleasures they passed from appetite to satiety and back to appetite (see p. 37f), and according to this principle one's yearning could never be satisfied. He makes the point by examining two verses in the Bible which seem to contradict each other. The first preacher of the church, as he describes Peter,[95] mentions God as being the one 'on whom the angels long to look',[96] and yet Christ says: 'Their angels in heaven always behold the face of my father who is in heaven' [Matt. 18:10]. Gregory holds that, despite appearances, each statement is true: the angels both see God and long to see him; otherwise put, they both thirst to look upon him and look upon him (*Mor.* 18.54.91). In one of his homilies, Gregory discusses the figure of Mary Magdalene at the empty tomb of Jesus, yearning to see him again; 'it is not enough for a lover to have one look, because the power of love increases the will to see.' He then turns to another female figure, the one who symbolized the church in the Song of Songs: 'Upon my bed at night I sought him whom my soul loves; I sought him but did not find him. I will arise now and go about the city, in the streets and in the squares, and seek him whom my soul loves' [S. of S. 3:1f.]. Holy longings, Gregory felt, grow as their fulfilment is delayed; if there were no delay, they would not be longings. From this he passes naturally to the words of a psalm: 'My soul thirsted for the living God. When shall I come and appear before the face of God?' (Ps. 42:2; *Hev.* 25.2). In this emphasis, Gregory may have pointed away from Benedict, who, as far as we can tell from his Rule, was not particularly interested in longing for God, and the sense of experience which was ever incomplete. Amid the gloomy and negative aspects of Gregory's views, there was a firm centre which gave him something positive to hold onto: 'Someone who longs for God with his whole soul certainly already possesses the one he loves' (*Hev.* 30.1).

This translation

One circumstance, in particular, makes the words of Gregory difficult to translate: he writes expecting his words to be listened to. The play of sounds we have noticed lying behind his comment that the lamb can walk and the elephant swim in the Bible is a feature of his style, in which runs of vowels can be used to lovely effect (*sed leniter veniens recidiva febris*, *Reg. past.* 3.9.156). He is also prone to alliteration, often using a series of words beginning with an emphatic consonant, such as on the numerous occasions in the *Dialogues* when he describes a remarkable person as 'a man of venerable life' (*vir vitae venerabilis*; the initial letter must be pronounced in the medieval and not the classical fashion). Alliteration could be used in direct speech to give added point to something which was already exciting: 'I have been given to a dragon to be eaten up!' (*draconi ad devorandum datus sum*, *Hev.* 19.7). Sometimes echoes can be heard across a series of sentences. In the preface to the *Moralia*, Gregory describes Job as a man strengthened by the highest virtues (vir*itaque iste summis* vir*ibus fultus*). The following sentence explains that his virtue was exercised quietly, but was stirred up when he was whipped (virt*us* quidem *etiam per* quietem *se exercuit sed* virt*utis opinio commota per* flag*ella* flag*ravit*). Shortly afterwards, Gregory refers to burning heat (flag*rantiam*), although the word is used in the context of aromas being spread about, and is presumably meant to suggest fragrance (*fragrantiam*) as well. Several sentences later, he speaks of Job's misfortunes being turned into a virtuous fervour (*in* fervorem virtutis vertitur). While this stylistic trait does not affect his ideas, the sounds which are similar occur within units of sense, so Gregory must have chosen to express himself using words the sounds of which allow him to reinforce his meaning. The notes appended to the translation may help readers see just a little of the oral quality of his prose, but much of Gregory's quality as a writer can be appreciated only by reading it in Latin, and out loud, as he doubtless anticipated his writings would be read.

The issue of sexist language is a vexed one, which has proved more difficult than I anticipated to deal with. On numerous occasions I began casting long sentences into gender-free English, only to be ambushed by a third person singular pronoun which proved impossible to avoid translating into natural English in a gendered way. Beyond this purely technical issue, it has increasingly seemed to me that, because the society in which Gregory lived was one which predisposed him to think of males, rather than females and males, as active agents, forms of English which could be thought carelessly or insultingly gendered in the contemporary world may be appropriate when rendering the thought of someone who lived in a very different world. For these reasons, it has seemed both convenient and fitting to use expressions which I would be less happy with in other contexts.

A large part of Gregory's writings consists of quotations from the Bible. I have translated the text given by Gregory, although its meaning sometimes differs from that found in modern translations. It has sometimes seemed worthwhile to use the words of traditional translations of the Bible into English, rather than using other, and perhaps more current expressions. The numbering of verses and psalms follows that found in most modern English Bibles, rather than that of the Vulgate.

Gregory's writings have been described as being so unsystematic that it is of no real consequence where you begin and where you finish reading them.[97] More than once it has occurred to me that it would be interesting to open Gregory's works at random and begin translating whatever passages presented themselves. It is also true that few passages in his writings stand out as making decisive contributions to the articulation of Christian thought; rather, Gregory's noteworthiness emerges from a sustained tone and way of doing things. Otherwise put, few people will read Gregory with a view to finding compelling statements of Christian teaching; rather, they will be interested in the example he provides of thinking and living as a Christian. I have therefore sought to introduce some of the areas in which he may be of most interest to readers of the twenty-first century. We begin with passages illustrating his way of handling the Bible, which seems much more current than it did a short while ago, and two of his homilies on the Gospels, these being examples of popular preaching which repay close attention. Then we move on to passages showing Gregory's insight into human psychology. Beyond this, in the interest of letting Gregory's voice be heard on matters not suggested by issues for the second matters which may be of contemporary interest, I have chosen some passages with the aim of conveying something of the general tone of his thinking and writing, for this purpose selecting portions from his greatest work, the *Moralia in Job*, in particular ones which illustrate his inner life.

The immense difficulties under which Gregory worked and his awareness of the unfathomable depths of the human heart meant that he was never tempted to an easy optimism. An image which frequently came to his mind was that of the sea. The Christian writers of antiquity often saw this as being a turbulent and dangerous element, doubtless thinking back to the story of Jesus stilling a storm at sea, and perhaps beyond this to troubling references to waters in different parts of the Hebrew Bible. It was easy for Gregory, fascinated as he was by the workings of the human mind, to see this as a deep sea (*Mor.* 29.15.27). He was attracted by the metaphor of dangerous waves, which even a seasoned sailor could find it hard to cope with (*Reg. past.* 1.9.31f.). One of the ways in which Gregory expressed his own situation was by the metaphor of a man at sea. Tossed as he was on the waves of sin, who was he to be directing others towards salvation? In the shipwreck of this life, his hope was that a friend would hold out towards him the plank of prayer (*Reg. past.* 4, ad fin; the same metaphor occurs at *Reg.* 1.7). And whereas the sea, with its rolling breakers and waves, represented the present world, the firm shore stood for the quiet of eternity (*Hev.* 24.1). As he came towards the end of his mighty exposition of Job, Gregory naturally thought of himself as a sailor on a vast sea, who was now in sight of the shore (*Mor.* 35.1.1).

But the image was the more poignant for Gregory, because it also recalled his own past in a monastery, when he had known happiness. In his early days as pope he described himself as weeping when he remembered the loss of the peaceful shore where his life had been one of quiet, and as looking with sighs towards the land which he was now unable to gain, as the winds blew against him (*Reg.* 1.41, to bishop Leander of Seville). Tossed on the waves of a great sea in a tiny boat, he would sigh at the recollection of his past life, as if he were looking over his shoulder towards a shore (*Dial*. prol. 5). One thinks of a man in a storm at sea, from which he can see the shore. Tossed as he is in a continuous heaving motion, he knows from his own experience that there is a place of stability. But it is beyond his power to reach it, and he must satisfy himself with yearning. Many people in the contemporary West are attracted to Buddhism, and seek to eradicate desire from their lives. The spiritual tradition from which Gregory speaks points in the reverse direction. In the midst of transience and turbulence, it was yearning that enabled him to keep functioning, in the hope that that which was now unattainably distant would in the end be the object of his loving contemplation, face to face.

2

THE BIBLE

Gregory is a man of the Bible: the book stood at the very centre of his life. In one sentence of extraordinary length he explains why he loves it so much.

Moralia

20.1.1 Although holy scripture incomparably transcends all knowledge and teaching, so that there is no need for me to say that it preaches the truth, that it issues a summons to the heavenly country, that it turns the heart of someone who reads it from earthly desires to embracing the things which are above, that it provides the strong ones with exercise in its obscure sayings and treats the little ones gently in its lowly speech, that its meaning is neither so inaccessible as to instil fear nor so obvious as to be held in contempt, that use of it takes away any dislike and that, the more it is meditated upon, the more it is loved, that it helps the mind of its reader with lowly speech and lifts it up with lofty meanings, that in some sense it grows with those who read it, that, while it can to some extent be investigated by ignorant readers, the learned can nevertheless always find it new, so, to say nothing about the importance of its subject matter, it nevertheless transcends all kinds of knowledge and teachings by the very way in which it says things, because in one and the same mode of discourse the piece of material it presents expresses a mystery, and it knows how to speak of the past in such a way as to be able to predict the future by the same subject, and without changing its way of speaking it knows how to describe things which have happened and to announce things which should be done in the same language, just as is the case with these very words of blessed Job,[1] who, in speaking of his affairs, speaks of ours in advance, and in making his own griefs known in speech, gives voice through its meaning to the circumstances of the holy church.

A passage in one of his homilies on Ezekiel provides a clear statement of the way the Bible is to be understood:

Homiliae in Hiezechihelem prophetam

1.9.30   It goes on, referring to this book: *Which was written on the inside and the outside* [Ezek. 2:10]. For the book of the Bible is written on the inside through allegory and the outside through history; on the inside through a spiritual understanding, on the outside through a mere literal sense suited to those who are still weak; on the inside, because it promises things which cannot be seen, on the outside because it lays down visible things through its upright precepts; on the inside because it promises heavenly things, on the outside because it orders in what way earthly things are worthy of contempt, whether we put them to use or flee from desiring them. For it says some things about heavenly secrets, and ordains other things concerning outward actions. And those things which it orders on the outside are quite clear, but those things which it tells of interior things cannot be understood in full. And so it is written: *You stretch out heaven like a skin, you who cover its upper parts in the waters* [Ps. 104:2f.]. For what is indicated by the word heaven but holy scripture? From it shine forth the sun of wisdom and the moon of knowledge, and the stars of examples and virtues from the ancient fathers. It is stretched out like a skin because, having been formed by its writers through the tongue of the flesh, it is explained before our eyes in words through the exposition of learned people. But what are indicated by the word waters but the most holy choirs of angels? It is written of them: *And the waters which are above the heaven, let them praise the name of the Lord* [Ps. 148:4f.]. And so it is that the Lord covers the upper parts of heaven in the waters, because the high things of the Bible, that is what it tells of the nature of God or eternal joys, are known only to the angels in private, while we are still ignorant of them. Therefore heaven is also stretched out before us, and nevertheless its upper parts are concealed, because some things in the Bible are already clear to us through the disclosure of the Spirit, while other things which can only be made known to the angels are still kept hidden from us. Nevertheless we already discern a part of these hidden things through a spiritual understanding, we have already received the pledge of the Holy Spirit, because while we do not know these things in their fullness, nevertheless we love with our deepest being, and we are fed with the nourishment of truth through the many spiritual understandings which are already known to us.

9.31 It therefore rightly says *which was written on the inside and the outside*, because in the Bible the strong are made content by its obscure and lofty sayings, while we little ones are nourished by its plain precepts. And so it is written: *The high mountains for the deer, the rock is a refuge for the hedgehogs* [Ps. 104:18]. For the mountains of understanding should belong to those who already know how to make leaps in contemplation. But the rock may be a refuge for the hedgehogs, because those of us who are little and covered with the spikes of our sins, even if we cannot understand high things, may be saved in the refuge of our rock, that is, in the faith of Christ.[2] As if to say: Because I considered you were unable to grasp the mysteries of his divinity, I have told you only of the weakness of his humanity.

Much of Gregory's deepest reflection on the Bible is contained in his homilies on the book of Ezekiel. Many people who encounter Gregory's speculations wonder on what basis he says such unexpected things. In the introduction to one of his homilies he takes his hearers into his confidence:

2.2.1 In case some people rebuke me in the silence of their thoughts for presuming to discuss the deep mysteries of the prophet Ezekiel which great expositors have left untouched, they should know in what frame of mind I am undertaking this. For this is a task I approach not with rashness but in humility. For I know that I have understood very many things in holy scripture when in the company of my brothers which I was not able to understand by myself. I have tried to understand it by one kind of understanding, and from this as well, so that I may know from the merit of the understanding of these people which is given to me. For it is clear that this is given to me for the benefit of those people in whose presence it is given to me. From this circumstance, by the generous gift of God it happens that, when I am teaching in your presence what I am learning on your behalf, my understanding becomes greater and pride smaller, because, to tell the truth, I am hearing with you many of the things which I say. Therefore, whatever I have understood imperfectly in this prophet comes from my own blindness, while if I have been able to understand anything correctly, it comes from a gift God has given you, venerable people. But often, through the grace of the almighty Lord, some things among those he says are better understood when the word of God is read in private and the mind, conscious of its failings, when it considers what it has heard, strikes itself with the dart of grief and pierces itself with the sword of remorse, so that all it can do is weep and wash the stains with streams of tears.[3] While this is going on, the mind is sometimes carried away to the contemplation of sublime things, and in its longing for them it is tortured by a kind of weeping which it enjoys. The soul feels pain at still being here where it continues to lie helpless, brought to the ground through its lack of strength, and not yet being there, where it would flourish amid bright light and not be already turning the eye of the mind back to the darkness of our mortal condition. From this, yes from this a warm glow is born in the mind, and from this glow sorrow arises. And because it is not yet strong enough to cling to heavenly things, the mind rests, worn out by its ardour, amid tears. But the progress of an individual is one thing, and the edification of many is another. Therefore, God being the giver, the word of instruction has to put forward things which set in order the lives and conduct of those who listen. Now, therefore, let us seek out in the words of the prophet, just as we have begun to do, whatever may build us up, so that we are eager for good works.

In his second homily on the book of Ezekiel, Gregory discusses the circumstances in which the word of the Lord came to the prophet, who was by the river Chebar [Ezek. 1:3], paying particular attention to the significance of the proper nouns used in the text. The meanings of the words in Hebrew had been explained by Jerome, a scholar of that language whose explanations Gregory largely follows.[4] Gregory treats the names in the Old Testament in the same way he does events: in his understanding, everything is related to Christ.

1.2.6 These Hebrew words are most useful in our understanding the mystery. For Chebar means weightiness or heaviness, Ezekiel the strength of God, Buzi despised or looked down on, and Chaldeans those who bring into captivity, like demons. And so, Ezekiel came by the river Chebar, and because Chebar means weightiness or heaviness, what corresponds to the river Chebar but the human race? It is something that flows down from its origin towards death, and it makes itself heavy through sins, those it commits and those it is carrying, because, as it is written, *Wickedness takes its seat in a weighty piece of lead* [cf. Zech. 5:7f.]. Every sin is heavy, because it does not allow a soul to be lifted up towards higher things. And so it is said through the psalmist, *Sons of men, for how long will your hearts be heavy?* [Ps. 4:3 Vulg.]. But it is written of the Lord: *He is the power of God and the wisdom of God* [1 Cor. 1:24]. And so Ezekiel came by the river Chebar because, through the mystery of his incarnation, the strength of God condescended to draw near to the human race which, carrying the burdens of its sins, was flowing down from its origin towards death every day, just as it is said of him through the psalmist: *And he will be like a tree planted by the rivers of water.*[5] Yes, he was planted by the rivers of water, because he became incarnate alongside the steady movement of the peoples who were flowing downward.[6] Now we have said that Ezekiel has the meaning strength of God, and Buzi despised. But Ezekiel is the son of Buzi, because God's only-begotten condescended to take flesh from that people whom the Lord despised because of their sin of unbelief. Therefore, the strength of God is born from that which is held in contempt and despised, because our Redeemer condescended to assume humanity from a misbelieving and despised people. He came into the land of the Chaldeans. As we have said, Chaldeans means those who bring into captivity, like demons. It cannot be doubted that wicked people, who do wicked things themselves and beguilingly persuade others to act wickedly, are those who bring into captivity. They are also rightly understood as being like demons, because, although they are not demons by nature, those who entice others to wickedness are taking upon themselves the function of demons in order to promote wickedness. And so the strength of God came into the land of the Chaldeans, because the only-begotten of the Father appeared among people who were flowing downward towards sin in their own right, and drawing others along towards sins, bringing them into captivity.

Working from what may seem unpromising material, Gregory uses passages in the book of Ezekiel to state some key principles of biblical interpretation. The prophet reported receiving a vision of a wheel upon the earth beside living creatures, which had four faces [Ezek. 1:15]. If this were not hard enough to understand, he went on to describe more than one wheel:

1.6.12 *And the appearance of the wheels and their function was like a vision of the sea; and the four had one likeness, and their appearance and operation was like that of a wheel in the middle of a wheel* [Ezek. 1:16]. What is this thing, spoken of as one wheel, to which is added a little later *like a wheel in the middle of a wheel*, unless the New Testament, which lay hidden allegorically in the letter of the Old Testament? So it is that the same wheel which appeared beside the living creatures is described as having four faces, because over the two testaments holy scripture is divided into four parts, the Old Testament into the law and the prophets,[7] and the New into the gospels and the acts and sayings of the apostles. We know that, wherever we turn our face, we see what is to be seen there. Therefore the wheel has four faces, because first it sees among the peoples wrong deeds which have to be restrained through the law, later it sees among human failings those things which should be restrained through the prophets, then with greater subtlety through the gospel, and finally it looks upon them through the apostles. It can also be understood that the wheel should have four faces for this reason: holy scripture, having been spread through the grace of preaching, has become known in the four parts of the world. And so one and the same wheel is well described as having first appeared beside the living creatures and later having had four faces, because were the law not in harmony with the gospel, it would not have become known in the four parts of the world.

13   There follows: *And the appearance of the wheels and their function was like a vision of the sea* [Ezek. 1:16]. The holy utterances are rightly said to be similar to a vision of the sea, because they contain great ideas which roll, and meanings like waves. And sacred scripture is not undeservedly said to be similar to the sea, because the ideas it expresses are confirmed by the sacrament of baptism. Now we must bear in mind that we sail in ships at sea when we are on our way to the lands we long for. And what is it that we long for but that land of which it is written: *My portion in the land of the living* [Ps. 142:5]? But as I have said, someone who crosses the sea is carried on wood. And we know that through the law holy scripture gives us advance notice of the wood of the cross, when it says: *Cursed is everyone who hangs on wood* [Deut. 21:22]. Paul attests this of our Redeemer, saying: *He was made a curse for us* [Gal. 3:13]. It also speaks of wood through the prophets, when it says: *The Lord reigned from the tree*,[8] and again: *Let us cast wood into his bread*.[9] But through the gospel, where the passion of the Lord which had been prophesied is revealed, the wood of the cross is displayed openly. Through the apostles this same cross is insisted upon in both words and deeds, as when Paul says: *The world is crucified to me, and I to the world*, and again: *Far be it from me that I should glory, save in the cross of our Lord Jesus Christ* [Gal. 6:14]. Therefore, for we who are making our ways towards our eternal homeland, holy scripture is a sea because of its four faces. It speaks of the cross, because it carries us to the land of the living by means of wood. Had not the prophet seen holy scripture as being like the sea, he certainly would not have said: *The earth has been filled with the knowledge of the Lord, as the waters cover the sea* [Isa. 11:9]. It goes on:

14   And these four had one likeness, and their appearance and operation was like that of a wheel in the middle of a wheel [Ezek. 1:16]. These four had one likeness, because what the law predicts, the

prophets do as well; what the prophets make known in advance the gospel brings out in the open; what the gospel brought out in the open the apostles have preached throughout the world. Therefore the four have one likeness, because the books of the Bible, despite being separated by time, are nevertheless united in their meaning.

15 *And their appearance and operation was like that of a wheel in the middle of a wheel.* The wheel in the middle of a wheel is, as we have said, the New Testament within the Old Testament, because the New Testament makes clear what the Old Testament indicated. For, to mention just a few things among many, what is Eve brought forth from the side of Adam as he slept but the church being formed from Christ as he was dying?[10] What is Isaac, who was led to the sacrifice, carried wood, placed on the altar, and lived [Gen. 22:6–13], but our Redeemer, who was led to the passion and carried the wood of the cross himself? And so he died as a sacrifice for us in accordance with his human nature, while nevertheless remaining immortal in accordance with his divine nature. What is the murderer freed after the death of the high priest and returning to his own land [Num. 35:25–8; Josh. 20:6] but the human race which, after it had brought death on itself by sinning, was freed from the chains of its sins after the death of the true priest, that is our Redeemer, and restored to the possession of paradise? Why is it ordered that there be a place of atonement inside the tabernacle, with two cherubim of pure gold placed upon it, one at each end, stretching their wings and covering the mercy seat, looking towards each other with their faces turned towards the mercy seat, unless the two Testaments are concordant concerning *the Mediator between God and humanity* [1 Tim. 2:5], so that what one signifies, the other brings out in the open [Exek. 25:17–20]? What is indicated by the place of atonement, but the Redeemer of the human race himself? Of him it is said through Paul: *Whom God has set forth to be a propitiation through faith in his blood.*[11] What is meant by the two cherubim, which are called the fullness of knowledge, but both Testaments? One of them stands at one end of the mercy seat, the other at the other, because what the Old Testament begins to promise concerning the incarnation of our Redeemer by way of prophecy, the New Testament states has been fully accomplished. The two cherubim are made of pure gold, because what is written down in both Testaments is the pure and unadulterated truth. They stretch their wings and cover the mercy seat, because we, people through whom almighty God speaks, are protected from the failings which threaten us by the strengthening teaching of sacred Scripture. When we consider its teachings attentively, we are protected by its wings from the error of ignorance. But the two cherubim look

towards each other, their faces turned towards the mercy seat, because neither Testament disagrees from the other in any respect. And as it were they keep their faces turned towards each other, because what one promises the other reveals, looking as they do upon *the Mediator between God and humanity* placed between them.[12] The cherubim would have turned their faces away from each other, if one Testament denied what the other promised. But since they speak in agreement about *the Mediator between God and humanity*, they face the mercy seat so that they are looking at each other. Therefore, the wheel was in the middle of a wheel, because the New Testament is present within the Old Testament. And, just as we have often remarked already, the New Testament makes clear what the Old promises, and what the one brings news of in a hidden way, the other shouts out as being having been openly revealed. Therefore, the Old Testament is a prophecy of the New Testament, and the New Testament an exposition of the Old Testament. It goes on:

16 *Where they went, they went on their four sides, without turning* [Ezek. 1:17]. Where else do the divine scriptures go, but to human hearts? But they go along on their four sides, because sacred scripture goes to human hearts through the law as it points to the mystery. It goes a little more openly through the prophets as it prophesies the Lord. It goes through the gospel, by showing forth what it prophesied. It goes through the apostles, by preaching the one whom the Father showed forth for our redemption. Therefore the wheels have both faces and paths, because the holy scriptures make us aware of precepts and give us examples of how to carry them out. And they go on their four sides because, as we have said above, they speak at different times, or at any rate because they preach the incarnate Lord in all the regions of the earth. Concerning them it immediately adds, in a very clear way:

17 *and they did not turn back when they went* [Ezek. 1:17]. These things above were said with reference to the living creatures, but the things which can be understood of the living creatures cannot be understood of the wheels. Now the Old Testament indeed made its way forward, because it came to human minds through preaching, but afterwards it moved backwards, because its precepts and sacrifices were not able to be observed in their fullness according to the letter. For it did not remain without being changed, because it was not understood in a spiritual way. But when our Redeemer came into the world, he made that which he found being observed in a carnal way able to be understood in a spiritual way.[13] Therefore, when its letter is understood spiritually, every carnal thing displayed within it is given

life. But the New Testament is also called the eternal testament, even through the pages of the Old Testament,[14] because its meaning is never changed. It is therefore well said that the wheels went and did not turn back when they went, because, with the New Testament not being annulled when the Old comes to be observed with a spiritual understanding, the testaments do not turn back after themselves, and remain unchangeable until the end of the world. Therefore they make their way but are not turned back, because they come to our heart spiritually in such a way that their precepts and basic thrust are never changed. There follows:

18 *The wheels were also upright, high and frightening to look at* [Ezek. 1:18]. Why is it that these three things are recorded as pertaining to the language of holy scripture, it being said that it is upright, high, and frightening to look at, that is terrifying? We need to find out in what respects the divine scriptures are spoken of as upright, high and frightening to look at. It should be known that an upright stance is appropriate for someone doing well, so it is said through Paul: *The one who stands should take heed lest he falls* [1 Cor. 10:12]. He also said to his disciples: *So stand fast in the Lord, my dearly beloved* [Phil. 4:1]. And the prophet, who saw himself standing before the Lord by virtue of his life and conduct, said: *The Lord lives, in whose sight I stand* [2 Kgs. 3:14]. But height is the promise of the heavenly kingdom, which is attained when everything which can corrupt in mortal life has been brought under control. And hell, which tortures the reprobates endlessly and keeps them in their tortures for ever, so dreadful, is frightening to look at. Therefore, holy scripture is upright because of its righteous instruction, high because of the loftiness of what is promised above, and frightening to look at because of the threats and terrors of the judgment which will follow. Consequently, holy scripture has uprightness, for it directs us to stand firm in our conduct, so that the minds of those who hear it are not bent over in earthly desirings. It has height, for it promises the joys of eternal life in the homeland of heaven. It is also frightening to look at, for it threatens all the reprobates with the punishments of hell. Therefore, it displays uprightness in the way it builds up conduct, height in its promise of rewards, and a frightening appearance in the terrifying punishments. For it is upright in its precepts, high in its promises, and frightening in its threats. It has uprightness when it says through the prophet: *Put aside your perverse deeds, learn to do well, seek judgment, relieve the oppressed, judge the orphan, plead for the widow* [Isa. 1:16f.]. And again: *Break your bread for the hungry, and bring the needy that are cast out into your house, cover the naked person that you see, and do not hide yourself from your*

own family [Isa. 58:7]. It has height when it says through the same prophet: *No longer will the sun be your light by day, neither will the brightness of the moon give you light, but the Lord shall be for you an everlasting light; your God shall be your glory* [Isa. 60:19]. It has a frightening appearance when, describing hell, it says: *The day of the Lord's vengeance, the year of recompense when Zion is judged, and its streams shall be turned into pitch and its soil into brimstone, and its land shall become burning pitch; it will not be extinguished, day or night, for ever* [Isa. 34:8–10]. Blessed Job also describes this, saying: *The darkened land covered with the blackness of death, the land of woe and darkness where the shadow of death lies, chaotic, the dwelling place of everlasting terror* [Job 10:21f.]. Scripture has height when the Lord makes a promise through it, saying in a kindly fashion: *Just as the new heaven and new earth, which I am making to stand before me, says the Lord, so shall your seed and your name stand* [Isa. 66:22]. They in truth stand before the Lord, who do not squander their lives in perverse behaviour. It has height when it continues immediately: *And from one month to another, and one Sabbath to another, all flesh shall come to worship before me, says the Lord* [Isa. 66:23]. What is a month but a perfect fullness of days?[15] And what is a Sabbath, but a time of rest when the work done by slaves is not permitted? And so *from one month to another*, because those who are living perfectly here are led to perfect glory there. And from *one Sabbath to another*, because those who desist from perverse work here rest there in the reward of heaven. Scripture also has a frightening appearance when it immediately adds: *And they will go forth and see the carcasses of men, those who walked crookedly against me. Their worm shall not die, neither shall their fire be quenched* [Isa. 66:24]. Could anything more frightening be said or imagined, than to receive the wounds of damnation and for the pain of wounds never to be finished? Concerning the frightening appearance of the wheels it was well said through Sophonia, when it was made known that a day of judgment was going to catch up with the hard hearted: *The great day of the Lord is at hand, at hand and coming quickly. Bitter is the voice of the day of the Lord, when the strong will be sorely troubled. A day of wrath, that day, a day of trouble and affliction, a day of disaster and wretchedness, a day of darkness and murkiness, a day of cloud and whirlwind, a day of the trumpet and the clang of metal* [Soph. 1:14–16].

19 But as we have been speaking of the outer wheel, there remains a need to speak concerning the uprightness, height and frightening appearance of the inner wheel. Now the inner wheel has height when it prohibits us through the holy gospel from bending over to earthly desires, saying in the words of our Redeemer: *Take heed lest your hearts be made heavy with dissipation and drunkenness, and in the cares of this life*

[Luke 21:34]. It has height when it gives a promise concerning the same Redeemer, saying: *As many as believed in him, to them he gave power to become the children of God* [John 1:12]. Could anything higher than this power be spoken of, anything more lofty than this height, through which a created being is made the child of the Creator? It has a frightening appearance when it speaks of the reprobate, saying: *These shall go away into everlasting punishment* [Matt. 25:46]. It has height when Truth admonishes his disciples, saying: *Sell what you have and give alms. Provide yourselves with purses which will not grow old* [Luke 12:33]. It has height in promising, when it says: *They will come from the east and the west, and recline with Abraham and Isaac and Jacob in the kingdom of heaven* [Matt. 8:11]. It has a frightening appearance when it adds: *The sons of the kingdom shall be cast forth into outer darkness; there shall be weeping and the gnashing of teeth* [Matt. 8:12]. Again, it is said to these people in the voice of the Truth: *You shall die in your sins* [John 8:21, 24]. It has height when it says in the words of the first shepherd: *Add to your faith virtue, and to virtue knowledge, and to knowledge abstinence, and to abstinence patience, and to patience due respect, and to due respect love of the brothers, and to love of the brothers charity* [2 Pet. 1:5–7]. It has height when it says a little afterwards: *For there will be provided for you in abundance an entrance into the eternal kingdom of our Lord and Saviour Jesus Christ* [2 Pet. 1:11]. Again, a promise is given to good shepherds, saying: *When the chief shepherd shall appear, you will receive an unfading crown of glory* [1 Pet. 5:4]. It has a frightening appearance, when it says: *The day of the Lord is coming like a thief, in which the heavens will pass away with great violence and the elements melt with the heat* [2 Pet. 3:10]. And so, since all these things must melt away, what kind of people is it right for you to be, who are engaged in holy actions and proper conduct, awaiting and hastening the coming of the day of God, through which the burning heavens will melt, and the elements be consumed by the heat of the fire? It has height when it raises us up from earthly desires through Paul, saying: *Mortify your members which are upon the earth, fornication, uncleanness, inordinate affection, evil concupiscence, and covetousness, which is idolatry* [Col. 3:5]. It has height when it gives a promise, saying: *Your life is hidden with Christ in God. For when Christ your life shall appear, then shall you also appear with him in glory* [Col. 3:3f.]. It has a frightening appearance when it threatens, saying: *In the revealing of our Lord Jesus Christ from heaven, with his mighty angels, taking vengeance in the flaming fire on those who do not know God, and those who do not obey the gospel of our Lord Jesus Christ, who will experience everlasting punishments of destruction, away from the presence of the Lord, and from the glory of his power* [2 Thess. 1:7–9]. It has height when it admonishes us, saying: *See that no-one return evil for evil to any person, but always follow what is good, towards each other and towards everyone* [1 Thess. 5:15]. It has height when it gives a promise, saying: *If we be dead with him, we shall live with him; if we suffer, we shall also reign with him* [2 Tim. 2:11f.]. And again: *The sufferings of this present time are not worth comparing with the glory which shall be revealed in us* [Rom. 8:18]. It has a frightening appearance when it threatens, saying: *A frightening prospect of judgment, and a fiery indignation, which shall devour the adversaries* [Heb. 10:27]. Again, he says: *It is a frightening thing to fall into the hands of the living God* [Heb. 10:31]. He also brings all these things together in a short statement, saying: *So that you might be able to comprehend with all the saints what is the breadth, length, height and depth* [Eph. 3:18]. Charity is indeed broad, for it has room for the love of enemies and tolerates them with patience, through the same love with which almighty God loves us so broadly. We ought therefore to show to our neighbours this quality which we see shown to us, in our unworthiness, by our Creator. Therefore, the breadth and length pertain to height, which expands our way of living through love, so that brotherly love tolerates bad things with patience. Height is being recompensed with eternal rewards, concerning the immensity of which it is said: *The eye has not seen, nor the ear heard, nor has there risen up into the heart of man, the things which God has prepared for those who love him* [1 Cor. 2:9]. It therefore has elevation in height, because no process of thinking is now able to gain an idea of the everlasting joys of the saints. And its depth is that condemnation, incalculably great, to punishment, which will plunge into the bottommost part of those it receives. In these respects the holy scriptures have a frightening appearance, because when they speak of the punishments of hell they strike terror beyond reckoning into those who hear them. And so it is well said: *The wheels were upright, high and frightening to look at* [Ezek. 1:18], because in both testaments holy scripture is of upright stance when it admonishes, high when it promises, and frightening when it threatens.

Let it be enough, dearest brothers, for us to have said these things today by the gift of God, so that, refreshed by a rest, we may return to discuss the material which follows, trusting in Jesus Christ, God the author of all things and Our Lord, who lives and reigns with the Father in the unity of the Holy Spirit, God for ever and ever. Amen.

The emphasis on moral instruction in Gregory's preaching on the Bible may suggest that he was not concerned with preaching doctrine. As the following passage indicates, this is not true. It shows Gregory arguing from the Bible, as well as examples from the natural world, for the resurrection of the body. He begins with the resurrection of Jesus.

Moralia

14.55.69 Therefore we derive hope for our resurrection from reflecting on the glory of our Head. But in case someone, quietly thinking things over, should say that he, being both God and man together, overcame the death which he incurred from his humanity by virtue of his divinity, whereas we, being merely human, are unable to rise from the condemnation of death, it was right that at the time of his resurrection the bodies of many saints rose as well, so that he might both give us an example in himself and strengthen us through the resurrection of others who were like us in being merely human, since, should a man despair of receiving what the one who was both God and man showed forth in himself, he would be able to assume that something which he knew had occurred to people who were beyond doubt merely human could also take place in himself.

70 But there are some people who, observing that the spirit is released from the flesh, that the flesh becomes rotten, that what is rotten is turned into dust, and that the dust is so completely dissolved into its elements that human eyes are utterly unable to see it, abandon hope in the possibility of the resurrection; and when they look upon dry bones, they are not confident that they can again be clothed in flesh and become green with life. If these people do not hold onto faith in the resurrection because of obedience, they ought certainly to hold onto it because of reason. For what does the world imitate in its elements every day if not our resurrection? Yes, as the moments of the day pass the light which lasts for a time undergoes a kind of death when, with the arrival of the darkness of night, the light which was looked upon is taken away, and it undergoes a kind of rising again, when the light which had been removed from our sight is restored as night is brought to an end. Moreover, as the seasons pass we see trees lose their green leaves and stop producing fruit; and suddenly, look, a kind of resurrection comes as we see leaves burst forth as if from withered wood, pieces of fruit growing, and the whole tree clothed with a beauty that lives again. All the time we see tiny seeds of trees entrusted to the damp earth, from which not long afterwards we behold great trees arising, bringing forth leaves and pieces of fruit. Let us therefore think about the tiny seed of some tree which is cast in the ground so that a tree may be produced from it, and let us see if we can understand whereabouts the huge tree which came forth from it, the

wood, the bark, the green leaves and the abundant fruit lay hidden inside such a tiny seed. Is it really possible that any such thing was to be seen in such a seed when it was lying in the ground? And yet, with the Maker of all things secretly arranging everything in a wonderful way, the hardness of bark was lying hidden in the soft seed, mighty strength was concealed in its weakness, and the bearing of abundant fruit in its dryness. So why be surprised if the one who forms great trees from very fine seeds should again, when he wishes, shape very fine dust which was reduced into its elements away from our sight into a human being?[16] And so, because we have been created as beings with reason, we should derive hope for our resurrection from what we see of things and turning them over in our mind. But because the sense of reason has become sluggish in us, the grace of the Redeemer has come towards us as an example. For indeed our Creator came, experienced death, and showed forth the resurrection, so that we who were reluctant to have hope in the resurrection on the ground of reason would hold onto it through his help and example. Therefore blessed Job can say: *I know that my Redeemer lives, and at the last day I shall rise from the earth.*[17] And any one who despairs of experiencing the power of the resurrection in himself ought to blush at the words of a faithful person among the gentiles, and consider how heavy a penalty should be borne by someone who, knowing that the Lord's resurrection has already taken place, still does not believe in his own, when someone who was still hoping in that of the Lord believed that his own would take place as well.

71 But consider, I hear the word 'resurrection', yet I am enquiring into how this resurrection is effected. For truly, I believe that I shall rise again, but I want to hear in what way. In fact, I want to know whether I shall rise in some other body, perhaps a very fine one, like the air, or that in which I die. But if I rise in a body like the air, it will not be really me who rises again. For how is it a true resurrection, if the flesh cannot be real? Reason clearly suggests that, if the flesh is not real, beyond doubt the resurrection will not be real. For it cannot properly be called a resurrection, if that which rises again is not that which fell. Take these clouds of doubt away from us, blessed Job, and because, through the grace of the Holy Spirit which you have received, you have begun to speak to us of the hope of our resurrection, show clearly if our flesh truly rises again.

There follows:

56.72 *And again I shall be enclosed within my skin* [Job 19:26 Vulg.]. When the word skin is used so clearly, every doubt about a true resurrection is removed, because in that glorious resurrection our bodies will not be incapable of being touched and more subtle than the wind and air, as Eutychius, bishop of the city of Constantinople wrote. For in that glorious resurrection our body will indeed be subtle because of the operation of a spiritual power, but it will be able to be touched because of its very nature. So it was that our Redeemer showed the disciples who doubted his resurrection his hands and side, and exposed his bones and flesh so they could touch them, saying: *Touch and see, because a spirit does not have flesh and bones such as you see I have* [Luke 24:39]. When, having been placed in the city of Constantinople, I brought forth this testimony of the truth from the gospel to that Eutychius, he said: 'The Lord did this for a reason: to remove doubt as to his resurrection from the hearts of his disciples.'[18] I said to him: 'What you are arguing is amazing, for it turns something which cured the hearts of the disciples from doubt into a cause of doubt for us! For could anything worse be said than something which turns that which brought his disciples back from all their doubt to faith into a source of doubt for us as to his true flesh? For if it is argued he did not have what he showed, something which strengthened the faith of his disciples destroys ours.' He went on to say: 'He had a body which could be touched and he showed it; but after he had strengthened the hearts of those who touched it, everything in the Lord which could be touched was turned into something subtle.' I replied to this, saying: 'It is written: *Christ rising again from the dead dies no more; death has no more dominion over him* [Rom. 6:9]. Therefore, if there was something in his body which could be changed after the resurrection, the Lord returned to death after the resurrection, contrary to the true statement of Paul. What fool could take it upon himself to say this, other than someone who denied the reality of his resurrection in the flesh?' Then he taunted me, saying: 'Since it is written *Flesh and blood cannot possess the kingdom of God* [1 Cor. 15:50], we have no reason to believe that the flesh truly rises.' I said to him: 'In sacred scripture the word flesh is sometimes used in its natural meaning and sometimes refers to sin or corruption. Flesh is used in its natural meaning when it is written: *Now this is bone of my bones, and flesh of my flesh* [Gen. 2:23], and *The Word became flesh and dwelt among us* [John 1:14]. But flesh refers to sin when it is written: *My spirit shall not remain among men, because they are flesh* [Gen. 6:3], and when the psalmist says: *He remembered that they were but flesh, a wind that passes away and does not return* [Ps. 78:39]. So it is that Paul said to his disciples: *But you are not in the flesh, but in the Spirit* [Rom. 8:9]. For it was not the case that those to whom he sent epistles were not in the flesh, but because they had overcame the passions of fleshly desires and were already free in the strength of the Spirit they were not 'in the flesh'. Therefore, when the apostle Paul said *Flesh and blood cannot possess the kingdom of God* [1 Cor. 15:50], he wanted the word flesh to be understood with reference to sin, not with reference to nature. And so, shortly after, he shows that he used the word flesh with reference to sin, saying *Neither shall corruption inherit incorruption* [1 Cor. 15:50]. Therefore, in the glory of the kingdom of heaven there will be flesh according to nature, but it will not be according to the desires of passion, because when the sting of death has been overcome it will reign in everlasting incorruption.'

73 Eutychius immediately responded that he agreed with what I said, but he still denied that a body could rise again and be able to be touched. In the treatise he wrote concerning the resurrection he had also made use of the evidence of the apostle Paul, who says: *What you sow will not come to life unless it first dies, and what you sow is not the body that is to be, but a bare kernel* [1 Cor. 15:36f.]. Drawing too hasty a conclusion, he said that the flesh will either be able to be touched or not be itself, since the holy apostle, when treating the glory of the resurrection, said that the body that is sown is not the body that is to be. But here he is answered quickly. For the apostle Paul, in saying *What you sow is not the body that is to be, but a bare kernel*, is describing something we can see, that a kernel sown without a stem and leaves comes up with a stem and leaves. Therefore Paul, making more of the glory of the resurrection, did not say that a kernel of seed lacked what it had been, but that there was present something which it had not been. But Eutychius, when he denies that the true body rises again, does not at all say there is present what had been lacking, but that something which had been there was lacking.

74 Having become embroiled in a lengthy dispute on this matter, in our bitter controversy we were beginning to avoid each other when the emperor Tiberius Constantine of good memory, receiving myself and him in private, informed himself as to the nature of our disagreement. Weighing the arguments made on either side, he demolished the book he had written about the resurrection with arguments of his own and ordered that it was to be destroyed by fire. On departing from him, I straightaway came down with a serious illness, and Eutychius became ill and died. After his death, as there was scarcely anyone who followed his teachings, I decided to take what I had begun no further, in case I seemed to be hurling words into ashes. But while he was still alive and I had come down with violent fevers, he used to hold the skin of his hand before the eyes of all my acquaintants who went to him bearing greetings, as I knew from what they told me, and said

'I confess that we shall all rise in this flesh.' Previously, he used to deny this utterly, as they themselves said.

75   But, putting aside these things, let us examine with great care in the words of blessed Job whether there will be a true resurrection and a true body in the resurrection. For look, we cannot now be in any doubt concerning hope for the resurrection, when he says: *And at the last day I shall rise up from the earth* [Job 19:25]. He also takes away doubt concerning the true restoration of the body, when he says: *And again I shall be clad in my skin* [Job 19:26].

Now he adds, to take away anything we do not understand clearly:

76   *And in my flesh I shall see God* [Job 19:26]. See how he speaks in plain words of the resurrection, the skin, and the flesh. Is there anything left which could cause our mind to doubt? If, therefore, this holy man believed, prior to the fact of the Lord's resurrection, that the flesh would be brought back to a state of completeness, what guilt will attach to our doubting, if the true resurrection of the flesh is not believed in even after there is the example of the Redeemer? For if the body will not be able to be touched after the resurrection, assuredly someone other than the person who died will rise and something which is wicked to say is believed, that I shall die and someone else rise again. And so I ask you, blessed Job, add what you feel and take away from us any doubt on this point.

There follows:

77   *Whom I shall see for myself and my eyes shall behold, and not another* [Job 19:27]. For if, as certain followers of errors think, after the resurrection the body will not be able to be touched but a subtle, invisible body will be called flesh, although it may not be the substance of flesh, it will obviously be one person who dies and another who rises again. But blessed Job destroys their opinion with a voice which conveys the truth, when he says: *Whom I shall see for myself and my eyes shall behold, and not another.* Let us, following the faith of blessed Job and believing that the body of our Redeemer was truly able to be touched after the resurrection, confess that our flesh will be both the same and different after the resurrection: the same in nature but different in glory; the same in truth but different in power. And so it will be subtle, because it will also be incorruptible. It will be able to be touched, because it will not lose the essence of its true nature. But the holy man adds with what confidence he is able to possess faith in this resurrection, with how much certainty he can anticipate it.

There follows:

58.78 *This my hope is placed in my lap* [Job 19:27 Vulg.]. We believe that we possess nothing more securely than that which we hold in our lap. Therefore the hope he held was placed in his lap, because his hope in the resurrection was one of complete confidence. But, having indicated that the day of the resurrection would come, now, whether speaking in his own person or as a symbol of the holy and universal church, he rebukes the deeds of evil people, and predicts the judgment which follows on the day of the resurrection.

For he immediately adds:

59.79 *Why then do you now say: Let us pursue him and find the root of a word against him? Therefore flee from the face of the sword, since the sword is the avenger of iniquities, and know there is a judgment* [Job 19:28f. Vulg.]. Now in the first statement he rebukes the deeds of wicked people, and in the second he reveals the punishments which come from the divine judgment. For he says: *Why then do you now say: Let us pursue him and find the root of a word against him?* Perverse people who listen with the wrong kind of keenness to things which are spoken fittingly and try to find in the speech of a just man a means of accusing him, what do they seek against him other than the root of a word, from which they may derive a starting point for what they say, and broaden the branches of evil chatter when they accuse him? But when a holy man sustains such things from evil people, he does not speak against them, but rather grieves for them and rebukes their wrongful ideas, and shows them the evils from which they should flee, saying: *Therefore flee from the face of the sword, since the sword is the avenger of iniquities, and know that there is a judgment.* Any person who acts perversely, even in not being bothered to fear it, does not know that there is a judgment of God. For if he knew that this was to be feared, he would not do those things which must be punished in it. For there are very many who are aware that there is a last judgment in theory, but by their perverse behaviour they indicate that they do not know about it. For a person who does not dread this as he should, has not yet found out about the whirlwind of alarm with which it will come. For if he knew how to weigh up the heaviness of the trial which we must dread, in his fear he would most certainly take precautions against the day of wrath. To *flee from the face of the sword* is to appease the sentence of strict punishment before it appears. For the awe inspired by the Judge can only be avoided before the judgment. Now he is not seen, but he is appeased by prayers. But when he is seated in that fearful judgment, he will then be able to be seen but not to be appeased, because in his wrath he will all at once repay all the deeds of the wicked which he long tolerated in silence. And so we must fear the Judge now, when he is not yet exercising judgment, when he maintains his long-held toleration, when he continues to put up with the evils he sees, in case, when he stretches out his hand in vengeful retribution, the strictness with which he executes judgment is proportionate to the period during which he was waiting before the judgment.

3

SERMONS TO THE PEOPLE

Sometimes Gregory's teaching, with its resolutely allegorizing tendency and the great interest he displays in the introspective concerns of elite groups, can seem remote from the lives of ordinary people. But in his capacity as bishop, Gregory found it necessary to preach regularly to a congregation of decidedly ordinary believers. In the following two homilies we see him pitching his message to such an audience. The first was delivered following a reading in the liturgy of John 21:1–14, three days after Easter, in the basilica of the martyr Laurence, the church now known as San Lorenzo fuori le Mura, to the south-east of the city. The church had recently been the object of papal interest, for Gregory's predecessor pope Pelagius II had rebuilt it, and a mosaic still to be seen in the church shows him offering a model of it to Christ.

Homitiae xl in Evangelia

24.1   The passage from the holy gospel which has just been read out in your hearing, my brothers and sisters, raises a question in the mind, but the very raising of it should indicate a need to be discerning.[1] For it can be asked why Peter, who was a fisherman before his conversion, went back to fishing; and in the light of what the Truth says, *No-one, having put his hand to the plough, and looking back, is fit for the kingdom of God* [Luke 9:62], why he went back to that which he had left? But if discernment is employed, it is quickly seen that there was no guilt in going back to an occupation which, having been without sin before his conversion, was so after his conversion as well. For we know that Peter was a fisherman, but Matthew a tax collector, and after his conversion Peter went back to fishing, but Matthew did not sit again at the tax office, because it is one thing to seek food by fishing, and another to increase one's wealth by profits made from collecting tax. For there are many kinds of work which can scarcely, if at all, be engaged in without sins. And so it is necessary that after conversion the mind does not run back to things which entangle it in sin.

2   It can also be asked why the Lord, who had walked on the waves of the sea in the presence of his disciples before his resurrection, stood on the shore as the disciples were toiling at sea after his resurrection. The reason for this is quickly grasped, if thought is given to the relevant circumstances. For what does the sea signify but the present world, its crashing breakers the tumults of affairs and the waves of a life subject to corruption? What is represented by the firmness of the shore but an eternal, everlasting quiet? Therefore, because the disciples were still caught up in the waves of mortal life, they were toiling in the sea. But because our Redeemer had by then passed beyond the corruptible nature of the flesh, after his resurrection he stood on the shore, as if he were speaking to his disciples of the mystery of his resurrection through what was happening, and saying: 'Now I do not appear to you at sea, because I am not with you amid the tossing waves.' Hence in another place he says to his same disciples after his resurrection: *These are the words which I spoke to you while I was still with you* [Luke 24:44]. Now it is obvious that he was with those people to whom he appeared in person in his body, but nevertheless he said he was now not with them, the immortality of his flesh set him apart from the mortality of their bodies.[2] And so what he asserts there when he is placed with them; that he is not with them, he reveals here by the location of his body as well, when he shows those still at sea that he is already on the shore.

3   It was brought about that the disciples found the fishing very hard, and this was so that there would be the highest wonder at the teacher as he came along. Immediately he said: *Cast the net on the right side of the boat and you will find* [John 21:6]. Twice in the holy gospel we read that the Lord ordered nets to be cast for fishing, once before his passion and once after his resurrection [cf. Luke 5:4–6]. But whereas our Redeemer, before he suffered and rose again, simply ordered that the net be cast for fishing, without ordering that it be cast to the right or to the left, when he appeared to the disciples after his resurrection he ordered that the net was to be cast to the right. In the first haul of fish so many were caught that the nets were broken; in the second as well many were caught, but the nets were not broken. Now who does not know that good people are represented by the right hand side, and bad people by the left? Therefore the first haul of fish, for which no order was given as to the side to which the net was to be cast, denotes the church of the present day, gathering together the good and the bad at the same time and not choosing who is pulled in, because it does not know those whom it is able to choose. But the second haul of fish,

which took place after the resurrection of the Lord, was directed only to the right, because only the church of the elect, which will have nothing in common with bad work,[3] attains the vision of his glorious brightness. In the first haul the quantity of fish meant that the net was broken, because many reprobates, people who break the church asunder with heresies, are now coming to the confession of faith together with the elect. But in the second haul many large fish are caught and the net is not broken, because the holy church of the elect, reposing in the uninterrupted peace of her Creator, is not torn by any controversies.

4   When fish of such a size had been caught, *Simon Peter went up and pulled the net to land* [John 21:11]. I believe that your charity can already see why it was Peter who pulled the net to land.[4] Yes, the holy church has been entrusted to him; to him in particular it is said: *Simon son of John, do you love me? Feed my sheep* [John 21:17]. And so what is revealed later in words is now signified in deed. Therefore, because the church's preacher separates us from the waves of this world, it is most necessary that Peter pulls the net full of fishes to land. He is the one who drags the fishes to the firmness of the shore, because with the voice of holy preaching he reveals to the faithful the stability of the eternal homeland. He did this by speaking, he did it by letters, and he does it every day by miracles.[5] Whenever we are converted through him to the love of everlasting quiet, whenever we are separated from the turbulence of earthly things, what are we but fish, placed inside the net of faith, being pulled to the shore?

But having said that the net was full of large fish, it adds how many there were, one hundred and fifty-three. The number contains a great mystery, but the mystery that lies in wait there for your eager attention is very deep. The fact is, the evangelist would not have taken the trouble to state the exact number, had he not considered it full of mystery. Now you know that in the Old Testament everything good we do is enjoined by the ten commandments, but in the New the strength to do the same good things is given to the larger number of the faithful through the sevenfold grace of the Holy Spirit. The prophet, in making him known in advance, says: *The Spirit of wisdom and understanding, the Spirit of counsel and fortitude, the Spirit of knowledge and goodness, and the Spirit of the fear of the Lord will fill him.*[6] But that person obtains a good work in the Spirit, who acknowledges the faith of the Trinity, so that he believes that the Father and the Son and the same Holy Spirit are of one power, and confesses they are of one substance. Because, therefore, the seven things of which we spoke above are expressed more broadly through the New Testament, but the ten commandments through the Old, all our strength and the good we do is fully comprised by the number seventeen. Therefore, let us multiply seventeen by three, and it comes to fifty-one. This number certainly does not lack a great mystery, because we read in the Old Testament an order that the fiftieth year was to be called a jubilee, in which the whole people would rest from all toil [Lev. 25:11]. But true rest is an undivided unit. Now a single unit cannot be divided; where there is a process of division, there is no true rest. Let us therefore multiply fifty-one by three, and it comes to a hundred and fifty-three. Because, therefore, everything we do which shows forth the faith of the Trinity tends towards rest, we multiply seventeen by three, which must give fifty-one. And it is then our true rest, when we already perceive the brightness of the Trinity, which we hold most certainly to exist in the unity of divinity. We multiply fifty-one by three, and we have the full number of the elect in the land above, just like the number of fish, one hundred and fifty-three. It was therefore appropriate after the resurrection of the Lord for the net to be cast to catch the number of fish which would indicate the elect, the citizens of the country above.

5   In the midst of these things the portions of the holy gospel read out yesterday and today prompt us to consider with due care why it is that we read that our Lord and Redeemer ate broiled fish after his resurrection. For something which took place twice is surely not lacking in mystery. For in the passage which has been read out now he ate bread and broiled fish, while in that which was read out yesterday he ate some honeycomb as well as broiled fish [cf. Luke 24:42]. Now what are we to believe the broiled fish indicates, if not that *Mediator between God and humanity* [1 Tim. 2:5], who suffered? For it was he who condescended to lie hidden in the waters of the human race, allowed himself to be caught by the snare of our death, and at the time of his passion was broiled, as it were, in his affliction. But the one who condescended to become a broiled fish in his passion, showed himself to us as a honeycomb in his resurrection. Or perhaps he who allowed the affliction of his passion to be represented by broiled fish wished to express the two natures of his person through a honeycomb. Yes, a honeycomb is honey in wax, but the honey in the wax is the divine nature in human nature. Moreover, this is consonant with today's reading, in which he ate fish and bread. For he who could be broiled like a fish in his human nature strengthens us with bread in his divine nature, as he says: *I am the living bread which came down from heaven* [John 6:51]. And so he ate broiled fish and bread, so that he might show us by the very food he ate that he endured the passion in accordance with our human nature, and brought about our restoration in accordance with his divine nature. If we consider this carefully we can

also see how suitable it is for us to imitate this. For the Redeemer draws attention to what he has done in such a way as to make a smooth path for us, his followers, to imitate. For look, our Lord wished to associate honeycomb with broiled fish in what he ate because the people who do not withdraw from the love of interior sweetness when they experience tribulations for God here below are the ones he receives to eternal quiet in his body. Honey is taken with broiled fish, because those who experience pain here below for the sake of the truth are satisfied with true sweetness there.

6   It should also be noticed that the Lord is described as having had his last banquet with seven disciples, for Peter, Thomas, Nathaniel, the sons of Zebedee, and two of his other disciples are said to have been present. Why did he celebrate his last banquet with seven disciples, if it was not to indicate in advance that only those who were full of the sevenfold grace of the Holy Spirit would enjoy everlasting refreshment with him? All this takes place over a period of seven days as well, and perfection is often indicated by the number seven. Therefore, those who have passed beyond earthly things in their zeal for perfection feast upon the presence of the Word at the last banquet. They are not held fast by love of this world; even if it causes them trouble through temptations in one way or other, it does not weaken the longings which they have begun to experience. Concerning this last banquet it is said elsewhere through John: *Blessed are those who are called to the marriage supper of the Lamb* [Rev. 19:9]. He says they are called not to lunch but to a supper, for this reason: supper is a banquet at the very end of the day. Therefore, when the time of this present life is over and they come to the refreshment of contemplation above, they are not called to the lunch of the Lamb but his supper. This supper is clearly indicated by the last meal, at which seven disciples are mentioned as having been present, because as we have said at that time interior refreshment restores those who now, filled with sevenfold grace, are panting in their love of the Spirit.

Go after these things for yourselves, brothers and sisters; long to be filled with the presence of this Spirit. Give careful thought to the future which must follow for you from the realities of the present. Consider whether you are full of this Spirit, and you will learn whether you will be able to arrive at that banquet. For anyone whom that Spirit does not restore, will assuredly go hungry when the eternal banquet is providing refreshment. Remember what Paul says of that same Spirit: *Anyone who does not have the Spirit of Christ, is not his* [Rom. 8:9]. The Spirit of love is a kind of token of being held by God. Does someone whose mind is reduced to fragments by animosities, puffed up by pride, provoked by anger to the point of being cut into pieces, tortured by avarice and weakened by loose living, have the Spirit of Christ? Consider who the Spirit of Christ is. Assuredly, he is the one who brings it about that friends and enemies are both loved, earthly things are despised, desire for heavenly things burns, the flesh is ground down on account of its vices, and the mind is restrained from passionate desire. And so, if you want to know what rights you have in being held by God, consider the character of the one who holds you. For behold, what we have said is what Paul cries out in a truthful voice: *If someone does not have the Spirit of Christ, this person is not his* [Rom. 8:9]. As if to say openly: Anyone who is not ruled by God dwelling within him now will not rejoice in the divine brightness when it is made manifest later. But we who are too weak to accomplish these things which have been said and are unable to attain the summit of perfection, let us place the footsteps of our holy longing on the road towards God every day. Speaking through the psalmist, Truth offers us consolation: *Your eyes have seen my imperfection, and all will be written in your book* [Ps. 139:16]. Our imperfection will not be entirely harmful to us if, having set out on the journey towards God, we do not look back to the things which have taken place and hasten to make our way past those things which remain. For he who was good enough to inflame the imperfect with longings makes these stronger over time until they come perfection, through Jesus Christ our Lord, who lives and reigns with him in the unity of the Holy Spirit, God for ever and ever. Amen.

The following homily was also preached in the basilica of the martyr Laurence, but on a date which cannot be determined. It is a powerful piece of preaching, which followed a reading of Luke 16:19–31.

40.1   In the language of the Bible, dearest brothers and sisters, historical truth is the thing we need to deal with first, and then the spiritual understanding of an allegory is to be sought. For the fruit of allegory is plucked with all its sweetness when it is first strongly rooted in the truth by way of history. But because allegory sometimes builds up faith, and history morality, we who by God's initiative are now speaking to the faithful do not believe it would be foreign to our purpose to disregard that order of speaking. You who are already strong in the faith you hold should first hear a short discussion concerning the allegory; something concerning morality which arises from the history which you definitely need to know will be kept to the end of our exposition, because the things which happen to be heard last are generally better remembered.

2   Therefore we shall run over the allegorical meanings quickly, so as to arrive more quickly at the broad expanses of moral teaching. *There was a certain rich man who was clothed in purple and fine linen, and each day he feasted sumptuously* [Luke 16:19]. Whom, dearest brothers and sisters, whom does this rich man clothed in purple and fine linen who feasted sumptuously each day indicate, other than the Jewish people who, having the visible trappings of a fine life, put the delights of the law they had received to the use of their own splendour rather than any good purpose? And whom does Lazarus, full of sores, stand for in a figurative way, but the people of the gentiles? When converted to God it was not ashamed to confess its sins; its wound was just a sore. Now poison is conveyed from the internal organs and comes out through a sore. So what is the confession of sins, but a kind of breaking open of wounds? Because when confession is made the poison of sin, which had been lying hidden unwholesomely in the mind, is uncovered so as to bring health. For sores bring filth to the surface. And what else do we do when we confess sins but uncover the evil which was lying hidden within us?

But the wounded Lazarus *longed to be fed by the crumbs which fell from the rich man's table* [Luke 16:21], and no-one gave him any, because that proud people disdained to admit any gentile to knowledge of the law. It viewed the teaching of the law as a matter not of charity but of self-regard, puffing itself up, as it were, on account of the riches it had been given. And the words of knowledge which came down to him were like crumbs falling from a table.

On the other hand, dogs licked the wounds of the poor man as he lay. In sacred scripture dogs can sometimes be understood as preachers. For the tongue of a dog makes a wound healthy by licking it, just as, when holy doctors teach us as we confess our sins, it is as if they touch our wounded mind with their tongues, and, because they snatch us from sin by what they say, it is as if they lead us back to health by touching the wounds. For because the tongue of preachers is designated by the word 'dogs' it is said to the Lord through the psalmist: *The tongues of your dogs out of the enemies, from himself* [cf. Ps. 68:23]. Indeed, holy preachers were chosen from among the unfaithful Jews who, coming to assert the truth against thieves and robbers [cf. John 10:8], were as it were barking loudly on behalf of the Lord. On the other hand, it is said to the condemnation of certain people: *Dumb dogs that cannot bark* [Isa. 56:10]. And so, because holy preachers condemn sins but approve the confession of sins, saying *Confess your sins to one another and pray for each other, that you may be healed*,[7] the dogs lick the sores of Lazarus. The fact is, when holy teachers receive the confessions of gentiles, they restore their wounded minds to health. For this reason Lazarus is appropriately understood to mean 'helped', because the people who cured his wounds by correction of the tongue were the very ones who helped him to gain deliverance.[8] The licking of dogs can also indicate the tongues of people who slobber over us. It is obvious that such people lick our wounds, because very often, with improper partiality, they praise the bad things which we find fault with in ourselves. But it came to pass that they both died. The rich man who was clothed in purple and fine linen was buried in hell, but Lazarus was carried by angels to Abraham's bosom. What does the bosom of Abraham signify but the secret rest of the Father, concerning which the Truth says: *Many shall come from the east and west and shall sit down with Abraham and Isaac and Jacob in the kingdom of heaven; but the children of the kingdom shall be cast into outer darkness* [Matt. 8:11f.]? Someone described as being clothed in purple is rightly called a child of the kingdom. From far away he raised his eyes to see Lazarus, because while those who do not have faith are placed deep down in the punishment of damnation, prior to the day of the last judgment they look upon the faithful who are waiting in rest above them; their subsequent joys they are quite unable to behold. But what they look upon is far away, because they do not deserve to get there.

It is shown that he burned more fiercely in his tongue when he says: *Send Lazarus to dip the tip of his finger in water and cool my tongue, because I am tormented in this flame* [Luke 16:24]. The people without faith kept the words of the law in their mouths, but did not bother to observe them in their deeds. He will therefore burn more fiercely in the place where he shows that he was well aware of that which he did not want to do. And so it is appropriately said through Solomon concerning those people who are learned yet negligent: *The whole labour of man is in his mouth, yet his soul will not be filled* [Eccles. 6:7], because whoever labours for just one purpose, that of knowing what he ought to say, is fasting with an empty mind from feeding on what he knows.

He longed to be touched by the tip of his finger because, having been delivered to eternal punishments, he wished to have a share of the very least of the good deeds of the just. He was told in reply that in this life he had received good things, having thought that passing happiness constituted his whole joy. To be sure, just people are able to have good things here, but they do not receive these as a reward, because while they seek things that are better, that is eternal, whatever good things are present do not seem at all good in their opinion, on fire as they are with holy longings. And so the prophet David, who enjoyed the wealth of the kingdom and widespread deference, although he regarded these things as good, indeed he could not do without them, was nevertheless on fire in his eagerness for just one good thing, saying: *For me it is good to draw near to God* [Ps. 73:28].

Among these things it should be noticed what is said to him: *Remember, son* [Luke 16:25]. Look, Abraham calls him son and yet does not free him from his torment, for no impulse of compassion induces the faithful fathers who went before this unfaithful people to pull those whom they acknowledge as sons according to the flesh away from their torments, for they bear in mind that many had wandered away from their faith. In the midst of his torments the rich man says that he has five brothers, because the same proud Jewish people, which has for the greater part already been damned, knows that the successors it left behind on the earth are given over to the five senses of the body. He therefore uses the number five for the brothers he left behind. Placed as he was in hell, he laments that they do not rise to spiritual understanding, and asks for Lazarus to be sent to them. He is told that they have Moses and the prophets. But he says that they would not believe unless someone rose from the dead. He receives an immediate answer: *If they do not hear Moses and the prophets, neither will they believe if someone should rise from the dead* [Luke 16:31]. Indeed, the Truth says concerning Moses: *If you had believed Moses, you would also have believed me. For he wrote of me* [John 5:46]. And so what is said through the reply of Abraham has been fulfilled. For the Lord rose from the dead, but the Jewish people, who did not want to believe Moses, were too proud to believe even one who rose from the dead. And since it was too proud to understand the words of Moses in a spiritual way, it failed to come to the one of whom Moses spoke.

3 Let it suffice, dearest brothers and sisters, for us to have passed over these things in a speedy and concise fashion while investigating the mysteries of the allegory; now let our minds run back so we can understand the more general moral significance of the story. *There was a certain rich man clothed in purple and fine linen, and each day he feasted sumptuously. And there was a beggar named Lazarus, who lay before the gate of the rich man, full of sores* [Luke 16:19f.]. Some people think that the precepts of the Old Testament are more strict than those of the New, but they have been deceived by a failure to think carefully enough. For in the former taking the goods of others, not keeping hold of what you have, is punished. There, the unjust taking of property is punished by fourfold restitution [cf. Exod. 22:1, 2 Sam. 12:6]. But here, the rich man is rebuked not for having taken away the property of other people, but for not giving his own away. And it is not said that he oppressed anyone by force, but that he extolled himself because of the things

he had received. From this, therefore, from this in particular can be gathered the kind of punishment which is to be inflicted on someone who takes the property of other people, if someone who does not distribute what is his own is struck down by being condemned to hell. And no-one should think that that he is safe, saying 'Look, I don't take other people's things, but I enjoy the things I've been given lawfully', because that rich man was punished not for having taken away other people's things, but because when he had received things he forsook himself in a bad way. It was this which delivered him to hell, because in his prosperity he feared nothing, because he perverted the gifts he had received to feed his pride, because he knew nothing of the depths of kindness, because he was unwilling to redeem his sins, even though he could easily afford the price.

Now there are some who do not consider it a sin to be concerned with finely worked and expensive clothes. But if this were not a sin, the word of God would definitely not have been so careful to specify that the rich man who was tormented in hell had been clothed in fine linen and purple. Now no-one seeks out clothes which will attract attention except for a feeling of empty pride, with the aim of appearing more distinguished than other people. The deed itself bears witness that more expensive clothing is sought out only for the sake of empty pride, because no-one wants to wear expensive clothes when he cannot be seen by others. We are better able to gather that this is a sin from the reverse case: if humble clothing were not a virtue, the evangelist would not have taken care to say of John: *He had a garment of camel's hair* [Matt. 3:4].

But it is most important for us to observe how the story of the proud rich man and the humble poor man unfolds, as it comes from the mouth of Truth. For see, it says: *There was a certain rich man*, and then it goes on: *And there was a certain beggar named Lazarus* [Luke 16:19f.]. Obviously, the names of rich people are better known among the general public than those of the poor. Why is it then that the Lord, talking of a poor man and a rich man, utters the name of the poor man and not the name of the rich man, unless God knows and approves the humble, and does not acknowledge the proud? And so at the end it will be said to certain people who take pride in the miracles they have worked: *I do not know where you are from; depart from me, all you who work iniquity* [Matt. 7:23]. On the contrary, it is said to Moses: *I have known you by name* [Exod. 33:12]. Therefore he says *a certain man* of the rich man, and *a destitute person named Lazarus* of the poor man.[9] It is as if he were to say openly: A poor person who is humble is known to me; a rich person who is proud is not. I recognise the former and approve of him; the latter I do not recognise, and hold him worthy of reprobation.

4 We should also consider with what care our Creator arranges all things. For things do not happen only for a single reason. For look, the beggar Lazarus is lying before the gates of the rich man, covered in sores. From this one circumstance the Lord accomplished two acts of judgment. For perhaps the rich man would have had some excuse, if Lazarus, poor and full of sores, had not been lying before his gate, if he had been far away, if his destitution had not been so in-your-face. On the other hand, if the rich man had been far away from the eyes of the poor man who was full of sores, the poor man would have had to endure less temptation in his mind. But when he placed the destitute man full of sores before the gate of the rich man who abounded in pleasures, from this one circumstance, on the one hand he added to the damnation of the rich man who did not feel mercy at the sight of the poor man, and on the other hand every day he put the poor man to a thorough test, tempted as he was at the sight of the rich man. You can well believe that this destitute man, beset with sores, was forced to experience powerful temptations when he considered his circumstances, lacking as he did bread and not even having good health, while he could see in front of him the healthy rich man enjoying his pleasures with gusto; he saw himself afflicted with pain and cold, but the other rejoicing, clothed in fine linen and purple; himself oppressed with sores, the other overflowing with what he had received; himself in want, but the other unwilling to give. Dearest brothers and sisters, let us imagine how great a tumult of temptation must then have taken place in the heart of the poor man, whose poverty would certainly have been enough of a punishment, even if he had been well, and whose sickness would have been enough, even if assistance had been to hand. But so that the poor man would be put to the test even more, poverty and sickness were simultaneously causing him to waste away. And he saw above him the rich man stepping out, surrounded by a tightly packed throng of deferential people, while no-one visited him in his weakness and want. For the dogs who freely licked his wounds are evidence that no-one came to visit him. And so from this single circumstance of allowing Lazarus to lie before the gate of the rich man, almighty God manifested two acts of judgment: the uncaring rich man increased the damnation with which he was punished, and the poor man who was tempted advanced towards his reward. Every day the former used to gaze upon someone for whom he felt no pity, while the latter could see the person through whom he was being tested. Here below there were two hearts, but there was one who looked

upon them from above, training the one for glory as he tempted him and awaiting the punishment of the other as he tolerated him.

5   For it goes on: *It came to pass that Lazarus died and was carried by the angels into Abraham's bosom. But the rich man died and was buried in hell.*[10] Very clearly the rich man, having now been placed in a state of punishment, seeks the one for whom he had felt no pity in this life as his patron. For look, it continues: *Lifting up his eyes when he was in torments he saw from afar Abraham, and Lazarus in his bosom. And crying out he said: Father Abraham, have pity on me, and send Lazarus to dip the tip of his finger in water and cool my tongue, because I am tormented in this flame* [Luke 16:23f.]. Oh, how subtle are the judgments of God! With what discrimination does he reward our good and bad deeds! To be sure, it was said above that in this life Lazarus sought the crumbs which fell from the table of the rich man, and no-one gave them to him; now, referring to the punishment of the rich man, it is said that he longed for water to trickle down into his mouth from the tip of Lazarus' finger. From this, brothers and sisters, from this you can gather how severe the strictness of God is. For when the rich man who refused to give even the smallest thing from his table to the poor man in his distress was placed in hell, he came to the point of asking for the smallest things. Someone who refused to give crumbs of bread asked for a drop of water! Note carefully what it was that the rich man placed in the fire asked for: that his tongue be cooled. Now it is the practice of holy scripture sometimes to say one thing, but to mean something different from what is said. The Lord did not say earlier that this proud rich man was given to talking too much, but that he feasted in a wasteful way. He did not say that this man sinned because he talked too much, but because of gluttony, together with pride and holding on to what was his. But because people generally talk too much at feasts, someone who is said to have feasted improperly here below is spoken of as experiencing serious burning in his tongue in hell. For the fault of talking too much waits first upon those who feast improperly, and after too much talking there follows a light-hearted friskiness. Sacred scripture bears witness that friskiness follows gluttony, for it says: *The people sat down to eat and drink, and rose up to play* [Exod. 32:6]. But before the body can be moved to play, the tongue is moved to jokes and empty words. What, therefore, is indicated when the rich man, placed in torments, asks for his tongue to be cooled, if not that someone who had sinned by talking too much while feasting, experienced very painful burning in his tongue as a just reward?

6   But we need to consider with the greatest fear what was said to him in reply through Abraham: *Son, remember that you received good things*

in your life, and likewise Lazarus evil things. Now he is consoled, but you are tormented [Luke 16:25]. This statement, dearest brothers and sisters, requires dread rather than exposition. For if you, whoever you may be, have received some external good in this world, I have to say that you need to be thoroughly afraid of that outward gift, in case it has been given to you as a reward for some things you have done, in case the Judge who has given outward goods here below holds back from repaying with an inward good, in case honour or wealth here below turns out to be not an aid to virtue but a reward for your labour. For look, when he says *you received good things in your life*, he shows that there had been something good about the rich man, because of which he received good things in this life. Conversely, when it is said of Lazarus that he received bad things, it is clearly shown that there had been something bad about Lazarus which needed to be cleansed. But the fire of destitution cleansed the bad behaviour of Lazarus, and the happiness of a passing life was the reward for the good behaviour of the rich man. The affliction of poverty wiped the former clean; the only reward the latter received was wealth. And so, any of you who are doing well for yourselves in this world, whenever you recall having done good things, they should fill you with alarm, in case the prosperity you have been given turns out to be the reward for your good deeds. And when you catch sight of poor people doing various things which are blameworthy, do not look down on them and do not despair of them, because it may be that the forge of poverty is making clean something which was made dirty by indulging too much in a very slight evil. Concerning yourselves, you must certainly be afraid, because a prosperous life can follow even the doing of some bad things. But give careful consideration to these, because poverty is a teacher which makes peoples' lives wretched until it brings them to uprightness.

7 It goes on: *And beside all this, between us and you a great gulf has been established, so that those who wish to pass over to you are not able, neither can they come across from there to here* [Luke 16:26]. In this passage it is necessary for us to ask why he should say *those who wish to pass over to you are not able*. For there can be no doubt that those who are in hell long to pass over to the portion assigned to the blessed. But how can it be said that those who have already been received into the condition of blessedness wish to pass over to those being tormented in hell? Well, just as those who have been condemned desire to pass over to the elect, that is to move away from the affliction of their sufferings, so it is in the minds of the just to pass over to those who are afflicted and placed in torments in a merciful way and seek to free

them. Nevertheless, those who wish to pass over from the dwelling-place of the blessed to those who are afflicted and placed in torments are not able to do so, because the souls of the just, while they may possess the quality of mercy through the goodness of their nature, are already operating in harmony with the justice of their Creator, and are so constrained by what is just that they cannot be moved by any compassion towards the condemned. Indeed, their hearts are at one with the Judge to whom they cleave, and tender-heartedness does not lead them to stoop down to those whom they are unable to pluck out, because they then see that the distance to which these people have been driven away by the Author whom they love is the very distance which separates them from themselves. So it is that the unjust do not pass over to the portion of the blessed, because they are bound by everlasting damnation, nor are the just able to pass over to those who have been condemned, because, having already been raised up through the justice of the Judge, they in no way feel any merciful compassion towards them.

8   But after any hope for himself has been taken away from the rich man in the fire, his mind turns to the members of his family he had left behind, because punishment sometimes teaches the minds of the condemned charity, although it does them no good, so that people who, here below, held their sins dear and did not love themselves, at that time come to hold their relatives dear, in a spiritual way. And so it is now said: *Therefore I ask you, father, that you would send him to my father's house, for I have five brothers, that Lazarus may bear witness to them, lest they too come into this place of torments* [Luke 16:27f.]. We need to notice here what great things have been piled up to torture the rich man in the fire. For his knowledge and his memory serve to punish him. He recognizes Lazarus whom he had despised, and he also remembers his brothers whom he left behind. Now his punishment regarding the poor man would not have been complete, if he did not recognize him by way of retribution. And the punishment in the fire would not have been complete if, in the midst of his own sufferings, he did not fear for his relatives as well. Therefore, so that sinners may be punished still more amid their sufferings, they see in glory those they despised, and they are tormented because of the punishment of those whom they loved, to no good purpose. But we need to believe that before the recompense made at the last judgment they are able to look upon some of the just as they rest, with the result that, as they see them in joy, they are tormented not only by their own punishment, but also by the good which the others enjoy. And the just are always looking upon the unjust in their torments, so that their joy is thereby increased,

because they can see the evil from which, thanks to God's mercy, they escaped, and the more they see others undergoing what they could have suffered themselves, had they been forsaken, the more they give thanks to the one who snatched them away from it. And when the just look upon the punishment of the condemned, the shining blessedness of their souls is not darkened, because it cannot be doubted that, where compassion for suffering does not exist, this could not diminish the happiness of the blessed ones. Why be astonished if looking upon the torments of the unjust is a source of joy for the just, when in a picture black pigment is spread in the background to make the white and red appear more bright? And although their joys are quite enough to satisfy them completely, nevertheless there can be no doubt that the evils of the condemned are always in front of them, because there is nothing which occurs within the creation which those who look upon the brightness of their Creator cannot see.

9   When the rich man asks for Lazarus to be sent, Abraham's answer follows swiftly: *They have Moses and the prophets, let them hear them* [Luke 16:29]. But he who had despised the word of God considers that those who came after him would be unable to hear them. And so the rich man answered: *No, my father, but they will believe if someone comes to them from the dead* [Luke 16:30]. He is quickly told, in a declaration full of truth: *If they do not hear Moses and the prophets, neither will they believe someone who rises from the dead* [Luke 16:31], because it is clear that those who despise the words of the law will find the precepts of the Redeemer who rose from the dead more difficult to fulfil, these being more subtle. For whatever is said through the law is less than what is commanded through the Lord. The former directed that tithes were to be given, but our Redeemer orders that those who follow perfection are to let go of everything. The former puts a stop to sins of the flesh, but our Redeemer even condemns bad thoughts. Therefore, *if they do not hear Moses and the prophets, neither will they believe someone who rises from the dead*, because how could those who neglect to fulfil the lesser precepts of the law grow strong enough to obey the loftier commands of our Saviour? And it is evident beyond any doubt that they will refuse to believe someone whose sayings they are unwilling to fulfil. Let it be enough for us to have said these things in reflecting upon this story.

10   But you, dearest brothers and sisters, who are aware of the rest of Lazarus and the punishment of the rich man, be sensible: seek those who will intercede for your sins and look after poor people who may be your advocates on the day of judgment. For now you have many Lazarus's; they are lying before your gates, and they stand in need of

those things which fall from the table every day when you have had enough. The words of the holy reading should instruct us to fulfil the commands to act with kindness. If we go looking for Lazarus we can find him each day; if we do not seek Lazarus we see him every day. Look, the poor who may then come forward as our intercessors are shamelessly offering themselves, they are asking us. By rights we should be the ones asking, yet we are asked. Consider whether we ought to deny what is sought from us, when those who are seeking are our patrons. So do not waste the opportunities to receive mercy, do not turn a blind eye to the means of help you have been given. Think about the punishment before the punishment comes. When you see people who have been cast down in this world, even if their deeds seem to be blameworthy, do not look down on them, because the medicine of poverty may cure those whose weak behaviour did them harm. If they have done the kinds of things which ought with justice to be rebuked, you can turn these things, if you want to, to the advantage of your reward, so that from their very vices you will accumulate additional opportunities for doing good, since you can give words as well as bread, the word of correction with the bread which will restore them, and the person who sought one kind of nourishment from you may receive two kinds, being satisfied outwardly by food and inwardly by speech. And so when a blameworthy poor person is seen, he ought to be advised and not looked down on. But if there is nothing to be rebuked, he ought to be held in the highest veneration as an intercessor. But look, there are many people we see of whose merits we are unaware. Therefore they should all be venerated, and you must make yourself humble before all of them, because you do not know who may be Christ [cf. Matt. 25:40].

11   Let me mention, brothers and sisters, something which is well known to my brother and fellow priest Speciosus, who is here present.[11] At the very time when I was seeking life in a monastery an old woman named Redempta, clothed in the habit of a nun, was living in this city by the church of Blessed Mary Ever Virgin. She had been a disciple of that Herundo, abundant in her mighty virtues, who was said to have lived the life of a hermit on the hills of Praeneste.[12] Two disciples wearing the same habit lived with her, one named Romula and another, still alive, whose face I know although I do not know her name. And so these three remained together in one dwelling place, leading a life rich in the way it was conducted, yet materially poor. But this Romula whom I mentioned surpassed her fellow disciple of whom I spoke by the great merits of her life. Indeed, she was marvellous in her patience and obedient to the highest degree; by watching over her

mouth she maintained silence, and she was most assiduous in the practice of continuous prayer.

But because people who we believe are already perfect very often still have some imperfection in the eyes of the craftsman on high, just as it often happens that those of us with no experience can look upon and praise as having already been brought to perfection still unfinished carved figures which the carver, although he hears them being praised, continues to work on and file away, and keeps on hammering them to improve them, this Romula of whom we have spoken came down with an affliction of the body which doctors call by the Greek word paralysis, and she lay stretched out on her bed over many years, having almost completely lost the use of her limbs. Nevertheless these sufferings did not lead her mind towards impatience. For the loss of her limbs was turned into a gain in virtues, because the less she was able to do anything else, the more devoted she grew in the practice of prayer.

One night she called out to that Redempta I have mentioned, who cared for both her disciples as though they were her daughters, saying 'Mother, come! Mother, come!' She quickly arose with her other disciple; this is well known from what both of them and many other people have said, and I knew about it at the same time as well. And when, in the middle of the night, they were standing by the bed of the person who was lying there, suddenly, a light sent from heaven filled the entire dwelling-place, and so dazzling was its brilliant brightness that the hearts of those who were present were seized with a dread beyond reckoning. As they themselves said afterwards, their whole bodies became stiff, and they remained in a state of numbed shock. For a sound like that of some great multitude approaching began to be heard, and the entrance to the dwelling place was shaken as if a throng of people were pressing against it as they made their way in. And, as they said, they were aware of a multitude of people coming in, but owing to their great fear and the brightness they could see nothing, because their dread had made them lower their eyes, and the brightness of the great light prevented them. A wonderfully fragrant scent immediately followed this light, and such was its nature that the sweetness of the scent reinvigorated the minds which the light that had been given off had filled with terror. But since they were unable to endure the power of that brightness, that same Romula began to comfort Redempta, her teacher in how to live, who was trembling as she stood by, with a soft voice: 'Do not be afraid, Mother, I am not dying now.' And as she continued to say this, little by little the light which had been given off was taken away, although the scent which had followed it lingered. And so the scent which had been diffused remained, while a second and a third day passed.

So it was that on the fourth night she again called that same teacher of hers. When she came she asked for and received the viaticum.[13] Before the same Redempta and her other disciple had departed from the bed of the person who was lying down, suddenly, behold! two choirs singing psalms positioned themselves in the space before the entrance to the dwelling place, and they said they could distinguish the voices of both sexes, the males reciting the chants of the psalms and the females the responses. And while the heavenly funeral solemnities were being celebrated before the door, that holy soul was freed from the flesh. As she was being conducted to heaven and the choirs of psalm singers ascended, the psalmody began to be heard more softly, until both the sound of the psalm singing and the scent of sweetness were so far away that they came to an end.

12   Now who held this person in high regard while she lived in the body? She seemed unworthy to all, everyone looked down on her. Who deigned to approach her, who went near her? But in a heap of manure a pearl of God was lying hidden. A heap of manure, brothers and sisters, is what I call this corruptible body, a heap of manure is the name I give to the meanness of poverty. And so the pearl which had been lying hidden was taken up and, having been placed as an ornament of the heavenly King, she now shines amid the citizens on high, glittering amid those glowing stones of the everlasting diadem. O you who are in this world, you who believe that you are rich, or really are, compare, if you can, false riches to the true riches of Romula. You are going to lose everything you possess along the way of this world; she sought nothing for the journey and found everything when she arrived. You lead a happy life, you fear a sorrowful death; she endured a sorrowful life, she came to a happy death. You seek passing human respect; she, looked down on by other people, found that choirs of angels were her companions. So learn, brothers and sisters, to look down on all temporal things, learn to disdain the honour which is transient and to love the glory which is everlasting. Honour the poor whom you see, and consider people outwardly despised by the world to be friends of God inwardly. Share what you have with them, so when the time comes they may deign to share what they have with you. Think of what is said through the mouth of the teacher of the gentiles: *At this time your abundance may supply their want, so that their abundance also may be a supply for your want* [2 Cor. 8:14]. Think of what the Truth says in his own person: *Inasmuch as you have done it to one of the least of my brethren, you have done it to me* [Matt. 25:40]. So why are you reluctant to give,

when what you hold out to someone who lies on the ground you are giving to the one who is seated in heaven? May almighty God himself speak within your minds these things which he has spoken in your ears through me; who lives and reigns with the Father in the unity of the Holy Spirit, God for ever and ever. Amen.

4

HUMAN TYPES

Ancient philosophers taught that an unexamined life is not worth living, and Gregory was highly introspective. He felt that a just person would look upon his life with anxiety, carefully considering whether he was growing or lessening in good every day, placing himself in front of himself and walking in his own company, seeing whether he was rising or flowing downwards.[1] But some people can examine their lives more acutely than others, and some process of analysis of himself and others which we cannot trace made Gregory one of the masters in examining the motions of the human heart. His insight can be unnerving, and no reader will be under any illusion as to the difficulty of living in a manner which would have pleased him. But one cannot help feeling that the territory he describes is known from his own experience and inhabited by him, and that his demands are possible.

Gregory is very alert to the enormous variety of human types. Take his analysis of various sins. Apart from the few words in Job which suggested the passage which follows, it is completely lacking in biblical references. This is highly unusual for Gregory, and may indicate that to a greater extent than usual he is not reacting to the biblical text as much as reporting his own experiences.

Moralia

7.28.34 *The paths of their way are turned aside* [Job 6:18]. Everything which is turned aside is twisted back on itself. Now there are some people who undertake to withstand the sins which draw them astray with their whole strength, but when the critical moment of temptation arrives they do not remain firm in their purpose. For one person, puffed up with the perverse insolence of pride, when he considers that the rewards of humility are great, rises up against himself and, as it were, lays aside his inflated, swollen arrogance, and promises to display humility in the face of all insults. But on being suddenly struck by just one insulting word, he straightaway returns to his old pride, and he is brought back to his swollen headedness to such an extent that he completely forgets having aspired to the virtue of humility. Someone else, stirred by avarice, is panting to increase his possessions. When he sees that all things swiftly pass away, he firmly fixes his mind which was roaming because of its desires, and determines that now he will now try to get nothing and possess the things he has got only under the bridle of great control. But when attractive things are suddenly presented to his eyes, his mind immediately begins to pant with eagerness, he is unable to control himself, he looks for a way to get them and, forgetful of the self-control he had promised himself, his desires for gaining them cause him to harass himself with the rods of his thoughts. Another person, polluted by the corruption of loose living, is held captive by prolonged habit. But he sees how great the cleanness of chastity is and realizes he has been overcome by the foulness of the flesh. He therefore resolves to hold in check the stream of pleasures and prepares himself to resist his habit, apparently with all his strength. But in a sudden temptation he is struck by some eye-catching thing that he sees or is presented to his memory, and straightaway his state of preparedness falls apart,[2] and the one who had taken up the shield of resolve against delight lies pierced by its javelin, and, loose living having defeated him, it was as if he had never prepared the weapons of intention against it. Someone else is kindled by flames of anger and is so headstrong that he hurls insults at his enemies. But when no occasion for rage is disturbing his mind he considers how great the virtue of mildness is and how high the loftiness of patience, and he holds himself back in the face of insults; nevertheless, when some tiny occasion for strife is born, he is suddenly inflamed in his inmost part to words and insults, so that not only does the patience he had promised escape his recollection, but also his mind is not aware of itself and the loud reproaches it utters. And when he has fully given vent to his rage, he returns to tranquillity as if he had been taking exercise, and he then pulls himself together in the privacy of silence, his tongue having been restrained not by patience but because he has satisfied his shamelessness. And so, when he is just able to exercise restraint after his abusive language, it is too late, just as it is often not the right hand of the person in charge of them which checks the foaming horses from their rush, but the end of the field. It is therefore well said of the condemned *the paths of their way are turned aside*, because while they certainly desire right things on due consideration, they always twist themselves back to their bad old ways, and the people who indeed desired good but never departed from evil turn back to themselves in a circular motion, being as it were stretched out beyond themselves. Yes, what they want is to be humble without being looked down on; to be content with what is theirs without being in need; to be chaste without mortifying the body, and to be patient without having to endure insults. And what are they doing while they seek to gain these virtues when fleeing from the labours associated with them but desiring to have triumphal processions in cities at the end of a war while being unacquainted with the struggles of war in the field?

35 Nevertheless, what is said of their paths being turned aside can also be understood in another way. For it often happens that people energetically prepare themselves against particular vices, but neglect to overcome others, and having failed to position themselves against the latter they also allow the former, which they had overcome, to come back against them. For one person who has already subdued his flesh against loose living has yet to restrain his mind from avarice, and while he obliges himself to remain in the world through avaricious conduct and does not withdraw from earthly actions, when an opportune moment presents itself he sinks as well into the loose living which he gave the appearance of having already overcome. Someone else defeats the passion of avarice but has completely failed to subdue an impulse towards loose living, and when he gets ready what he has to spend on his loose living, he makes the neck of his heart submit to the yoke of the avarice, which he formerly vanquished, as well. Someone else has already thrown to the ground rebellious impatience but has not yet defeated futile ambition, and when this makes him become entangled with the honours of the world, pierced with the goads of human affairs he is brought back to impatience as a captive; whenever futile ambition eggs on his mind to defend itself, he is overcome and has to submit himself to that which he had defeated. Someone else has already subdued futile ambition but has still to throw impatience to the ground, and when his impatience makes him threaten those who stand in his way, he blushes at being unable to do what he said he would, and is summoned back under the yoke of futile ambition; having been overcome by something else, he has to submit to something which he had rejoiced to have overcome completely. So it is that vices operating on behalf of each other keep their hold over an escapee: they receive someone, apparently already lost, who is in the power of their lordship, and hand him over one to the other to be punished. And so *the paths of their way are turned aside* in the case of perverse people, because if, having defeated one kind of wickedness,

they take to their heels while another is holding supremacy, the latter becomes tangled up with the one which they had defeated.

Gregory is struck by the immense variety of human beings. The Devil, he feels, often tempts people in ways appropriate to the kinds of people they are. In the following passage, he comments on a portion of the book of Job describing Leviathan, a monster living in the sea. Modern scholars tend to identify Leviathan with the crocodile, but Gregory felt it represented the Devil.

Moralia

33.24.44 *Who can discover the face of his garment?* [Job 41:13]. Leviathan tempts the minds of religious people in one way, and those given over to this world in another. For he casts before wicked people the bad things which they desire in an obvious way, but, lying in wait for good people in secret, he deceives them under an appearance of holiness. To the former he shows his wickedness more overtly, as if to members of his household; to the latter, as if to strangers, he cloaks himself with a feigned integrity, so that, under the covering veil of respectability, he can introduce by stealth the bad things which are not in his power to do so in the open. And so his members, when unable to bring about harm with overt wickedness, often clothe themselves with a good deed, and although they show that they are wicked by what they do, they deceive by their appearance of holiness. For if evil people were openly bad, they would completely fail to be received by the good. But they take upon themselves an appearance of being good, so that when good men receive in them something which resembles what they love, they are receiving as well, mixed up with it, the poison which they shun. Hence the apostle Paul, seeing that some were serving the belly under the cover of preaching, said: *For Satan himself is transformed into an angel of light. So why should we be surprised if his servants are transformed to be like servants of justice* [2 Cor. 11:14f.]? This was the transformation Joshua feared when, seeing an angel, he asked on whose side he was, saying: *Are you for us, or our enemies?* [Josh. 5:13]. This was so that, if he were of the enemy power, the knowledge that he was held in suspicion would make him recoil from his deceit. Because, therefore, Leviathan, labouring at his work of wickedness, is often clothed with an appearance of holiness, and because the garments of his pretence can only be detected through divine grace, it is well said: *Who can discover the face of his garment?* [Job 41:13]. The answer is, none other than the one who breathes the grace of a most subtle discernment into the minds of his servants, so that, when his malice is laid bare, they may see the face which he had hidden, covered by the appearance of holiness, naked.

The difference between human beings was not only a convenience to Satan, allowing him to tempt individuals in ways to which they were vulnerable. It also meant that within the church there could be mutual responsibility. Here, Gregory is considering a portion of the book of Job in which the stricken man enumerates his good deeds.

Moralia

19.25.42   *And with great care I investigated a cause which I did not know* [Job 29:16]. In these words we should consider all the things which are said and how they are put forward, item by item, because there is no reward which he omits. He is indeed just in his deeds, kind when his neighbours are weak, and vigorous in the affairs of the poor. For anyone who considers the goods of the eternal reward must exert himself to do everything which will bring about this reward. For it is said concerning this through Solomon: *Who fears God neglects nothing* [Eccles. 7:18 Vulg.]. Paul also says concerning this: *Prepared for every good work* [2 Tim. 2:21]. But among these things, it should be known that lesser things which it is within our power to do are sometimes to be passed over in the interests of greater ones. For who does not know that burying the dead constitutes a good work? And nevertheless it was said to someone who asked to be allowed to go to bury his father: *Let the dead bury their dead, but you go, and preach the kingdom of God* [Luke 9:60]. Carrying out this duty was to be neglected for the task of preaching, because the former activity involved burying in the ground those dead in the flesh, but the latter raising up to life those dead in the soul. It is also said by the prophet to the chiefs of the synagogue: *Seek judgment, relieve the oppressed* [Isa. 1:17]. And nevertheless, the apostle Paul says: *Set up as judges those who are looked down on in the church* [1 Cor. 6:5]. For he was rousing his listeners to the good of wisdom, to tongues of various kinds, and also to searching out the mysteries of prophecy, saying: *Desire spiritual gifts, and especially that you may prophesy* [1 Cor. 14:1]. But because they would not be able to receive spiritual gifts if earthly affairs weighed them down, he said in advance, long before: *Set up as judges those who are looked down on in the church* [1 Cor. 6:4]. As if he were to say openly, let those people who are of less merit in the church and who do not show themselves strong by powerful and mighty gifts give judgment concerning earthly matters, since lesser goods can be supplied by those who are incapable of great ones.[3] Yet those whom he mentions as being looked down upon he nevertheless calls wise, when he says: *Is there not a wise one among you who can judge between his brothers?* [1 Cor. 6:5]. What can be concluded from this, other than that people who have received wisdom in exterior things should judge earthly cases? But those endowed with spiritual gifts should certainly not be involved with secular affairs, so that, when they are not being forced to set in order lesser goods, they may be well practised in devoting their energy to the service of higher goods.

43 But great care should be taken so that those who shine with spiritual gifts should by no means totally abandon the affairs of their weak neighbours; rather, they should entrust these things to other people for whom it is suitable to deal with them. So it was that Moses appointed seventy men of the people [Num. 11:16f., 24f.], so that, hiding himself away from secular matters, he might penetrate internal things with greater ardour. And so it happens that the highest men make progress towards spiritual gifts when lowly things do not crush their minds; and again, the men who are least in the church do not live without doing good, when they find in exterior affairs things which they may carry out with virtue. For the holy church subsists in the unity of the faithful, just as our bodies are unified by the joining together of their limbs. For there are some parts in the body which allow us to look upon the light, and others which are hardly separated from the touch of the earth. Now the eye is directed towards the light and is protected from dust, in case it goes blind. But the foot is carrying out its task properly when it does not hesitate to receive the dust of the earth. Nevertheless these parts of the body are joined together by an exchange of functions, one with another, so that the foot runs on behalf of the eye and the eye keeps watch on behalf of the foot.

44 The limbs of the holy church ought therefore to be distinct in their tasks yet joined together in charity, so that the highest men look after the lives of those who are busy with earthly affairs, just as the foot walks by the light of the eyes; conversely, let those involved in earthly affairs apply whatever they do to the use of those who are greater than they, just as the foot does not keep watch for itself as much as take steps on behalf of the eyes. And so, when they combine their forces in mutual service, something wonderful happens: because each of the elect devotes himself to what he is able to do on behalf of someone else, their works achieve what they are unable to do by themselves.

45 But amid these things it should be known that when people who might appropriately devote themselves to the external affairs of

their neighbours cannot be found, those who are full of spiritual gifts must lower themselves to the weakness of these people and, with the stooping motion of charity, serve their earthly needs as much as they fittingly can. The mind should not become weary if its understanding, always intent upon the contemplation of spiritual things, at some time becomes bent over in the management of little things and as it were becomes smaller, when that Word through whom all created things cohere [cf. Col. 1:17], with the intention of being of service to human-kind, having taken human nature upon himself, willed to become *a little lower than the angels* [Heb. 2:7]. What is there to wonder at if someone drags himself along for the sake of another person, when the Creator of people and angels received a human form for the sake of people? And nevertheless, the understanding is not lowered by being dragged along, because the more subtle its penetration of the things which are above is, the more humbly it fails to condemn the things which are lower, for the love of its Creator. Why is it beneath our dignity or something difficult for us, we who wash our faces with the same bodily hand we use to put shoes on our feet, to direct our mind upwards and downwards? Therefore let blessed Job, because he did not despise little things while he was carrying out great ones, say: *And with great care I sought out a cause which I did not know* [Job 29:16].

46   In this regard I see a need to note that we never ought to be hasty in pronouncing judgment, that we should not judge things rashly and without consideration, that any evil things we may have heard should not influence us, and that we should not believe things which are spoken of far and wide without proof. We shall dread doing this if we think with proper care about what our Creator has done. Yes, so that he might restrain us from pronouncing judgment immediately, he himself, although *everything was naked and open to his eyes* [Heb. 4:13], still did not wish to judge the evils which had been heard of Sodom. He said: *The cry of the people of Sodom and Gomorrah has increased, and their sins are piled up. I shall go down and see whether their behaviour conforms to the cry which has come unto me, or whether it is not so, so that I shall know* [Gen. 18:20f.]. Why was it that the Lord, almighty and all-knowing, gave the impression of being uncertain before he had proof, if it was not to place before us an example of serious behaviour, lest we presume to believe evil of people before we have proof? And look, he descended by means of angels to investigate the evils, and straightaway struck those atrocious people, he who is patient and mild, and of whom it is written *But you, Lord, you judge with tranquillity* [Wisd. 12:18] and of whom it is written elsewhere *The Lord repays with patience* [Eccles. 5:4]. Finding them implicated in such a great crime, as it were he laid

his patience aside and, deciding not to wait for the day of the last judgment to punish them, he anticipated the day of judgment in their case with the fire of judgment. Observe! It is as if he found it hard to believe what he heard, and nevertheless when he learned the truth he made no delay in striking them down. Obviously this was to give us an example: when we hear of great crimes we should be slow to believe in them, but when the truth is established we should be quick to punish them. Therefore blessed Job, discharging this watchful concern, says: *And with great care I investigated a cause which I did not know.* We can also appropriately apply these words, through an interpretation according to a type, to the voice of the church. Yes, when she judges the evil deeds of fleshly people through her elect, she seeks out that which she does not know, because she seeks out evil deeds which she did not know about when they were being committed by correcting them in her judgment. And so the holy church, when she has been hindered by the wickedness of unjust people for a time, will remember, and say: 'And with great care I sought out a cause which I did not know.' As if she were to say openly: The evils which I did not know in the behaviour of my elect I punished with strict judgment in wicked people.

In the third book of his *Pastoral Rule*, Gregory recommended how different types of people should be advised. He did so by setting up a series of binary oppositions. This schematic approach may seem overly black and white, but as the panorama of human types unfolds Gregory's insight and sensitivity become ever clearer. Just under one-third of the third book is translated here.

Regula pastoralis

3.2 How men are to be admonished in one way and women in another. Men are to be admonished in one way and women in another, because heavier things are to be imposed on the former and lighter on the latter, so that great things may exercise the former and easy ones convert the latter by means of gentleness.

That the young are to be admonished in one way and the elderly in another.

The young are to be admonished in one way and the elderly in another, because a stiff admonition often guides the former towards making progress, whereas a gentle request prepares the latter for good works. Indeed, it is written *Do not rebuke an older person, but entreat him as a father* [1 Tim. 5:1].

That the poor are to be admonished in one way and the wealthy in another.

The poor are to be admonished in one way and the wealthy in another, for we ought to offer the former consoling comfort in the face of their distress, and inspire among the latter fear in the face of their pride. Indeed, it is said to a destitute person by the Lord through the prophet: *Fear not, because you will not be put to confusion* [Isa. 54:4]. And not long afterwards he speaks to her in a kindly way: *Poor little woman tossed in a storm* [Isa. 54:11]. Again he comforts her, saying: *I have chosen you in the furnace of poverty* [Isa. 48:10]. But on the other hand Paul says to his disciple concerning the rich: *Enjoin the rich of this world not to be high-minded and not to trust in the uncertainty of their riches* [1 Tim. 6:17]. Here it should be particularly noted that the teacher of humility, when he refers to the rich, does not say 'Ask' but 'Enjoin', because while kindness is to be displayed towards weakness, respect is definitely not owed to pride. Therefore what needs to be said to such people is correctly expressed as an order given to those who swell up in their lofty imaginings even in passing circumstances. Concerning them the Lord says in the Gospel: *Woe to you that are rich, you have received your consolation* [Luke 6:24]. It is because they do not know the joys which are eternal that they console themselves with the abundance of the present life.

Therefore consolation is to be provided to those people who are being roasted in the furnace of poverty; and fear inspired in those who are being lifted up by the consolation of passing glory, so that the former may learn that they possess riches which they cannot see, and the latter come to know that they can by no means hold onto the riches which they can see. Nevertheless, the quality of their lives can completely change the order in which people are ranked; a rich person may be humble, or a poor person proud. And so the voice of the preacher ought to be adjusted to correspond to the life of the listener, so that he chastises the pride of a poor person with a strictness appropriate to the way in which it is not the poverty with which he is inflicted which makes him bend over, and that he beguiles the humility of rich people with a gentleness appropriate to their not being lifted up by the abundance which supports them.

Yet sometimes even a rich person who is proud can be appeased by kindly exhortation, because on most occasions even serious wounds are soothed by mild treatments, and people who are raving mad are often brought back to health by a kindly doctor, their state of madness being alleviated when he stoops down to them in a kindly way. We should pay careful attention to the fact that when an evil spirit laid hold of

Saul, David took a harp and caused his madness to subside [cf. 1 Sam. 16:23]. What is indicated by Saul but the pride of the powerful, and what by David but the humble lives of the saints? And so, when Saul was snatched by an unclean spirit and his madness was alleviated by the singing of David, this was because, when the reason of powerful people is turned into madness through their pride, it is appropriate that the calmness of our speech, as if it were the sweetness of a harp, calls it back to soundness of mind. But sometimes, when the powerful of this world are being censured, they should first be asked about situations which are similar, as if they applied to other people. And when they have pronounced the correct judgment, as if against another person, then, in ways that are fitting, they are to be chastised concerning their own offence, so that a mind swelling with worldly power which has trampled on the neck of its pride by its own judgment will be unable to lift itself up against the person who reproves; having been bound by a verdict from its own mouth, it will not be able to busy itself with its own defence.

So it was that the prophet Nathan, having come to rebuke the king, sought from him a judgment which was apparently to do with the case of a poor person against someone who was rich, so that the king would first give a judgment and then learn of his own guilt [cf. 2 Sam. 12:1ff.] since he would be completely unable to speak against a verdict which he had justly pronounced against himself. And so the holy man, seeing him as a sinner as well as a king, in wonderful stages took care, first to bind the bold wrongdoer by his own declaration, and then, moving to the attack, to operate on him. For a short while he concealed the identity of the one he was pursuing, but when he was in his grasp he suddenly struck him. Perhaps he would have fallen upon him less effectively if he had sought to chastise his guilt overtly when he began to speak with him, but, having opened with a case that was similar, he made the rebuke which he had kept hidden sharper. The doctor came to the sick person and saw the wound which was to be healed, but he was unsure what the sick person could tolerate. So he concealed the surgeon's knife under his clothes, and then, having pulled it out, suddenly plunged it into the wound, so that the sick person felt the knife with which he was operating before he saw it; otherwise, having first seen it, he may have refused to feel it.

3 How the happy are to be admonished in one way and the sad in another.

The happy are to be admonished in one way, and the sad in another. There should be placed before the happy the sorrows that punishment brings, but there should be placed before the sad the joys of the kingdom that are promised. Let the happy learn from bitter threats what they should fear; let the sad hear of the joyous rewards which they can look forward to. Indeed, it is said to the former: *Woe unto you who laugh now, because you will weep* [Luke 6:25], but the latter will hear that same Teacher say: *I will see you again, let your heart rejoice, and let no-one take your joy from you* [John 16:22]. But there are those who are not happy or sad because of their possessions; they are this way because of the types of people they are. It has to be explained to such people that certain vices exist in association with certain types of people. For happy people are not far removed from loose living, nor are sad people from anger. And so each person has to consider not merely the situation in which he is placed because of the type of person he is, but also something worse of a similar nature which presses hard upon him, in case, failing to fight against that which he has to put up with, he succumbs as well to a vice from which he thinks himself free.

4   How subordinates are to be admonished in one way, and superiors in another.

Subordinates are to be admonished in one way, and superiors in another: the former, so that their lower state does not grind them down; the latter, so that their higher place does not lift them up; the former, in case they fail to carry out what they are ordered to do; the latter, in case they order that more than is just is to be carried out; the former, that they be subordinate in humility; the latter, that they exercise command with moderation. For there is said to the former something which can be understood in a figurative way: *Children, obey your parents in the Lord* [Eph. 6:1; cf. Col. 3:20.]. But there is enjoined upon the latter: *And fathers, do not provoke your children to anger* [Eph. 6:40; Col. 3.21]. Let the former learn how to set their inward dispositions in order before the eyes of the hidden Judge; the latter, how to provide those entrusted to them with visible examples of good living.

For superiors ought to know that if they ever do things which are wrong, they will deserve to die as many times over as the number of examples of perdition they pass on to their subordinates. And so it is necessary for them to restrain themselves from wrong with particular care, because they are not the only ones who die because of the wrong things they do. In cases where conduct which is not blameless is found, subordinates are to be admonished, lest they are punished with greater strictness, and superiors, lest they are judged for the faults of their subordinates, even if they find they have nothing to fear as far as their own conduct goes; the former, that they live with as much attention to themselves as befits those who do not have to care for others; but the latter, that they discharge their cares for others while not ceasing to care for themselves, and not to be so passionately concerned with themselves that they become indolent in watching over the people entrusted to them.

It is said to the former, who is free to attend to himself: *Go unto the ant, you sluggard, and consider her ways, and learn wisdom* [Prov. 6:6]. Whereas the latter is admonished in a frightening fashion, when it is said: *My son, if you make a solemn promise on behalf of your friend, you have pledged your hand on behalf of a stranger, you are trapped by the words of your mouth, and held captive by your own speech* [Prov. 6:1f.]. For to make a solemn promise on behalf of a friend is to receive someone else's soul, to the danger of your life. The hand is pledged on behalf of a stranger, because the mind is bound by a duty of care which it had not previously had. Someone is trapped by the words of his mouth and held captive by his own speech, because when he has to declare what is good to those who have been entrusted to him it is necessary that he first live in accordance with the things which he says. Therefore, someone is trapped by the words of his mouth when necessity constrains him not to let his life become slack so that it contradicts his admonitions. And so he is forced, in the sight of the strict Judge, to enact in his deeds the very things people have seen him urge upon others with his voice. An appropriate exhortation immediately follows, as it says: *And so do what I say, my son, and deliver yourself, because you have fallen into the hand of your neighbour; run, make haste, awaken your friend; do not allow your eyes to sleep, and let not your eyelids slumber* [Prov. 6:3f.]. For anyone who is placed above others to give an example of how to live is admonished not only to keep watch over himself but also to awaken his friend. For it is not enough for him to keep watch over himself by living well if he does not separate someone over whom he is placed from the lethargy of sin. To be sure, it is well said: *Do not allow your eyes to sleep, and let not your eyelids slumber.* For to give sleep to the eyes is to let one's attention wander and forget about the care of one's subordinates. Now the eyelids slumber when our thoughts, weighed down by laziness, pay no heed to those things in our subordinates which they know ought to be rebuked. We are fully asleep when we neither know about nor correct the deeds of those entrusted to us. We are not asleep but are slumbering when, knowing the things which ought to be censured, we are nevertheless held back by some weariness of the mind from correcting them with due rebukes. The eye is drawn from drowsing to deep sleep, because when a superior does not put a stop to an evil which is known to him, it generally comes about, thanks to his negligence, that he does not know about the wrong-doing of his subordinates.

Therefore, superiors are to be admonished to strive to become living creatures of heaven by looking carefully all around them. Yes, the living creatures of heaven are described as being full of eyes round about and within [cf. Rev. 4:6], and it is fitting that all who are superiors have eyes within and round about, since they should do their best to please the interior Judge within themselves and, giving examples of how to live outwardly, discover as well the things which need to be corrected in others.

Subordinates are to be admonished that, if they happen to see those placed above them acting reprehensibly, they should not be reckless in judging their lives, in case a justified rebuke of their evil deeds sees them plunged further into the deep because of their pride. These people are to be admonished in case the notice they take of the failings of those placed above them should move them to presumption against them; rather, they should judge those things which are really wicked in private so that, constrained by the fear of God, they do not refuse to bear the yoke of respect under them.

We will show this more clearly by bringing forward what David did. Now when Saul, his persecutor, had entered a cave to answer the call of nature, David, who had for a long time been enduring evil acts of persecution from him, went in there with his men. When his men egged him on to slay Saul, he restrained them, answering that he ought not lay his hand on the Lord's anointed. Nevertheless he went up in secret and cut off the edge of his cloak [1 Sam. 24:3f.]. Now what is designated by Saul but bad rulers, and what by David but good subordinates? Therefore, for Saul to answer the call of nature is for bad superiors to broaden the extent of the malice they have conceived in their hearts to the point of foul-smelling works, and to make public the wicked things they had thought of in private by carrying them out in the open. Yet David was afraid to slay him, because the minds of subordinates, when they are virtuous, refrain from any carping disparagement, and the sword of their tongues never strikes the lives of their superiors, even when they find fault with their weakness. Even when, because of their lack of strength, they simply cannot restrain themselves from speaking, even in a humble way, about the dreadful wrongs which their superiors have committed on the outside, as it were they silently cut off the edge of a cloak; because clearly, when they disparage a higher dignity, even without causing harm and in secret, it is as if they made the clothing of a king who was placed above them dirty; nevertheless, they return to themselves and bitterly blame themselves for the slightest wounding word. And so it is well written in this case: *Afterwards David struck his heart, because he had cut off the edge of Saul's cloak* [1 Sam. 24:5]. Yes, the deeds of superiors are not to be struck with the sword of speech, even when they are rightly judged to be worthy of censure. But if someone's tongue is loosened against them, even in a small way, the heart of that person must endure the hardship of penitence, so that by this means it may return to itself; having committed an offence against a superior power, it should be in dread of judgment being passed against it by the one who placed it in a higher position. For when we commit offences against those placed above us, we set ourselves against the ranking established by the one who placed them above us. Hence Moses too, when he saw the people complaining against himself and Aaron, said: *For what are we? Your murmuring is not against us, but against the Lord* [Exod. 16:8].

5   How servants are to be admonished in one way and masters in another.

Servants are to be admonished in one way and masters in another. Servants, that they never lose sight of their lowly rank, but masters, that they do not forget that they were created equal in nature to their servants. Servants are to be admonished not to despise God by being so proud as to speak against the ranks he has established; masters are also to be admonished, because if they do not recognize those whom they regard as their inferiors to rank as being their equals of the nature they share, they are showing pride against God because of some function he has given them. The former are to be admonished to think of themselves as servants of their masters; the latter are to be admonished to recognize that they are the fellow servants of their servants. For it is said to the former: *Servants, obey your masters according to the flesh* [Col. 3:22]. And again: *Let all those servants who are under the yoke think their masters worthy of all honour* [1 Tim. 6:1]; whereas it is said to the latter: *And you, masters, do the same to them, forgoing threats, knowing that he who is both their Lord and yours is in heaven* [Eph. 6:9].

6   How the wise of this world are to be admonished in one way and the foolish in another.

The wise of this world are to be admonished in one way and the foolish in another. For the wise are to be admonished to let go of knowing what they know; the foolish are also to be admonished, to strive to know what they do not know. Among the former one thing has to be destroyed right away, their estimation of themselves as being wise; among the latter, whatever someone may know of the wisdom above needs to be consolidated at this time, because through their lack of pride they have, as it were, prepared their hearts to be built upon. With the former it is necessary to labour so that, for them to become foolish in a fashion that is more wise, they may abandon foolish wisdom and learn the wise foolishness of God; but it should be proclaimed to the latter that they need to pass from that which is thought foolishness in order to draw nearer to true wisdom. For it is said to the former: *Whoever among you seems to be wise in this world, let him become a fool, that he may be wise* [1 Cor. 3:18]; but to the latter it is said: *Not many wise according to the flesh.*[4] And again: *God has chosen the foolish things of the world, to confound the wise* [1 Cor. 1:27]. Arguments based on reason generally convert the former; sometimes examples work better with the latter. With the former it is advantageous for them to end up lying on the ground, their arguments having been defeated; but for the latter it is sometimes enough for them to know of the praiseworthy deeds of others.

And so that outstanding teacher, *a debtor to the wise and unwise* [Rom. 1:14], when he admonished the Hebrews, some of whom were wise but others slow, when speaking to them of the fulfilment of the Old Testament, overcame their wisdom by an argument, saying: *For what is becoming obsolete and growing old is ready to vanish away* [Heb. 8:13]. But when he perceived that some had to be won over by examples alone, he added in the same letter: *The saints experienced mockings and floggings, bonds and imprisonment as well; they were stoned, sawn in two, tempted, slain when struck by the sword* [Heb. 11:36f.]. And again: *Remember those who are placed over you, who spoke the word of God to you, and, observing the outcome of their conduct, imitate their faith* [Heb. 13:7]. As can be seen, triumphant reason would vanquish the former, while gentle imitation would persuade the latter to rise to higher things.

7   How those lacking in shame are to be admonished in one way and the sensitive in another.

Those lacking in shame are to be admonished in one way and the sensitive in another. For nothing less than a harsh rebuke restrains the former from their vice of shamelessness; but gentle encouragement is usually enough to turn the latter in a better direction. The former do not know they are doing anything wrong unless many people rebuke them; a teacher who reminds them of their evil deeds in a mild way is usually enough to convert the latter. One who censures the former with firmness straightens them out with greater success, whereas the latter make better progress if that which is to be censured in them is, as it were, touched on in a roundabout way. For the Lord rebukes the shameless people of the Jews openly, saying: *You had the forehead of a prostitute and refused to blush* [Jer. 3:3]. On the other hand he encourages the sensitive, saying: *You shall forget the disorder of your youth, and you shall not recall the shame of your widowhood, because he who made you shall be your ruler*.⁵ Paul as well rebuked the Galatians who were shamelessly doing wrong in an outspoken manner, saying: *O foolish Galatians, who has bewitched you?* And again: *Are you so foolish that, having begun with the Spirit, you are now coming to your fulfilment in the flesh?* [Gal. 3:1–3] But he rebuked the faults of the sensitive as if he was suffering with them, saying: *I have rejoiced in the Lord greatly, since your care for me has at last flowered again; you used to care, but lacked opportunity* [Phil. 4:10]. Hence, a rebuke would bring to light the faults of the former, and softer speech veil the negligence of the latter.

8 How the arrogant are to be rebuked in one way and the timid in another.

The arrogant are to be rebuked in one way and the timid in another. For the former, in their utter self-confidence, pour scorn on others with reproaches; but the latter, who are all too aware of their own weakness, quite commonly fall into despair. The former have the highest opinion of everything they do; the latter, thinking that what they do is beneath contempt, are broken by despair. The works of the arrogant must therefore be carefully analysed with a sharp eye by the person who censures them, so that it might be shown how they displease God in thinking well of themselves.

For we better correct the arrogant when we show that the things which they believe they did well were really done badly, so that in the place where glory was believed to have been gained, there follows a confusion which may be to their benefit. But sometimes, when they are completely unaware of committing the vice of boldness, they can be corrected more efficiently by being thrown into confusion when another, more glaring fault is brought up in a roundabout way and reproached, so that they may know from something they are unable to defend that what they are defending is something improper. And so, when Paul saw each of the Corinthians puffed up against the others in his pride, so that one said he was of Paul, another of Apollos, another of Cephas, and another of Christ [1 Cor. 1:12], he placed before them a case of incest which had been committed among them and remained uncorrected, saying: *It is reported that there is fornication among you, and fornication of a kind unknown among the gentiles, that someone should have the wife of his father. And you are puffed up, and have not mourned deeply, so that the one who has done this deed might be removed from among you* [1 Cor. 5:1f.]. As if he were to say openly: Why are you so proud as to say that you are this person's or that person's, when you show through your laid-back indifference that you are no-one's?

On the other hand, we lead the timid to the path of proper conduct more appropriately if we try to identify in a roundabout way some good deeds of theirs, so that when we reprove and censure some things in them, we can praise others which we cherish, since when they hear praise their gentle nature, which the rebuke of a fault castigates, is strengthened. We generally have more success with them if we mention those good things which they have done and, if there are some things which have been done by them in an improper way, we should correct them not as if they had already been done but as though we are forbidding them to do something which they should not do. In this way the goodwill which we display towards the timid can strengthen the conduct of which we approve, and a mild exhortation against those things which we rebuke will be more effective. And so the same Paul, when he realized that the Thessalonians, while standing firm in the preaching they had received, were troubled by faintheartedness at the apparently imminent end of the world, first praises them because of their strong qualities which he could plainly see, and then carefully the qualities which were weak strengthens by giving them advice. For he said: *We are bound to thank God always for you, brothers, as is right, because your faith grows more and more, and the charity of each of you towards the others abounds; so that we ourselves boast of you among the churches of God, for your patience and faith* [2 Thess. 1:3f.]. Having placed these positive commendations of their lives at the beginning, a little while later he went on to add: *But we ask you, brothers, through the coming of our Lord Jesus Christ, and our gathering together to him, that you be not quickly turned away from your reason, nor alarmed, whether by a spirit or a word or indeed a letter as if from us, as though the day of the Lord were at hand* [2 Thess. 2:1f.]. A true teacher, he acted so that first, when they were praised, they would hear what they would recognize as being true, and then, when they were exhorted, they would comply. In case the admonition which followed unsettled their minds, praise was placed at the beginning to strengthen them. Knowing that they were made anxious by a concern that the end was near, he did not rebuke their distress but, as though unaware of what had happened, forbade them to be anxious in the future; so that, when they thought their frivolous ideas were unknown to their preacher, they would fear being open to censure if he did find out about them.

9   How the impatient are to be admonished in one way and the patient in another.

The impatient are to be admonished in one way and the patient in another. For the impatient are to be told that when they neglect to restrain their spirit they are also seized and carried away across many dangerous paths of wickedness which they did not seek, because it is clear that when someone is enraged the mind is forced to go where desire does not lead it, and when it is stirred up it does things, unawares, which make it grieve later when it becomes aware. The impatient are also to be told that when, in obedience to a headstrong impulse, they do things as though they were out of their minds, later on they will scarcely be able to recognize the evils they have perpetrated as their own. When they offer scarcely any resistance to their emotions, they ruin the things which they did well when their minds were tranquil, and by their thoughtless impulse they destroy what it may have taken long and careful toil to construct. For the virtue of charity, she who is the mother and guardian of all the virtues, is lost through the vice of impatience. Indeed, it is written: *Love is patient* [1 Cor. 13:4]. Therefore, without patience there is no love. Moreover, through the vice of impatience teaching, the very nurse of virtues, is brought to nothing. For it is written: *A man's learning can be known by his patience* [Prov. 19:11 Vulg.]. Therefore, to the extent that someone is proven to be less patient, he is shown to be less instructed. For someone who does not know how to tolerate the evils of others with calmness of mind as he makes his way through life cannot, in truth, impart good things through his teaching.

Moreover, through this vice of impatience the fault of showing-off frequently comes to pierce the mind, because, when someone who cannot bear being looked down on in this world tries to make a public display of whatever good qualities may lie hidden in him, he is in this way brought from impatience to showing-off; being unable to bear being looked down on, he takes prides in exposing himself ostentatiously. And so it is written: *A patient person is better than someone who is proud* [Eccles. 7:9]. This is clearly because a patient person chooses to endure whatever evils occur rather than for his hidden merits to be made known by the vice of ostentation. But on the contrary, a person who shows off chooses to have his good qualities put on display, even if they are not genuine, so that he does not have to suffer evils, however small.

Because even good things which have been done in the past are destroyed when patience is left behind, it was fittingly revealed to Ezekiel that in the altar of God there was a furrow, where the burnt offerings which had been placed above it might be kept [cf. Ezek. 43:13f.]. For if the altar did not have a furrow, any wind which blew up would scatter whatever sacrifice it found on it. But what do we take the altar of God to be, but the soul of a just person, the good works it performs being as numerous as the sacrifices placed before the eyes of God above the altar? And what is the furrow of the altar but the patience of good people which, when it lowers its mind to tolerate adverse circumstances, shows that it is placed in the lowest place, something like a kind of pit? Therefore the altar had a furrow, in case the wind scattered a sacrifice placed above it; that is, the minds of the elect keep watch over their patience in case, moved by a wind of impatience, they lose even that which they had done well. And this furrow is fittingly said to have been of one cubit, because the quality of oneness is maintained for as long as patience is not abandoned. And so it is that Paul says: *Bear one another's burdens, and so you will fulfill the law of Christ* [Gal. 6:2].

Now the law of Christ is the love of unity, and the only people who carry this out are those who do not take themselves off when they are burdened. Let the impatient hear what is written: *A patient person is better than a strong man, and one who is lord of his soul better than one who takes cities* [Prov. 16:32]. Victory over cities is less important, because the things that are subjugated are external; what is defeated through patience is much greater, because the soul is overcome by itself, and subjects itself to itself, when patience forces it to restrain itself inwardly. Let the impatient hear what Truth says to his elect: *Possess your souls in patience* [Luke 21:19]. For we have been created in a wonderful manner, so that reason possesses the soul, and the soul the body. And the soul loses its jurisdiction over and possession of the body, if it is itself not first possessed by reason. Therefore the Lord, who taught us to possess ourselves in patience, showed that it is the guardian of our human condition. And so we learn how great is the fault of impatience; through it we lose possession of that very thing we are. Let the impatient again hear what is said through Solomon: *The fool utters his whole spirit, but the wise person holds it back and keeps it for later* [Prov. 29:11]. Yes, through the force of impatience the whole spirit is brought into the light of day; if someone is upset it comes out more quickly, when there is no practice of wisdom to shut it in. But a wise person holds it back and keeps it for later. For when he is wronged he does not immediately desire to take vengeance, in fact he puts up with what has happened and even wants it to be forgotten, but nevertheless he well knows that at the last judgment all things will be avenged with justice.

On the other hand, the patient are to be admonished not to grieve inwardly because of what they endure outwardly, in case, by an infection of ill will on the inside, they corrupt the unblemished sacrifice, so valuable, which they offer on the outside; although people cannot see it, nevertheless with respect to the divine judgment sin has been committed, and the more it claims for itself the appearance of virtue before men, the worse the crime becomes.

The patient should be told to go out of their way to love those whom they have to tolerate in case, if love does not accompany it, the virtue they have displayed is changed into the very serious sin of hatred. So Paul, when he said *Love is patient*, immediately added *it is kind* [1 Cor. 13:4], thereby showing that those whom he tolerates out of patience he does not cease to love out of kindness as well. So it is that the same excellent teacher, when commending patience to his disciples, said: *Let all bitterness, wrath, indignation, clamour and evil speaking be put away from you*; and then, having, as it were, set all exterior things in proper order, he turns to interior things, adding *together with all malice* [Eph. 4:31].

Indeed, indignation, clamour and evil speaking are put away on the outside in vain if malice, the mother of vices, is in control on the inside; wickedness is cut from the branches on the outside to no purpose if it is retained in the root on the inside, from which it may rise up in more numerous ways. And so the Truth says well, in his own person: *Love your enemies, do good to those who hate you, pray for those who persecute you and tell untruths about you* [Matt. 5:44]. People consider it a virtue to tolerate their enemies, but God considers loving them a virtue, because the only sacrifice God accepts is one which the flame of charity sets alight before his eyes on the altar of good work. So it is that again he says to people who are patient but do not love: *Why do you see the speck in your brother's eye and not the beam in your own eye?* [Matt. 7:3]. Now an impulse towards impatience is a speck, but malice in the heart is a beam in the eye. For a breath of temptation sets the former in motion, whereas wickedness which has come to fruition carries along the latter, with scarcely any movement. Rightly therefore does he go on: *Hypocrite, first cast the beam out of your own eye, and then you will see how to remove the speck from your brother's eye* [Matt. 7:5]. As if he were saying to an evil mind which was feeling aggrieved inwardly while representing itself on the outside as holy because of its patience: first cast the heavy weight of malice away from yourself, and then rebuke others for their minor failing of impatience, for if you do not make an effort to overcome your insincerity, tolerating someone else's bad deeds may turn out to be something worse for you.

It very often happens to patient people that, on occasions when things go wrong for them or they listen to abuse, they experience no resentment, and such is the degree of patience they demonstrate that they maintain watchfulness over the innocence of their hearts; but when, a little while later, they call to mind again the things which they have suffered, they kindle within themselves the fire of resentment, look for a means of vengeance, and, reconsidering things, they turn the gentleness which they possessed when they were suffering into malice. Aid is more promptly brought to them by the preacher if the agent which causes this change is disclosed to them. For the cunning enemy initiates warfare against two people: first he rouses one to utter insults; then he provokes the other, who has been wounded, to pay the insults back. But very often, when he has already defeated the one who was persuaded to inflict the injury, he is overcome by the one who bore what was uttered with tranquillity. Therefore, being the victor over one, whom he subjugated by playing on his feelings, he raises himself up against the other with all his strength, angry that this person was offering strong resistance and gaining the victory. Having been unable to throw him off balance by hurling insults, he withdraws for a while from open struggle and, playing on his thoughts by suggesting things in secret, awaits the right time to trick him. Having failed in public warfare, he is on fire to carry out his plots in an unseen way. For indeed, at a time of quiet he returns to the mind of the victor and brings back to his memory the goods he has lost or the darts of injuries, and, exaggerating them in an extreme fashion, demonstrates that all the things he experienced were intolerable; and he unsettles his mind with such powerful grief that after his victory a patient person is very often taken captive, blushes having tolerated what happened in tranquillity, regrets not having returned the insults, and looks for a way to retaliate with worse things, should the chance be given.

Whom do these people resemble, unless those whose bravery allows them to be victorious in the field of battle, but whose carelessness lets them later be taken captive inside the walls of the city? Whom do they resemble, unless those who do not lose their lives when a serious illness strikes them suddenly, but are killed by a recurrent fever which sneaks up on them stealthily? Patient people should therefore be admonished to put their hearts in a state of defence after a victory, to keep their eyes open for the enemy who, having been overcome in open fighting, is lying ready to ambush the walls of the mind, and to fear even more the illness which creeps back, in case the cunning enemy is later able to rejoice and take all the more pleasure in his deception, because he is trampling underfoot the necks of the victorious which had formerly been held upright against him.

10   How people of good will are to be admonished in one way and the envious in another way.
People of good will are to be admonished in one way and the envious in another. For people of good will are to be admonished to rejoice

in the good deeds of other people in such a way that they long to possess them as well. Let their praise for the deeds of their neighbours take the form of loving them, so that in the act of imitating these deeds they multiply them. Otherwise, if they are present in the stadium of this present life as no more than keen supporters of the contests of others, being themselves lazy spectators, after the contest they may remain without a prize; because they are not toiling in the contest now, with affliction they may then have to look upon the palms of victory won by people whose toils they are now too lazy to endure. To be sure, we sin seriously if we do not love the things that other people do well. But we receive no reward if we do not imitate the things that we love to the best of our ability.

Therefore, people of good will are to be told that, if they do not hasten to imitate the good deeds which they commend and praise, the holiness of virtues gives them pleasure in the same way that the contrived vanity of public entertainments pleases foolish spectators. For they loudly applaud the deeds of charioteers and actors, but nevertheless they do not wish to be the kind of people they see those whom they praise to be. They marvel that they have done the things which give them such pleasure, but still they refrain from giving pleasure in a similar way. People of good will are to be told that when they look upon the deeds of their neighbours they should return to their own hearts, and not take confidence from what other people do, in case they praise good deeds which they refuse to do. Those people who did not wish to imitate what pleased them will certainly be treated with greater harshness at the last judgment.

The envious are to be admonished to consider with due care how blind those people are who fail to make the progress that other people do and pine away at the exultation of others. How wretched those people are who become worse as their neighbour gets better! When they see the growing successes of other people, they become dejected and despondent, and die of an infected heart. Can there be a situation more unhappy than that of people who, having been made miserable at the sight of happiness, are made more wicked by their punishment? Nevertheless, if they had loved the good deeds of others which they were unable to possess themselves, they would have made them their own. Now this is what all those who stand firm in the faith are like: they are joined together like many limbs in one body, and while they obviously have different functions they become one, because they are combined in a harmonious manner. And so it comes about that the foot can see through the eye and the eyes walk through the feet, the hearing of the ears benefits the mouth and the tongue in the mouth helps the ears to do their job, and the stomach gives assistance to the hands while the hands work for the stomach [cf. 1 Cor. 12:14ff]. So we can deduce from the arrangement of the body what kind of behaviour we should practise. It would therefore be shameful if we did not imitate that which we are. The things which we love in others, even if we cannot imitate them, are ours as well; and whatever is loved in us becomes the property of those who love us. And so the envious should consider how great is the power of love, which turns someone else's work into ours, without any effort on our part.

And so the envious are to be told that when they fail to guard themselves from jealousy they are plunged into the ancient wickedness of the clever enemy. For it is written of him: *Death entered the world through the envy of the devil* [Wisd. 2:24]. Having lost heaven himself he envied the human who had been created and, lost as he was, piled up further damnation for himself by causing others to be lost. The envious are to be admonished to recognise that they are subject to many falls and a ruin which steadily accumulates, because from failing to dispel envy from their hearts they go downhill to the point of performing wicked deeds in public. For if Cain had not been envious when the sacrifice of his brother was accepted, he would certainly not have come to take his life. And so it is written: *And the Lord looked upon Abel and his offerings; but he did not look upon Cain and his offerings. And Cain was very angry, and his face fell* [Gen. 4:4f.]. Envy over a sacrifice was thus the seedbed of fratricide. In his grief that someone was better than he was, he put an end to him so that he simply did not exist. The envious should be told that when they are consuming themselves inwardly with the infection of envy, they are also putting to death anything good which can be seen in them. And so it is written: *A wholesome heart is the life of the flesh, envy is the rottenness of bones* [Prov. 14:30]. What is meant by the flesh other than weak and tender things, and what by bones other than strength in action? And it very often happens that some people whose hearts are innocent appear weak in some of their acts, while others who are already undertaking activities which appear mighty before human eyes are nevertheless wasting away on the inside, having been infected by envy of the good activities of others. It is therefore well said that *a wholesome heart is the life of the flesh*; because if the innocence of the mind is safeguarded, even those things which are weak on the outside are made strong at some time. And therefore it rightly goes on *envy is the rottenness of bones*, because through the vice of envy even those things which seem strong to human eyes perish before the eyes of God. For bones to rot because of envy is for things, even strong ones, to perish.

11 How people without guile are to be admonished in one way and false people in another.

People without guile are to be admonished in one way and false people in another. Those without guile are to be praised, because they take care never to say things which are false, but they are to be admonished so that they know they should sometimes keep silent about things which are true. For just as a falsehood always harms the one who utters it, so people can sometimes be hurt by hearing the truth. So it was that the Lord restrained his speech in the presence of his disciples by keeping silent, saying: *I have many things to say to you, but you cannot bear them now* [John 16:12]. And so people without guile should be admonished so that, just as they always avoid falsehood in a way that is beneficial, so they should also always speak the truth in a beneficial way. They are to be admonished to join prudence to the good of guilelessness, and to be firmly rooted in the latter in such a way that they do not lose the circumspection which prudence provides. For it is said on this matter through the teacher of the gentiles: *I want you to be wise in what is good, but innocent concerning what is bad.*[6] Truth himself admonishes his elect in his own voice, saying: *Be as prudent as serpents, and as guileless as doves* [Matt. 10:16]. This is because the slyness of the serpent ought to make the guilelessness of the dove more intense in the hearts of the elect, just as the guilelessness of the dove ought to hold the slyness of the serpent in check; this will mean that they are not led astray by prudence so that they become too smart, nor too lazy to think clearly because of their guilelessness.

On the other hand, false people are to be admonished to acknowledge how heavy is the toil of duplicity which they sustain, by their own fault. For in their fear of being detected they are always looking for shameless defences and always tossed about by their terrifying suspicions. But nothing can be defended with greater safety than something which is crystal clear; there is nothing easier to speak than the truth. For when someone is forced to defend his own intrigue, the hard work wearies his heart. Hence it is written concerning this: *The labour of their lips shall cover them.*[7] For what fills his lips now covers them then, because the one who now displays his heart behind a bland front of disquiet, then buries it away, in a harsh repayment. And so it is said through Jeremiah: *They taught their tongues to speak lies, they laboured to act wickedly* [Jer. 9:5]. As if it were said openly: those who could have been friends of the truth without any labour, labour so that they may sin; and when they turn away from a guileless life they wear themselves out so that they may die. For having been detected in a fault they shun being recognized for the kind of people they are and generally hide themselves under a veil of falsehood, and when the depth of their sin is apparent they do their best to excuse it; so that anyone who is trying to correct their faults often sees that what he believed to be certain about them has almost disappeared in the clouds of falsehood which have been scattered about.

And so it is rightly said through the prophet against a sinful soul making excuses for itself, in the form of Judaea: *There shall the hedgehog have its lair* [Isa. 34:15]. Now the word hedgehog designates the duplicity of a false-minded person who defends himself with cunning, because when someone takes hold of a hedgehog its head can be perceived, its feet seen, and its whole body made out, but scarcely has it been taken hold of it when it gathers itself into a ball, pulls its feet in and hides its head; something which could be seen in its entirety a moment before now completely disappears within the hands of the person holding it. False minds detected in their transgressions are just like this. The head of a hedgehog is perceived, because it can be seen from where the sinner began his approach towards wrongdoing. The feet of the hedgehog are made out, because it becomes clear through its footprints that evil was perpetrated. Nevertheless, when it suddenly makes excuses the insincere mind pulls in its feet, because it conceals all traces of its wickedness. It withdraws its head, because by the wonderful defences it makes it shows that it did not so much as begin to do anything wrong. And it remains like a ball in the hand of whoever holds it, because the person who rebukes it, suddenly losing sight of all the things which he had known, is left holding a sinner who is wrapped up inside his conscience, and the person who could see everything when he took hold of it, having been deceived by its shifty and wicked defence, comes to know nothing at all about it. Clearly, the hedgehog has its lair with the wicked, because the duplicity of a crafty mind gathers itself together and conceals itself behind a protective darkness.

Let the false hear what is written: *One who walks with guilelessness walks with confidence* [Prov. 10:9]. Yes, guileless conduct is a guarantee of great security. Let them hear what is said through the mouth of a wise person: *Our instructor, the Holy Spirit, flees from what is false* [Wisd. 1:5]. Let them hear what is again asserted by the witness of Scripture: *He converses with the guileless* [Prov. 3:32]. For God to converse is for him to reveal hidden things to human minds through the light provided by his presence. And so he is said to converse with the guileless because, through the shining ray with which he visits them, he enlightens their minds concerning the mysteries above which no shadow of duplicity can darken. For there is an evil specific to the duplicitous, because when they deceive others by their perverse and duplicitous behaviour they pride themselves in being more prudent than other people, and because the wretches give no thought to the strictness of retribution, they boast of what they have lost. But let them hear how strong is the divine punishment with which the prophet Sophonia threatens them, saying: *Lo, the great and terrifying day of the Lord comes, the day which is a day of wrath, a day of darkness and gloom, a day of cloud and whirlwind, a day of the trumpet and blaring noise above all the fortified cities and all the high cornerstones* [Soph. 1:14–16]. For what is meant by the fortified cities but suspicious minds, always surrounded by deceptive defences, which, whenever their wrongdoing is rebuked, prevent the javelins of truth from coming near? And, given that two walls always meet in a corner,[8] what is designated by the cornerstones but false hearts which, in their flight from the guilelessness of truth, are as it were twisted back towards themselves by a perverse duplicity. What is worse, in their private thoughts they are proud of themselves, considering that the very fault of falsity is in reality prudence. Therefore the day of the Lord, full of vengeance and punishment, is coming upon the fortified cities and upon the high cornerstones, because the wrath of the last judgment destroys human hearts enclosed within their defences against the truth, and breaks into pieces people who had been twisted in their duplicities. Then the fortified cities fall, because minds which were unyielding to God will be condemned. Then the high corner stones tumble down, because hearts which lift themselves up through a false prudence will be cast down through the sentence of justice.

12   How healthy people are to be admonished in one way, and those who are unwell in another.

Healthy people are to be admonished in one way, and those who are unwell in another. The healthy are to be admonished to make the health of the body work for the health of the mind, in case, if they turn the blessing of the good health they have received towards an evil purpose, this gift makes them become worse, and they go on to deserve punishments, the severity of which will reflect the extent to which they were not afraid to put God's abundant gifts to bad use. The healthy are to be admonished not to despise the opportunity of deserving everlasting salvation.[9] For it is written: *Behold, now is the acceptable time, behold now is the time of salvation* [2 Cor. 6:2]. They are to be admonished in case, having not wanted to please God when they were able, they will not be able to when, all too late, they want to. For this is why wisdom later abandons those whom she had previously been calling over a long period, despite their refusals, saying: *I called, and you refused; I held out my hand, and there was no-one to look upon it; you despised all my counsel and paid no attention to my rebukes; I shall laugh at your destruction and mock when what you feared comes upon you* [Prov. 1: 24–6]. And again: *Then they will call upon me, and I shall not listen to them; they will arise in the morning, and not find me* [Prov. 1:28]. So it is that, when the bodily health one has been received as a means of doing good is despised, one becomes aware of the greatness of the gift only when it is lost. And at the end, something which was given and not put to good use at an appropriate time is sought fruitlessly.

And so it is again well said through Solomon: *Do not give your honour to strangers, and your years to a cruel person; in case perchance strangers are filled with your power, and your labours are in another's home, and you mourn at the end, when you have consumed your flesh and body* [Prov. 5:9–11]. For who are strangers to us, but the evil spirits, who have been excluded from a share in the heavenly country? And what is our honour but that we, created in bodies of clay as we have been, have nevertheless been made in the image and likeness of our Creator? And who else is the cruel person, but that apostate angel who, in his pride, brought ruin upon himself as he was punished with death and, when he was lost, did not hesitate to bring death upon the human race? Therefore, someone created in the image and likeness of God who devotes the period of his life to serving the pleasures of evil spirits, gives his honour to strangers. And someone who spends the lifetime allotted him doing the will of an enemy who lords it over him in a cruel way hands over his years to a cruel person.

And so it is well added: *In case perchance strangers are filled with your power, and your labours are in another's home*. For whoever employs the health of body he has received and the wisdom of mind which has been given to him not in the exercise of virtues but in the perpetration of vices is using his energies to increase the size not of his own home but of the dwelling places of others, that is the deeds of unclean spirits, whether it be by loose living or proud conduct, so that the number of the lost grows as this person is added to it. It therefore goes on appropriately: *And you mourn at the end, when you have consumed your flesh and body*. For the bodily health we have received is generally used up when we practise vices; but when it is suddenly taken away, when the flesh is weakened by afflictions, when the soul is on the point of being forced to go forth, the health, now vanished, which was long employed for evil will be looked for, as if for the purpose of living well. And, being completely unable able to regain through the service of God what they lost through carelessness, people then groan at not having wished to serve him. And so it is said elsewhere: *When he killed them, then they sought him* [Ps. 78:34].

On the other hand, when the whips of discipline chastise those who are unwell, they are to be admonished to consider themselves as children of God. For if he did not intend to give an inheritance to those whom he had punished, he would not have taken care to educate them by way of hardships. So it is that the Lord says to John through an angel: *Those whom I love I rebuke and chastise* [Rev. 3:19]. Again it is written: *My son, do not neglect the discipline of the Lord, and do not faint when you are rebuked by him. For the Lord chastises the one he loves, he scourges every child whom he receives* [Heb. 12:5f.]. Again the psalmist says: *Many are the tribulations of the just* [Ps. 34:19]. Again, blessed Job, crying out in his anguish, says: *If I have been just I will not lift up my head, being completely filled with affliction and misery* [Job 10:15]. The unwell should be told that if they believe in the heavenly country they have to suffer here hardships which cannot be avoided, as it were in a strange country. For stones were struck with blows away from the temple of the Lord for a reason: when it was being built they could be laid in place without any noise from a hammer [cf. 1 Kgs 6:7]. It is clear that we are struck by scourges on the outside now, so that later, in an interior way, we can be placed in the temple of God without being chastised by discipline, seeing that present chastisement curtails whatever is superfluous in us, and in the future the concord of charity alone will bind us together in the building.

Those who are unwell are to be admonished to consider how harsh the scourges of discipline are which chastise children of the flesh so that they may receive earthly inheritances. So is the pain of divine punishment, through which an inheritance which will never be lost is received and punishments which will last for ever are avoided, really heavy? Paul says on this matter: *Indeed, we have had fathers according to the flesh to bring us up, and we paid them respect; shall we not submit the more to the Father of spirits, and live? Indeed, the former brought us up according to their will for a few days, but the latter does so to profit us, so that we might receive his holiness* [Heb. 12:9f.].

The unwell should be admonished to consider how bodily discomfort can benefit the health of the heart, for it calls the mind back to knowledge of itself and brings back the memory of its weakness, which health generally drives away, so that when the flesh is struck forcibly the soul, which was led outside itself in its pride, is made to remember the condition to which it is subject. This was well shown when Balaam's journey was delayed – if only he had been willing to follow the voice of God in obedience! [cf. Num. 22:22ff.] For Balaam was making his way towards his destination, but the animal under his control would not let him go as he wished. Yes, the she-ass, stopped in her tracks by a command, saw an angel which the human mind did not see, because very often the flesh, slowed down by its troubles, reveals God to the mind through being chastised. The mind which was controlling the flesh did not see him, and so impeded a spirit anxiously wishing to advance in this world, as though it were making a journey, until the invisible being who barred the way was made known to it. And so it is well said through Peter: *A dumb animal corrected his insanity, speaking in a human voice and restraining the madness of the prophet* [2 Pet. 2:16)] Yes, a mad person is rebuked by a dumb beast of burden when a mind which has been raised up in its pride is brought, by an affliction of the flesh, to remember the good of humility to which it ought to hold fast. But Balaam did not obtain benefit from this reproof, because when he was about to curse it was his voice, but not his mind, that he changed.

The unwell should be admonished to consider how great a gift physical affliction is. It washes away sins which have been committed and prevents others which could have been committed; while it originates in external misfortunes, it inflicts the wounds of penitence on the mind it strikes. And so it is written: *A wound which is blue wipes away evils; so do misfortunes in the inward parts of the belly* [Prov. 20:30]. A wound which is blue wipes away evils because painful scourges wash away wicked things which have been thought of or carried out. But the word belly is usually taken to refer to the mind, because just as the belly digests food, so the mind breaks down cares by cooking them thoroughly. That the mind is indicated by the belly is taught by the phrase where it is written: *Human breath is the lamp of the Lord, which searches out all the inward parts of the belly* [Prov. 20:27]. As if to say: The illumination of divine inspiration, when it enters the human mind, casts light upon it and makes something which, before the coming of the Holy Spirit, was able to experience bad thoughts without being aware that it was thinking them, capable of seeing itself. *A wound*, therefore, *which is blue wipes away evils; so do misfortunes in the inward parts of the belly*, because when we are struck outwardly we are called back to remember our sins in silence and affliction; we bring back before our eyes all the wrong things which we have done, and what we suffer outwardly makes us the more afflicted inwardly because of what we have done. And so it happens that, amid the wounds of the body which can be seen, a blow against the belly which is hidden cleanses us to a greater extent, because a wound of affliction which cannot be seen heals the wickedness of a bad deed.[10]

The unwell are to be admonished to preserve the virtue of patience by constantly bearing in mind how great were the evil deeds which our

Redeemer endured from those whom he created: that the mean reproaches and insults he bore, being struck on his face by scoffers, were as many as the souls of the captives he snatches every day from the hand of the ancient enemy; that, cleansing us with the water of salvation, he did not hide his face from the spittle of those without faith; that, freeing us from eternal torments by speaking on our behalf, he bore the scourges in silence; that, giving us everlasting honours among the choirs of angels, he suffered blows from fists; that, saving us from the pricking wounds of sins, he did not refuse to submit his head to the thorns; that, intoxicating us with an everlasting sweetness, he drank in his thirst bitter gall; that he who adored the Father on our behalf while being equal to him in divinity remained silent when he was adored in mockery; that, preparing life for the dead, he, life itself, went so far as to die. Why, therefore, is it considered bitter for a human to endure scourges from God for doing wrong, if God endured such great evils from humans for doing good? What person of sound understanding will there be who is not grateful for being beaten, if the one who lived here without sin did not depart without being scourged?

13   How those who live without doing wrong because they fear punishment are to be admonished in one way, and those who have become so hardened in wickedness that they cannot be corrected even by punishment, in another.

Those who live without doing wrong because they fear punishment are to be admonished in one way, and those who have become so hardened in wickedness that they cannot be corrected even by punishment in another. For those who fear punishment should be told that they should by no means desire temporal goods, which they see that even wicked people have, as though they were something important; and that they should by no means flee, as though they were something unbearable, present evils with which, as they cannot be ignorant, even good people are generally afflicted here below. They are to be admonished that, if they truly desire to be free from evils, they should dread the punishments which are everlasting; and they should not continue in this fear of punishments but, nourished by charity, grow up into the graciousness of love. Indeed, it is written: *Perfect love casts out fear* [1 John 4:18]. And again it is written: *You have not received a spirit of bondage again to fear, but the Spirit of adoption as sons, whereby we cry: Abba Father* [Rom. 8:15]. And so the same teacher says again: *Where the Spirit of the Lord is, there is freedom* [2 Cor. 3:17].

If, therefore, the dread of some punishment continues to hold someone back from acting wrongly, it is clear that the freedom of the Spirit does not hold sway in the mind of a person who lives in such fear.

For it cannot be doubted that, if he did not fear punishment, he would have acted wrongly. And so a mind which is held fast by the bondage of fear does not know the grace of freedom. For good things are to be loved for their own sakes, and not pursued because punishments are threatened. For a person who does good deeds because he fears being tormented harshly really wishes that there was nothing to fear, so that he could brazenly do things which are forbidden. And so it is clearer than daylight that from the perspective of God, before whose eyes sin has been committed in desire, innocence of life has been lost.

On the other hand, those who are not restrained from acts of bad behaviour by scourges are to be handled with invective, its bitterness proportionate to the extent they have become hardened in their inability to feel. For in most cases they should be treated in a scornful manner, but without real scorn, and despaired of, but without real despair; in this way the despair which has been put on display may produce dread, and the admonition which follows it may bring them back to hope. And so God's strict pronouncements against them should be brought forward, so that by reflecting on eternal chastisement they may be called back to knowledge of themselves. For let them hear how what is written has been fulfilled in themselves: *If you were to pound a fool in a mortar, and he was ground like grains of pearl barley, his foolishness would not be taken away from him* [Prov. 27:22]. Against such people the prophet complained to the Lord, saying: *You have consumed them, and they have refused to receive correction* [Jer. 5:3]. Here is what the Lord says: *I have done away with this people and abandoned them, and yet they have not turned back from their ways* [Jer. 15:7]. And again he says: *The people have not returned to the one who strikes them* [Isa. 9:13].

Again, the prophet complains, in the voice of those who administer punishment, saying: *We would have cured Babylon, and she is not healed* [Jer. 51:9]. Yes, the cure of Babylon is sought, but she is not brought back to health, when a mind, ashamed of its bad conduct, hears the words of correction and receives the scourges of correction, but nevertheless disdains to return to the straight paths of salvation. And so the Lord reproached the Israelite people who, despite having been taken captive, were nevertheless not brought to turn from their wickedness, saying: *The house of Israel has become dross to me; they are all bronze and tin and iron and lead in the midst of the furnace* [Ezek. 22:18]. As if he were to say openly: I wanted to purify them through the fire of suffering, and I wished them to become silver or gold, but in the furnace they have become to me bronze, tin, iron and lead, because even in their time of trial they were eager to hurry not to virtue but to vices. Now when bronze is struck, it resonates more than other metals.

119

Therefore, a person who grumbles when he is beaten by way of punishment is turned into bronze in the midst of the furnace. But tin, when it is skilfully worked, looks deceptively like silver. Therefore, a person who, in the midst of his suffering, does not free himself of the vice of hypocrisy, becomes tin in the furnace. Someone who plots against the life of his neighbour makes use of iron. Therefore, a person who maliciously persists in causing harm in the midst of his suffering is iron in the furnace. Now lead is heavier than other metals. Therefore, someone who, even in the midst of suffering, is so burdened by the weight of his sin that he is not lifted up from earthly desires, is found to be lead in the furnace. Here again it is written: *Despite much sweaty toil, her rust has not gone forth from her, even through fire* [cf. Ezek. 24:12]. Yes, he brings upon us the fire of suffering, to free us from the rust of vices; but when we persist in vice, even when we are being scourged, we do not lose the rust through fire. And so a prophet says again: *In vain has the founder smelted, for their malicious ways have not been destroyed* [Jer. 6:29].

But it should be known that people who have remained uncorrected while being scourged harshly can sometimes be softened by a gentle admonition. For sometimes gentle blandishments can restrain people whom torments have failed to correct from committing wicked acts, because lukewarm water quite often recalls to their former health those whom a strong potion was unable to cure, and some wounds which cannot be cured by surgery are healed by a soothing application of oil. And a hard diamond which can scarcely be cut is made soft by the mild blood of goats.[11]

14 How quiet people are to be admonished in one way and those who talk too much in another.

Quiet people are to be admonished in one way and those who talk too much in another. For it should be pointed out to quiet people that, by fleeing certain vices without proper thought, in a roundabout way they become entangled in worse things. For often, when they restrain their tongues more than they should, in their hearts they support a kind of excessive talk, which is worse, so that the thoughts which they restrain with some violence by maintaining too great a silence are boiling the more furiously in their minds. These thoughts tend to flow more widely when people think that, because they cannot be seen outwardly by those who could censure them, there is no need to worry. And so the mind is sometimes lifted up in pride and despises those it hears speaking as being weak. And when someone shuts the mouth of his body he fails to recognize how much he lays himself open to vices by being proud. Truly, in restraining his tongue he lifts up his mind;

and while he is oblivious to his own wickedness, he is privately making accusations against everyone else, with the freedom that secrecy provides.

Quiet people are therefore to be admonished to be very careful to understand not only how they should present themselves outwardly, but also how they should display themselves inwardly, so that they fear incurring a hidden judgment because of their thoughts more than a rebuke from their neighbours because of their words. For it is written: *My son, be attentive to my wisdom, and incline your ear to my prudence, so that you may keep careful watch over your thoughts* [Prov. 5:1f.]. Now there is nothing in us more inclined to run away than the heart, which goes away from us as often as it flows downwards with evil thoughts. The psalmist says concerning this: *My heart has deserted me* [Ps. 40:12]. Again, on returning to himself, he says: *Your servant has found his heart, so that he may pray to you* [2 Sam. 7:27]. Therefore, when thinking is held in check through watchfulness, the heart which used to run away is found.

But quiet people, when they endure injustices, generally pass on to a resentment which is the more bitter because of their failure to talk about their sufferings. For if their tongues were to speak in a calm way of the hardships they were suffering, resentment would simply flow away from their consciousness. Wounds which have been staunched cause more pain. For when the festering which had been taking place on the inside is expelled, a wound lies open so that it can be healed. Therefore, people who are silent more than is profitable ought to understand that they should not become more resentful by holding their tongues amid the hardships they suffer. For they are to be admonished that, if they love their neighbours as themselves, they should by no means keep silent about things for which they could justly rebuke them. For the medicine of the voice is good for both of them: the person doing a bad deed is restrained, and by the opening of the wound the fervour of resentment is abated in the person who experienced it.

For people who watch their neighbours doing bad things yet hold their tongues in silence are like those who, when they have seen wounds, withdraw medical treatment, so that by their unwillingness to cure the infection when they were able to they become causes of death. Therefore the tongue should be held in check with discernment, not bound so tightly that it cannot be untied. For it is written: *The wise person will keep silent until an opportune time* [Sir. 20:7], so that when he considers the circumstances favourable he puts aside his self imposed silence and, by speaking appropriately, devotes himself to what may be useful. And again it is written: *A time for speaking and a time for silence*

[Eccles. 3:7]. Indeed, the alternation of times needs to be considered with discernment; otherwise, the tongue it may babble away uselessly when it ought to be bound, or it may hold itself back in laziness when it could usefully speak. The psalmist, thinking this over, says: *Set a watch-house, O Lord, over my mouth, and a door to stand by my lips* [Ps. 141:3]. It was not a wall he sought to place before his mouth, but a watch-house, which could be opened and closed. And so we must learn to be circumspect, so that the voice may open a mouth which has discernment, and silence may again close it, at times which are appropriate.

On the other hand, people who talk too much are to be admonished to consider with due attention how great is the upright stance which they lose when they let themselves flow away in a flood of words. For the human mind is like water; when enclosed on every side it moves upwards as it comes together, seeking again the place from which it came down. But when it is released it goes to waste, scattering itself to no purpose across the low ground. For the pointless words by which a mind which had been in self-imposed silence wastefully scatters itself are as many as the streams by which it is led outside itself. And so the mind lacks the strength to return to knowledge of itself inwardly because, having been scattered abroad through talking too much, it has shut itself outside the secluded place of private reflection. And, as no defensive watchfulness encloses it, it lies completely exposed to the wounds of the enemy who plots against it. And so it is written: *As a city lying open with no walls around it, so is the man who is unable to curb his spirit in speaking* [Prov. 25:28]. Lacking the wall of silence, the city of the mind lies open to the javelins of the enemy, and when it casts itself outside itself through what it says, it shows that it lies open to the enemy. He overcomes such a mind without effort, because that which is being defeated is fighting against itself through talking too much.

But because the lazy mind is impelled to its downfall step by step, it generally happens that, from failing to guard against words which are idle, we come to those which cause harm; so that at first the tongue takes pleasure in speaking about other people's business, then it slanderously criticizes the lives of those it talks about, and finally it breaks out into open abuse. From this point incitements to anger are sown, quarrels arise, torches of hatred are kindled, and the peace which had been in people's hearts is extinguished. And so it is well said through Solomon: *A person who lets water escape is the source of quarrels* [Prov. 17:14]. Now to let water escape is to loosen the tongue in a torrent of speech. But on the other hand, it is also said in a positive way: *The words of a man's mouth are as deep water* [Prov. 18:4]. Therefore, a person who lets water escape is the source of quarrels, because a person who does not curb his tongue breaks concord into pieces. And so it is written by way of contrast: *The person who makes a fool keep silent alleviates anger* [Prov. 26:10 Vulg.].

The prophet bears witness that anyone who is the servant of excessive speech is quite unable to adhere to justice in an upright way, saying: *A man with an idle tongue does not go in a straight line upon the earth* [Ps. 140:11]. Again, Solomon says on this topic: *Sin will not be lacking in excessive speech* [Prov. 10:19]. Isaiah says about it: *The concern for justice is silence* [Isa. 32:17], clearly indicating that justice of the mind is abandoned when people do not cease from talking immoderately. James says concerning this: *If anyone who does not restrain his tongue thinks that he is religious, he deceives his heart, his religion is vain* [Jas 1:26]. Again he says: *Let everyone be swift to hear but slow to speak* [Jas 1:19]. Here again, summing up the power of the tongue, he adds: *A restless evil, full of deadly poison* [Jas 3:8]. And here Truth admonishes us in his own person: *On the day of judgment, people will render account for every idle word which they speak* [Matt. 12:36]. Now a word which is not occasioned by some proper need or intended in a kind way to be useful, is idle. If, therefore, an account is demanded for an idle word, let us consider what punishment lies in store for talking too much, in which one sins as well through harmful words.

15　How the indolent are to be admonished in one way and the impulsive in another.

The indolent are to be admonished in one way and the impulsive in another. For the former are to be advised not to lose an opportunity of doing good by putting it off, whereas the latter are to be admonished in case, when in their haste they carelessly anticipate the time to do good, they change the merits of what they do. And so it should be pointed out to the indolent that when we do not want to do the things we are able to at an appropriate time, we later often find that it is beyond our power to do them when we want to. Indeed, a slothful mind which is not kindled with an appropriate fervour is afflicted with a listlessness which imperceptibly gains in strength, leaving it with no desire to do good things. And so it is aptly said through Solomon: *Indolence casts one into deep sleep* [Prov. 19:15]. For in that his feelings are good an indolent person keeps awake, as it were, while nevertheless being inactive and accomplishing nothing; but his indolence is said to cast him into a deep sleep because, before long, when his enthusiasm for doing good ceases, the feelings he had while he was awake are also lost. Rightly does it go on: *And the idle soul will be hungry* [Prov. 19:15].

For because it does not turn towards higher things by holding itself in check, in its neglect of itself it widens out in a desire for lower things; and when the mind is not held in check by the strength of its enthusiasm for things above, it is wounded through the hunger which comes from low covetousness, so that, having pretended to bind itself through discipline, it scatters itself in a hungry desire for pleasures. It is again written concerning this by the same Solomon: *In his desires he is utterly lazy* [cf. Prov. 21:26 Vulg.]. In the preaching of the Truth on this matter, a house is certainly said to be clean when one spirit departs from it, but when he returns in greater number that which had been left empty is occupied [Matt. 12:43–45].

Very often the lazy person, while he neglects to do necessary things, comes up with obstacles and suffers irrational fears; and when he seems to find what he was afraid of, apparently justly, he lets it be known that his inactivity was not at all unjustified. It is rightly said of him through Solomon: *Because it was cold the lazy man did not wish to plough; therefore he will beg in summer, and it will not be given to him* [Prov. 20:4]. Yes, the lazy man does not plough because it is cold when, having been bound fast by slothful torpor, he pretends not to notice the good things which he ought to do. The lazy man does not plough because it is cold when, in his fear of encountering unimportant things, he neglects works which are great. It is well said: *he will beg in summer, and it will not be given to him*. For someone who does not sweat now when he carries out good works begs in the summer, when the sun of judgment blazes more strongly, and he receives nothing, because he asks in vain to be admitted into the kingdom. It is again well said to this person through the same Solomon: *A person who observes the wind does not sow, and a person who observes the clouds never reaps* [Eccles. 11:4]. For what is expressed by the wind, if not the temptation of evil spirits? And what are designated by the clouds that are blown by the wind, if not the misfortunes suffered by perverse people? It is easy to see that clouds are driven by winds, because perverse people are roused to activity as unclean spirits breathe on them. Therefore, *A person who observes the wind does not sow, and a person who observes the clouds never reaps*, because whoever fears being tempted by malign spirits or persecuted by perverse men neither sows the grains of good work now, nor cuts the sheaves of a holy reward in the future.

On the other hand, when impulsive people anticipate the time for good works they ruin their worth, and when their discernment of what is good is very limited they often fall into what is bad. These people fail to consider what they ought to do and when they should do it, and they usually find out that they have done things which should not have been done in the way they did them. It is rightly said to these people, represented as a listener, by Solomon: *Son, do nothing unadvisedly, and you will not regret it after you do it* [Sir. 32:24]. And again: *Let your eyes go before your steps* [Prov. 4:25]. Yes, eyes go before steps when upright counsels precede what we do. For someone who neglects to look ahead with due reflection at what he is doing steps forward, closes his eyes, and moves briskly along his route. But he does not anticipate himself by looking ahead, and so quite soon he falls down, because he does not direct his attention through the eye of discerment to the place where he should have placed the foot of work.

The Pastoral Rule concludes with a brief fourth book, in which Gregory turns away from pastoral matters to address issues of importance to himself.

4   How the preacher, when everything has been done in a proper way, should return to himself, so that neither his life nor his preaching make him proud.

Now because it often happens that, when preaching has been poured forth abundantly and in an appropriate style, the soul of the speaker is lifted up in private by a secret joy at his performance, it is necessary that he take care to gnaw away at himself with a wounding fear, in case the person who brought others back to health as he cured their wounds with his remedies becomes puffed up through the neglect of his own salvation;[12] in case in helping his neighbours he neglects himself; in case, in the very act of lifting others up, he falls down. Greatness in virtue has frequently caused people to be lost, for when confidence in their strength makes them inordinately complacent, they perish unexpectedly through carelessness. For when virtue is in combat with vices, the soul is made to feel good by a kind of delight, and it comes to pass that the mind of a person who is doing well casts away any anxious fear for itself and takes its ease, secure and confident.

While the mind is in this somnolent state the cunning deceiver enumerates all the good things which it has done, and as its thoughts swell he praises it as though it were far superior to others. And so it happens that, in the eyes of the just Judge, the recollection of a mind's virtue can be a pit for it, because when the mind thinks over what it has done, in the act of lifting itself up in its own estimation it falls down before the Author of humility. Hence it is said to the prideful soul: *Since you are so beautiful, come down, and sleep with the uncircumcised* [Ezek. 32:19]. As if to say openly: because you lift yourself up on account of the comeliness of your virtues, you are setting yourself up for a fall through that very beauty of yours. And so the soul which takes pride in its virtue is condemned under the form of Jerusalem, when it is said: *You were made perfect in my comeliness, which I placed upon you, says the Lord; and having confidence in your beauty, you have played the harlot because of your renown* [Ezek. 16:14f.]. Yes, the mind is lifted up by confidence in its beauty, when it takes pride in the merits of its virtues, being pleased with itself and complacent. But through this very confidence it is led to play the harlot, because when a mind has been taken hold of and deceived by its own thoughts, evil spirits corrupt it, seducing it through vices beyond counting.

But it should be noted that it is said: *you have played the harlot because of your renown*, because when a mind ceases to have regard for the supreme Ruler it immediately seeks praise just for itself, and starts to claim as its own every good thing which it received to be employed for the renown of the one who gave it. It desperately wants its glorious reputation to be spread abroad; it busies itself so that it will become known to everyone as being worthy of wonder. And so it plays the harlot because of its renown, forsaking as it does the lawful marriage bed and, in its passionate desire for praise, submitting to a spirit which seduces it. David says concerning this: *He delivered their virtues into captivity, and their beauty into the hands of the enemy* [Ps. 78:61]. For virtues are delivered into captivity and beauty into the hands of the enemy when the old enemy becomes lord over a mind which has been led astray by its pride in doing good.

Nevertheless in one way or another this pride in virtue often tempts the minds of the elect, without completely overcoming them: a mind which had been lifted up is left alone, and having been left alone it is summoned back to fear. For David again says about this: *In my prosperity I said, I shall never be moved* [Ps. 30:6]. But because he was swelling up from confidence in his virtue, a little later he added that he was suffering: *You turned your face away from me, and I was troubled* [Ps. 30:7]. As if he were to say openly: When surrounded by my virtues I believed that I was strong, but having been abandoned I have come to understand how weak I am. And again he says: *I have sworn and am determined to observe your righteous judgments* [Ps. 119:106]. But since he was not strong enough to continue to observe that which he had sworn to do, on being thrown into confusion he immediately found how weak he was. And so he speedily gave himself over to the power of prayer, saying: *I am brought very low, Lord; give me life, according to your word* [Ps. 119:107].

But sometimes heavenly providence, before it moves someone forward by its gifts, calls a mind back to the memory of its weakness, to prevent it swelling up from the virtues it has received. And so the prophet Ezekiel, every time he was led to contemplate heavenly things, was first called *son of man* [Ezek. 3:1, 3 etc.], as if the Lord were admonishing him openly, saying: Do not lift up your heart in pride because of these things which you see, and consider carefully what you are, so that as you penetrate the heights you may recognize that you are human, for when you are transported beyond yourself you will be called back to yourself, troubled in mind, by the bridle of your weakness. And so it is necessary, when an abundance of virtues makes us feel good, for the eye of the mind to return to its weaknesses and lower itself in a way that will bring health. Let it look not upon the good things which it did but those which it neglected to do, so that when the heart has been weakened by remembering its infirmities it may, in the estimation of the Author of lowliness, be stronger and tougher in virtue. For almighty God, although he generally makes the minds of rulers perfect to a large degree, nevertheless leaves them imperfect in some small part, so that even when they are shining with wonderful virtues they feel wretched because of their loathsome imperfection. They certainly do not lift themselves up because of their great qualities while they are still striving laboriously against things that are very small; rather, as they are not able to conquer these tiny things, they do not dare to take pride in their exceptional achievements.

Behold, good man, compelled by the need to censure myself, while I have been staying up late in order to show what sort of person a pastor ought to be, I have been an ugly painter painting a beautiful person; I have been directing others to the shore of perfection while still being tossed in the waves of my offences. But amid the shipwreck of this life I ask you to support me with the plank of your prayer, so that while my own weight pulls me down, your well-deserving hand may lift me up.

5

MORALS ON JOB

The following passage provides a good introduction to Gregory's understanding of the human condition, the ways he dealt with the Bible, and the moralizing bent of his thinking. It is based on some words in the book of Job: *If I am asleep, I shall say: When shall I get up? And I shall await the evening again . . . My flesh is clothed in rottenness and clods of dust; my skin is dried and wizened* [Job 7:4f.].

Moralia

8.10.19 . . . The ease of indolence is represented by sleep, and physical labour by getting up. And the desire for rest is represented by the word evening, something associated with sleep. But the holy church, for as long as she continues in a life of corruption, unceasingly laments what she has lost through her mutability. For the first human was created for this purpose: that, with upright mind, he would lift himself up to the citadel of contemplation, and that no corruption would turn him away from the love of his Creator. But, because he moved the foot of his will away from his inborn security of standing, he immediately fell down from the love of the Creator into himself. But when he abandoned the love of God, that true citadel where he stood, he was unable to remain firm in himself either, because, through the power of slippery mutability, in his corruption he tumbled beneath himself to the point of being at variance with himself. Now, no longer held firmly by his secure place in the creation, he is always subject to change by the motion of alternating desire, so that when he is at rest he wants to be doing something and when he is busy he pants for rest. For because his mind, when firmly established, did not wish to stand when it was able, it is now unable to stand even though it may wish to. Yes, in abandoning the contemplation of its Creator it lost its good health and, always unwell, wherever it may find itself it wants to be somewhere else. Therefore, describing the inconstancy of the human mind, he can say: *If I am asleep, I shall say: When shall I get up? And I shall await the evening again* [Job 7:4]. As if he were to say openly: nothing which his mind experiences is enough, because it lost the one who would truly have been enough. For indeed, when I am asleep I want to get up, and when I get up I await the evening, because when I am quiet I want to be busy, and when I am occupied I seek quiet rest.

20   But this can also be understood another way. For to sleep is to lie in sins. If the word sleep did not designate sin, Paul would certainly not have said to his disciples: *Keep awake, you who are just, and do not sin* [1 Cor. 15:34]. And so he admonished his listener, saying: *Awake, you who sleep, arise from the dead; and Christ will give you light* [Eph. 5:14]. And again: *Now is the hour for us to rise from sleep* [Rom. 13:11]. So it is that Solomon as well admonishes the sinner, saying: *How long will you sleep, O sluggard?* [Prov. 6:9]. Therefore each of the elect, when the sleep of sin weighs down upon him, seeks to arise, to keep the watch of justice. But often, when he has arisen, he feels that he has been lifted up through the very greatness of his virtues. And so after his virtuous deeds he desires to be tempted by the adversities of the present life, in case his confidence in what he has done virtuously makes him fall into worse. For had the psalmist not known that temptation was good for him, he would certainly not have said: *Examine me, O Lord, and test me* [Ps. 26:2]. Therefore it is now well said *If I am asleep I shall say: When shall I get up? And I shall await the evening again* [Job 7:4], because even in the sleep of sin the light of justice is sought. And when virtuous achievements lift up a mind, it wishes adversity to come to its aid, so that a soul, having been lifted up more than it should have been through joy at its virtues, may immediately be strengthened as, through the changing circumstances of this present life, some sorrow emerges. And so it is said that the evening is not at all to be feared, but rather awaited. For we await good things and fear bad things. Therefore the just man awaits the evening because, when he needs to be exercised by tribulation, that very adversity becomes beneficial to him.

21   The temptation of sin is another thing which can be designated by the word evening. Often, the more painfully this wounds the mind, the higher is the level of the things of the spirit to which it raises that mind. For it is certainly not the case that an end is put to sin in this life through the practice of justice, so that one abides unshaken in that same justice, because, even if uprightness does already banish wrongdoing from the dwelling place of the heart, nevertheless the wrongdoing which has been driven away is sitting outside the door to our thoughts, knocking for it to be opened. Moses as well suggested

this in a spiritual sense when he told how the intervals of time were made in a bodily way, saying *there was light* [Gen. 1:3], and adding shortly afterwards *there was made evening* [Gen. 1:5]. Indeed, the Creator of all things, knowing in advance human sin, expressed then by means of time what now comes and goes in people's minds. Yes, light extends until the evening, because it is very clear that the shadow of temptation follows the light of uprightness. But because the light of the elect is not extinguished by temptation, it is said that not night but evening was made, because, while it is obvious that temptation often covers the light of justice in the hearts of the elect, it does not kill it; it brings it, so to speak, to an alarming paleness, but does not totally destroy it. Therefore the elect want to get up after sleep, and after they get up they look for the evening, because they keep watch from sin until the light of justice and, when placed in that light of justice, they are always preparing themselves against enticing temptations. They are not afraid of these but look for them, being aware that even temptations help them make progress in uprightness.

22   But however great may be the virtue with which they contend against their corruption, they cannot enjoy full health until the day of this present life draws to a close. And so it goes on: *And I shall be filled with sorrows until the darkness* [Job 7:4 Vulg.]. For sometimes troubles come rushing forward; sometimes things that turn out well give them pleasure and make them happy. Sometimes vices arise which stir up war in the flesh; sometimes, when they are defeated, they beckon the mind to pride. And so the life of good people is *filled with sorrows until the darkness*, because, for as long as the time of corruption continues, it is struck by afflictions coming from the inside and outside, and it finds its health guaranteed only when it departs for good from the day of temptation. And so the very same cause of sorrows is immediately added, when it says: *My flesh is clothed in rottenness and clods of dust.* For, as we have just said, of his own will the man put an end to his inborn firmness and plunged into the whirlpool of corruption, so that now he slides downwards through unclean works, or becomes dirty through improper thoughts. For it can be said that our nature, having become subject to its own sin by way of punishment, is no longer in accordance with nature; when set free it is led to the point of perverse works, but when tied fast it is darkened by thoughts of perverse works which will not go away. Therefore rottenness harms the flesh through the accomplishment of an illicit act, whereas dust, as it were, comes up before the eyes through the lightheadedness of bad thinking. When we consent to vices we are made weak by rottenness, whereas when we allow pictures of vices to come into our hearts we are made dirty by

clods of dust. Therefore he says: *My flesh is clothed in rottenness and clods of dust*, as if he were saying openly: the life of the flesh which I endure is either polluted by the corruption which comes from acting in a slimy way, or oppressed by the murk of wretched thoughts which come from the recollection of vices.

23 Nevertheless, if we take these words as having been said by the universal church, beyond doubt we find that she is sometimes weighed down with rotten flesh, and sometimes with clods of dust. Indeed, there are many within her who, giving themselves over to love of the flesh, become putrid with the stench of loose living. To be sure, there are some who abstain from fleshly pleasure, but nevertheless with their whole intent they are lying prostrate in earthly acts. Therefore, let the holy church say in the words of one of her members, let her say what she is putting up with from both kinds of people: *My flesh is clothed in rottenness and clods of dust*. As if she were to speak plainly, saying: There are many who are my members through faith, but they are not healthy and clean in what they do, either because, having been overcome by unclean desires, they are flowing downwards to the filth of corruption, or because, having given themselves over to earthly actions, they are covered by dust. In the case of the former, those slimy people I have to put up with, I sigh over flesh which is visibly rotting; in the case of the latter, those whom I endure as they go looking for the earth, what do I sustain but flesh which has been made dirty by dust?

24 And so it goes on appropriately with regard to each of them: *My skin is dried out and wizened* [Job 7:5]. Now in the body of the holy church those who give themselves over solely to exterior concerns are fittingly called skin.[1] As skin dries out, it is pulled together, because the minds of fleshly people, when they love things of the present and long for them to be placed nearby, so to speak, are unwilling for themselves to be stretched out through patience towards things of the future. When they neglect the richness of the hope which is within they become dried out so that their skin is drawn together, because if their lack of hope did not dry out their hearts this fevered smallness of spirit would certainly not have drawn their skin together. The psalmist dreaded this drawing together when, fearing a dryness of the mind, he said: *My soul shall be satisfied as with marrow and fatness* [Ps. 63:5]. Yes, marrow and fatness fill the soul when a hope from above is poured upon it and gives it comfort against the heat of present desires. Therefore the skin, when it dries out, is drawn together when a heart which has given over to external things and made parched through a lack of hope, is not extended towards the love of its creator but, in a manner of speaking, is folded back onto itself, by a wrinkled kind of thinking.

In the following passage Gregory is dealing with a speech made of Eliphaz, one of Job's comforters. It shows the importance of contemplation in his thought.

6.38.59 Those who are striving to gain the highest point of perfection, when they yearn to take hold of the stronghold of contemplation, should first test themselves through exercise in the field of work, so that with the necessary care they might come to know whether they are doing anything wrong to their neighbours, whether they are bearing with calmness of mind what their neighbours are doing to them, and whether their mind is neither set free so as to be joyous when temporal goods are placed before it nor wounded with great sorrow when they are taken away; after this, they should consider carefully whether, when they return to themselves inwardly for a thorough investigation of spiritual things, they are not drawing with them the slightest shadows of bodily things; or whether, if it turns out that they have been drawn, they are able to drive them away with the hand of discretion; whether, in their yearning to see the infinite light, they repress all images of what is finite and whether, given that they are striving to attain something that is above themselves, they overcome that which they are. And so it is now said rightly *Thou shall enter the tomb in abundance* [Job 5:26]. Yes, a perfect man enters the tomb in abundance because he first gathers together the works of an active life and then conceals completely from the world the capacity for feeling belonging to his flesh, which has died through contemplation. And so it fittingly goes on: *Like as a sheaf of grain cometh in his season* [Job 5:26].

60 For action comes at the beginning, and contemplation at the end. So it is necessary that whoever is perfect should first exercise the mind with virtues and then put it away in the barn of quiet. This was the case with the person from whom a legion of demons departed at the Lord's command. He sat down at the feet of his Saviour, received the words of his teaching, and ardently desired to depart from his country in the company of the one who had given him his health. But nevertheless that very Truth who bestowed health upon him said: *Return first to your own house, and declare the great things God has done for you* (Luke 8:39). For when we receive something, however little, of the knowledge of God, we are then unwilling to return to human affairs and are reluctant to be burdened with the needs of our neighbours. We seek the quiet of contemplation and love nothing other than that which restores us without toil. But Truth sends those of us who have been healed home, he orders us to tell of the things which have been

done concerning us, which clearly shows that the mind should first sweat in performing work, and then it ought to be restored through contemplation.

61 So it is that Jacob served on account of Rachael and received Leah, and he was told: *It is not the custom in our country to give the younger in marriage before the elder* [Gen. 29:26]. For Rachael means 'the beginning that is seen', but Leah 'toilsome'.[2] And what is indicated by Rachael but the contemplative life, and what by Leah but the active life? Yes, in contemplation the beginning, which is God, is what is sought; in working one toils under a heavy load of things which have to be done.[3] And so Rachael was beautiful but barren, and Leah bleary eyed but fruitful, because when a mind is keenly seeking the tranquillity of contemplation, it sees more, but does not generate as many children for God; whereas, when it directs itself to the toil of preaching, it sees less but brings forth more. Therefore, after he had embraced Leah, Jacob attained Rachael, because anyone who is perfect is first joined to the fruitfulness of the active life and is later coupled to the rest of the contemplative life. That the contemplative life lasts for a shorter time but is of greater merit than the active is shown by the words of the holy gospel in which two women are said to have done different things. Indeed, Mary, listening to the words of our Redeemer, was sitting at his feet, but Martha was busy with bodily services. And when Martha complained that Mary was resting, she heard: *Martha, Martha, you are anxious and disturbed about many things. Besides, one thing is necessary. Mary has chosen the better part which will not be taken away from her* [Luke 10:41f.]. What is expressed through Mary, who listened to the words of the Lord as she sat, but the contemplative life? And what through Martha, busy with outward services, but the active life? And while the concern shown by Martha is not rebuked, that of Mary is even praised, because while the merits of the active life are great, those of the contemplative life are preferable. And so it is said that the part of Mary is never to be taken away from her, because the works of the active life pass away with the body, while the joys of the contemplative become better after its close. The prophet Ezekiel expresses this well in a concise way when, having contemplated the living creatures which were flying, he says that *the form of a man's hand was under their wings* [Ezek. 10:8]. What can we understand by the wings of the living creatures but the contemplative activities of the saints, by which they fly to the heights and, forsaking earthly things, position themselves at the level of heavenly things? What do we take by the hands, unless acts of labour? This is because, when they stretch out in love of their neighbour, they also administer in bodily fashion

the good things which are worth more. But their hands are under their wings, because they transcend their active works in the strength of their contemplation.

62 By the grave there can be understood not merely contemplation in this life of ours, but the quiet of an eternal and innermost reward, in which, the more completely the life of corruption is killed within us, the more truly there is rest. Therefore someone who, having gathered together the works of the present life, has fully died to his own mutability and lies hidden in the secret of the true light, enters the tomb in abundance. And so it is said through the psalmist: *You shall hide them from human confusion in the secret of your face* [Ps. 31:20]. The comparison which follows also commends it well, when it goes on: *Like as a sheaf of grain cometh in his season.* Yes, grain in the field is touched by the sun because in this life the human soul is illuminated by being looked upon by the light above; it receives the rain because the word of truth fattens it; it is shaken by the winds because it is troubled by temptations; and it bears the chaff which grows with it because it tolerates every day the lives, increasingly wicked, of those who sin against it; and, when it is brought to the threshing floor, a heavy weight is brought to bear on it for the threshing, to separate it from the chaff with which it is mixed, because our mind, placed under heavenly discipline when it receives the scourges of correction, withdraws from the company of fleshly people in a cleaner state and, having left the chaff, it is brought to the barn, because, with the reprobates remaining outside, the elect soul is lifted up to the everlasting joys of the mansion above. Therefore it is well said: *Thou shall enter the tomb in abundance, like as a sheaf of grain cometh in his season*, because, when the just meet with the rewards of the heavenly country after their afflictions, it is as if the grains were brought to the barn after being pressed down; indeed, they experience blows at a time of someone else's choosing, but the time when they rest from the blows is their own. Now for the elect the time of the present life belongs to someone else, so that the Truth says to those who are still unbelievers: *My time has not yet come, but your time is always ready* [John 7:6]. And again: *This is your hour, and the power of darkness* [Luke 22:53]. Therefore he enters the tomb in his time like a sheaf of grain, because a person who first feels the weight of discipline here, so as to be made free of the chaff which will be burned, receives eternal rest.

But Eliphaz, having used in his speech the words tabernacle, stones, beasts, seed, vegetation and tomb, indicated that he did not speak of these things in a literal sense, when, after all these things, he immediately added:

63 *Lo we have searched this out; it is true* [Job 5:27]. It is indeed very clear that in these words nothing is said on a superficial level, because something which is searched out is certainly not lying before someone's face. And so he indicates he had searched out these things, because he shows that he looked for interior things in exterior words.

But after all these things he comes to the point of foolish boastfulness, because he straightaway adds:

39.64 *Apply your mind to the study of what you have heard* [Job 5:27]. However strong the teaching of the mind may be, a person who desires to teach someone who is better is simply ignorant. And so the points which Job's friends made correctly were not deemed correct by the Judge placed inside. When they are unsuited to the hearer they lose the force of their uprightness, because even medicinal remedies lose their potency when they are applied to healthy limbs. Therefore, in anything which is said the occasion, the time and the person have to be considered: whether the truth gives strength to the words which are said, whether a fitting time demands it, and whether the nature of the person does not stand in the way of the truth of what is said and the fittingness of the time. For it is the person who first of all sees the enemy whom he strikes who casts his darts in a praiseworthy way. Someone who strikes a fellow citizen when he fires an arrow in a sturdy fashion subdues the horns of a strong bow to no good purpose!

That Gregory saw the concluding words of Eliphaz as being significant is a reminder that ancient authors often devoted particular attention to the conclusions of their writings. It would be reasonable to expect Gregory to have made important statements towards the end of his massive exposition of Job, and this he did. The last part of the book of Job tells how, after his tribulations, he was blessed by God. Gregory used the text as the basis for a discussion of the Jews. The decades immediately following were to be of devastating significance in Jewish history. Persecution began in Visigothic Spain, while the ill-advised support Jews lent the Persians in their wars against the Byzantines led to forced baptisms when the Empire recovered the territory it had lost. And while modern scholarship is unclear as to relations between Jews and the prophet Muhammad, it was at this very time that the teachings of Islam were being first promulgated. Gregory thus speaks from within a situation which was soon to disappear for ever. The theme of preaching, always important for Gregory, plays a significant role.

Moralia

35.14.24 *And each one gave to him one sheep and one gold earring* [Job
42:11]. Although all these things are matters of historical truth,
nevertheless these gifts which are offered force us to turn again to the
mystery of allegory. We should not take it as being without significance
that it was just one sheep and just one golden earring that were offered.
And if there is nothing remarkable in the literal fact that one sheep was
offered, it is certainly astonishing that one earring was offered. But
what has a sheep to do with an earring, or an earring with a sheep? And
so we are forced by the particulars of these gifts to explore the things
which we have passed over rapidly when dealing simply with the
historical sense through the mysteries of allegory. Because Christ and
the church, that is the head and the body, is one person, we have often
said that blessed Job figuratively stands sometimes for the head and
sometimes the body. Therefore, with the truth of the history having
been preserved, let us interpret what is written in an allegorical way,
with reference to the holy church. *The Lord gave Job twice as much as he
had before* [Job 42:10]. Yes, the holy church, even if she now is losing
many people under the pressure of temptation, at the end of this age
nevertheless receives back twice as much as she had before when,
having received the gentiles in their fullness, all Judea which shall
then be found agrees to run to her faith as well. On this account it
is written: *Until the fullness of the gentiles should enter, and so all Israel
will be saved* [Rom. 11:25f.]. And hence Truth says in the gospel:
Elijah will come, and he will restore all things [Matt. 17:11]. For now the
church has lost the Israelites, having been unable to convert them
by preaching, but then, by the preaching of Elijah, she will receive
what she had lost in a fuller way, as she gathers together as many as she
can find.

25 Or: assuredly, for the holy church to receive double at her end
is for her to rejoice in both the blessedness of the soul and the
incorruptibility of the body of every one of us. For here is what is said
through the prophet concerning the elect: *In their land they shall possess
twice as much* [Isa. 61:7]. Here is what the apostle John says of the saints
who were asking for the end of the world: *A white stole was given to each
of them; and they were told to rest for a short while, until the number of their
fellow servants and brothers was fulfilled* [Rev. 6: 11]. For just as we said
long ago, each of the saints receives a white stole before the resurrection,
because they enjoy blessedness of soul alone, but at the end of the world
twice as much shall be given to them, because they shall possess glory
in their flesh as well as blessedness in their minds.

14.26   But the words which came after show us that they announce the conversion of the Jewish people at the end of this world. For it is added: *All his brothers came to him, and every one of his sisters, and all who had known him before, and they ate bread with him in his house* [Job 42:11]. His brothers and sisters indeed come to Christ then, when as many of the Jewish people as will be found are converted. For he took the substance of his flesh from that people. Then, therefore, his brothers and sisters draw near to him, when from that people which is joined to him through a blood relationship both those who are going to be strong, that is the brothers, and those who are going to be weak, that is the sisters, run to him together through knowledge of the faith with holy rejoicing.[4] Then they shall provide at his home a banquet of the utmost festivity when they no longer despise him as being merely human but, being mindful of his close relationship with them, rejoice in being closely connected to his divinity. Then they shall eat bread in his house, when, having put aside the observance of the superficial letter, they are so to speak fed in the holy church with the best part of mystical utterance, as if it were nourishing food. And it goes on well: *All who had known him before* [Job 42:11]. Indeed, they had known him before, when they despised him in his passion as one they did not recognise. For no-one who was fully acquainted with the law was ignorant that Christ would be born. Whence king Herod, alarmed by the visit of the wise men, was keen to have the priests and leaders seek out diligently where it was, according to what they knew already, that Christ was going to be born, and they immediately replied to him, *In Bethlehem of Judea* [Matt. 2:5]. Therefore, they had known previously the one they did not know when they despised him at the time of his passion. The blindness of Isaac provides clear and brief evidence for their earlier knowledge and subsequent ignorance. When he blessed Jacob he knew in advance what would happen in the future, while he did not know who was standing in front of him [Gen. 27:1–29]. The people of the Israelites, which accepted the mysteries of prophecy yet held its eyes shut when looking on him, was like this, because when the person of whom it had seen many things which were to happen was present before it, it did not see him. When he was placed right in front of it he was completely unable to see the person whose mighty coming Isaac announced long before! But look, at the end of the world they are coming, and they acknowledge the one whom they had known earlier. Look, they are eating bread in his house, because they are fed in the holy church on the nourishing food of holy scripture; look, they are shaking off all their old, sleepy failure to see. And so it goes on: *And they moved their head upon him* [Job 42:11 Vulg.]. What are we to take the head to mean, unless the governing authority of the mind? Just as it is said through the psalmist: *You have anointed my head with oil* [Ps. 23:5]. As if it were to say openly: You have poured over my mind, which was dried out in its thinking, an anointing of charity. And so the head is moved when the mind, touched by dread of the truth, is shaken from its failure to see. And so let his relations come to the banquet and, having banished their sleepiness, let them move their heads, that is, let those who were at one time connected to our Redeemer in the flesh receive in faith the refreshment of the word and lose their old unfeeling failure to see. Whence it is well said through Habakkuk: *His feet stand firm, while the earth is moved* [cf. Hab. 3:5f.]. For there can be no doubt that the earth is moved when the Lord is standing, because when he presses the footsteps of his fear into our hearts, every earthly thought which is within us trembles. Therefore, in this case to move the head is to shake off the immobility of the mind, and to hasten with the footsteps of belief to the knowledge of the faith.

27   But because the holy church, which now experiences aversion on the part of the Hebrews, will then be comforted by their conversion, it is rightly added: *And they comforted him for every evil which God had visited upon him* [Job 42:11]. Clearly, those who recover from the error of their former unbelief and give up the evil lives with which they had resisted those who taught what was right, comfort Christ and comfort the church. Surely to preach to hard hearts without fruit and undertake the toil of revealing the truth without deriving fruit from the toil in the conversion of the hearers is a matter of great grief? But, on the other hand, the progress which the hearers make later is a great comfort for preachers. Yes, change for the better is a relief to the speaker. And it should be noted that they were not prepared to comfort him while he was being scourged, but came to comfort him after the scourging, because at the time of his passion the Hebrews, despising the declarations of the faith, quite clearly disdained to believe that the person they proved to be human through his death was also God. And so the Lord says through the psalmist: *I have upheld one who would share my sorrow, and there was none; I sought one to comfort me, and found none.*[5] Indeed, in his passion he found no comfort at all, he who, scorning death, had to endure as his enemies the very people for whom he came to die. And so his neighbours came to comfort him after he had been scourged, because to this day the Lord suffers in his members; but at the end of time all the Israelites will run together to faith, having understood the preaching of Elijah, and return to the protection of the one from whom they fled; and then, as the different peoples come together, an extraordinary feast is celebrated. Then, so to speak, Job is

shown in good health after being scourged, when the Lord, after his passion and resurrection, is known to be living immortally in heaven with the certainty of faith by those who have been converted and now believe. Then, so to speak, Job is seen to be rewarded, when in the power of his majesty he is believed to be just as God is, and those who formerly resisted him are now seen to have been subjected to his faith. Therefore let the Hebrews who believe come together at the end of the world, and let them pay their vows to the Redeemer of the human race in the power of his divinity, as it were to Job in good health. And so it well goes on: *And each one gave to him one sheep and one gold earring* [Job 42:11]. What is indicated by a sheep but innocence, what by an earring but obedience? Indeed, a mind without guile is expressed by a sheep, and listening adorned with the grace of humility by an earring.[6]

28 But because this provides an opportune occasion for demonstrating the virtue of obedience, I am disposed to investigate this with a little more attention and care, and to show how meritorious it is. For obedience is the only virtue which plants the other virtues in the mind, and cares for them when they are planted. And so the first human received a command to keep and, if he had wished to subject himself to it in obedience, it would have enabled him to come without effort to eternal blessedness. On this account Samuel said: *Obedience is better than a sacrificial victim, and hearing better than offering the fat of rams, since resistance is like the sin of soothsaying, and failure to agree like the crime of idolatry* [1 Sam. 15:22f.]. Yes, in the law obedience is preferred to sacrificial victims, because while the flesh of another being is sacrificed through victims, one's own will is sacrificed through obedience. And so anyone who restrains the pride of his own judgment before God's eyes, sacrificing himself with the sword of the command, will correspondingly appease God the more quickly. In consequence, disobedience is, by contrast, called the sin of soothsaying, to show how great the virtue of obedience is. What should be felt in praise of it is therefore better shown by way of its opposite. For if resistance is like the sin of soothsaying, and failure to agree like the crime of idolatry, obedience is the only virtue which possesses the merit of faith; any person without it is found guilty of unfaithfulness, even if he should seem to be faithful. And so something which makes obedience manifest is said through Solomon: *An obedient man speaks of victories* [Prov. 21:28 Vulg.]. Yes, an obedient man speaks of victories, because when we humbly submit to the voice of another, in our heart we defeat ourselves. Hence Truth says in the Gospel: *He who comes to me, I shall not cast out, because I have come down from heaven not to do my own will but the will of*

him who sent me [John 6:37f.]. Why is this? Would he have driven away those who came to him if he were to do his own will? Is there anyone who does not know that the will of the Son differs in no way from the will of the Father? But since the first man, because he wished to do his own will, went forth from the joy of paradise, the second man, coming to redeem humanity, by showing that he did the will of the Father and not his own, taught us to remain where we are inwardly. Therefore, as he does not his own will but the Father's, he does not cast out those who come to him, because when he makes us subject to obedience by his own example, he closes the way out against us. Hence he says again: *I am not able to do anything by myself but I judge just as I hear* [John 5:30]. Indeed, steadfastness in obedience to the point of death is enjoined upon us. If he himself judges just as he hears, then he is obeying even when he comes to judge. Therefore, in case obedience until the end of this present life should appear wearisome, our Redeemer shows that he practises it even when he comes to judge. Need we be surprised that sinful man subjects himself to obedience during the short time of this present life, when the mediator between God and humanity does not depart from it even when he rewards the obedient?

29 But it ought to be known that while we should never do evil through obedience, something which is good has sometimes to be put aside through obedience. For the tree in paradise which God forbade the human to touch was not bad. But so that the human might advance from a good state to a better one through the merit of obedience, it was fitting that he be held back even from what was good, seeing that what he did would then be more truly virtuous, for by desisting even from what was good he would demonstrate in a more humble way that he was subject to his Creator. But observe what is said there: *Eat from every tree of paradise, but do not touch the tree of the knowledge of good and evil* [Gen. 2:16f.]. For someone who denies those who are subject to him one good thing has to grant them many things, in case the mind of an obedient person, if it abstains from all good things after being sent away unsatisfied, should utterly perish. But the Lord granted all the trees of paradise for food while prohibiting the use of one, in order to restrain the being he had created; his hope was that he would not be destroyed but rather advance; the more easily he held him back from one, the more latitude he had for all the rest.

30 But because sometimes the good things of this world are ordained for us and sometimes the bad, it should be particularly recognized that sometimes it is not real obedience if it is spontaneous, while sometimes it is not real obedience if it is not spontaneous. For when success in this world is enjoined, when a higher place is

commanded, someone who obeys in receiving these things lays aside the virtue of obedience if he is keen to have these things with his own desire as well. For the person who serves the lust of his personal ambition in gaining the good things of this life does not direct himself in accordance with obedience. On the other hand, when an order is given to despise the world and people are enjoined to undergo abuse and insults, unless the mind seeks these things of itself, it diminishes the merit of its obedience in descending reluctantly and unwillingly to things which are despised in this life. Indeed, obedience becomes a matter of loss when the desires of the mind do not accompany it in some way when it receives the abuse of this age. Obedience should therefore be spontaneous in things that turn out contrary to one's will, and vice versa not be spontaneous when things turn out well, so that when bad things occur it might be more glorious, being joined even in its desire to what God has arranged, and when things turn out well it might be more genuine, the mind being completely separated from the glory which it has received from God in the here and now.

31   But we shall be able to show the significance of this virtue better, if we think about the deeds of two people of the heavenly country. For Moses, when he was pasturing his sheep in the desert, was called by the Lord, who spoke to him through an angel in the fire, to be the leader who would deliver the whole multitude of the Israelites. But, being of humble disposition, he was immediately alarmed at the honour of the great command which had been placed before him, and he straightaway took refuge in his weakness. *I beseech you, Lord, I am not a man of words; from yesterday and the day before when you began to speak to your servant, I have become of slow and halting speech* [Exod. 4:10 Vulg.]. And, having sidelined himself, he earnestly asked for someone else, saying: *Send the one whom you will send* [Exek. 4:13]. Look! In speaking with the Creator of his tongue he represents himself as incapable of speech, to avoid receiving the power so great a command would bring. Paul as well had been instructed by divine inspiration to go up to Jerusalem, just as he says to the Galatians: *Then after fourteen years I went up to Jerusalem, taking Barnabas and Titus, but I went up according to a revelation* [Gal. 2:1f.]. On the way, having met the prophet Agabus, he heard how much hardship lay in store for him in Jerusalem. Indeed, it is written that the same Agabus, placing Paul's belt around his feet, said: *They will bind in the same way the man whose belt this is in Jerusalem* [Acts 21:11]. Paul immediately answered: *I am prepared not only to be bound, but also to die in Jerusalem for the name of Jesus, for I do not reckon my life as more valuable than myself* [Acts 21:13; 20:24]. And so, going to Jerusalem in accordance with the revelation, he knows misfortunes,

and nevertheless cheerfully went looking for them; when he heard of something to be afraid of, he panted for it with greater ardour. And so Moses does not spontaneously accept good things, because he resists becoming the leader of the Israelite people with prayers. Paul is even led to adversity according to his own wish, because he understands the impending evils, but in spiritual zeal he was on fire for even harsher things. The former wished to decline the glory of power in the here and now which God had ordered; the latter, when God ordained bitter and hard things,[7] was keen to prepare himself for things which were more harsh. We are therefore taught by the unbroken strength of these two leaders who have gone before us, that if we are truly striving to take hold of the palm of obedience, we should struggle for the good things of this world only because we are ordered to, and for bad ones as well because of our devoted obedience.

32   But it should be noted that in this place a sheep is offered with an earring and an earring with a sheep, clearly because the ornament of obedience is always associated with innocent minds. The Lord shows this, when he says: *My sheep hear my voice; and I know them, and they follow me* [John 10:27]. So no-one offered blessed Job an earring without a sheep, and no-one a sheep without an earring, because very clearly someone who is not innocent fails to obey his Redeemer, and one who disdains to obey cannot be innocent. But because this obedience is maintained not with the fear of a slave but through an impulse of love, and not out of dread of punishment but through love of justice, all those who come to the banquet are said to have given a golden earring, so that love, which surpasses all the virtues, just as gold does the other metals, might gleam in the display of obedience.

33   But because there can be no innocence and no true obedience among the heretics with their multiple divisions, those who come to knowledge of the faith ought to present a sheep, but just one, and they ought to present an earring, but just one; that is, let the people who come be such as will stand firm in innocence and obedience within the unity of the holy church. Yes, a unit cannot be divided numerically, because this unit of which we speak is not a number. And so let them present a sheep, but one; let them present an earring, but one; that is, coming into the holy church with innocence and obedience, let them bring to it a mind which the schisms of sects cannot divide.

34   I am disposed to open the eyes of faith and contemplate that last banquet of the holy church which marks the reception of the Israelite people. Yes, that great Elijah who is to come is called upon to invite the guests to that banquet, and neighbours and acquaintances come with gifts to the one whom they despised a little while earlier

when he was subjected to scourging. For as the day of judgment approaches the power of the Lord who is coming now shines on them in some way, whether by the words of the forerunner or by certain signs which suddenly appear. In their haste to forestall his wrath, they speed up the time of their conversion. But having been converted they come with gifts, because they revere the one whom they mocked in his passion a short while before, offering them works of virtue as though they were gifts. It cannot be doubted that by this offering of theirs they complete what we can see has in large part already been accomplished, but believe is still to be fully accomplished: *The daughters of Tyre shall adore him with gifts* [Ps. 45:12]. For the daughters of Tyre adore him with gifts more fully at the time when the minds of the Israelites, which are now subject to the desires of this world, bear as a sacrificial victim their acknowledgment of the one whom, in their pride, they had denied, at the time when he has become known. And although in some respects the lives of the faithful may appear to be less virtuous during the times in which the Antichrist approaches, although great dread may hold in check the hearts of even the strong in the struggle with that abandoned person; yet, strengthened by the preaching of Elijah, not only do all the faithful stand firm in the strength of the holy church but, just as we have said above, many of the unbelievers too are converted to knowledge of the faith, so that the remnants of the Israelite race which had earlier been utterly turned away, will run to the bosom of mother church with all kinds of tender devotion.

Whence it now goes on, appropriately:

15.35 *The Lord blessed the end of Job more than his beginning* [Job 42:12]. We believe that these things have taken place in a historical way; we hope that they are to take place in a mystical way. Job is blessed more at his end than his beginning because, as far as it pertains to the receiving of the Israelite people, as the end of the present world bears hard upon the holy church, the Lord comforts her in her grief by the widespread gathering of souls. Yes, she will be enriched more generously as it becomes increasingly clear that the end of the present, transient life is bearing hard upon her. For the psalmist had caught sight of the preachers of the holy church being enriched with a blessing at the end of time, when he said: *They shall still be multiplied in a fruitful old age; they shall endure well, so that they might announce* [Ps. 92:14 Vulg.]. They are certainly multiplied in a fruitful old age, because when their lives are extended their strength is continually enhanced and the profits of their merits become greater as well as there is more time. They indeed endure well so that they might announce, because, the more robustly those who preach heavenly things bear adverse circumstances, the richer are the benefits which come to their souls because of their sufferings.

16.36 *And he came to have fourteen thousand sheep and six thousand camels, and a thousand yoke of oxen, and a thousand she-asses; and he had seven sons and three daughters* (Job 42:12f.). The introduction to the story of Job reveals that he had seven thousand sheep, three thousand camels, five hundred yoke of oxen and five hundred she-asses before he was tested by being struck down [Job 1:3]; after he lost these things through being scourged, they were now restored to him twofold. But there were restored to him as many children as he had lost. Yes, he had seven sons and three daughters [Job 1:2], but he is now described as having received seven sons and three daughters. This is so that those who had died might be shown to be alive. For when it is said: *The Lord gave Job twice what he had had before* [Job 42:10], and yet he restored to him only as many children as he had lost, he also gave him twice the number of children, for he later gave him ten in the flesh again but kept the ten who had been lost in the hidden life of souls. But anyone who desires to be nourished as a living being with understanding by the fruits of mysteries concerning the aforesaid animals, leaving aside the straw of history, needs to know what we think. For we can understand that these animals designate the accumulated totality of the faithful. It is for this reason that it is said through the psalmist to the Father about the Son: *You have placed all things under his feet, all sheep and oxen, and the beasts of the field as well* [Ps. 8:6f.]. For this reason the same prophet, looking on all the people who dwell without guile in the holy church, says: *Your animals will dwell within her* [Ps. 68:10 Vulg.].

37 And so who should we take the sheep as being but the innocent, and who are the camels but those who outstrip the evils of other people by the twisted bulk of their abundant vices, and who are the yoked oxen but the Israelites subjected to the law, and who are the asses but the guileless minds of the gentiles? For the psalmist shows that all the innocent are designated by the name of sheep, he who says: *We are his people, and the sheep of his pasture* [Ps. 95:7]. And those who neglect to maintain their innocence are not filled with the food of inward pasture.

38 Sacred scripture sometimes uses the word camel to represent the Lord and sometimes the pride of the gentiles, being twisted as it were by the swelling which rises up on top. Because a camel lowers

itself voluntarily to receive burdens, not undeservedly does it designate the grace of our Redeemer who, in deigning to receive the burdens of our weakness, voluntarily came down from his lofty power. Whence he says through the Gospel: *I have the power of laying down my life, and taking it up again; no-one takes it from me* [John 10:18]. Similarly he says again: *It is easier for a camel to pass through the eye of a needle than for a rich man to enter the kingdom of heaven* [Matt. 19:24]. Who does he mean by the term 'rich man' but any proud person, and what by the expression 'camel' but his own stooping down? For a camel passed through the eye of a needle, when our Redeemer entered through the narrow straits of his passion, to the point of undergoing death. This passion was indeed like a needle, because it pricked his body painfully. But a camel enters through the eye of a needle more easily than a rich man does the kingdom of heaven, because had he, when he received the burdens of our weakness, not revealed to us through his passion the opening of lowliness, our proud stiffness would by no means have bent down to his lowliness. Again, the gentile people, which is twisted and full of vices, is designated by the word camel, just as it is said through Moses that when the day was already sinking, Rebecca, seated upon a camel, saw Isaac, who had gone out into a field, and straightaway that bashful woman came down from her camel and shielded herself from his sight with a veil [Gen. 24:64f.]. Who did Isaac designate, given that he had gone out in the field when the sun was already sinking, but the one who comes at the very end of this world, as if it were the end of the day, and goes out as if into a field? Although he is invisible, he revealed himself visibly in this world. Rebecca saw him when she was sitting on a camel, because the church which comes from the gentiles, while it was still involved in vices and cleaving to stirrings which were like those of animals, and not yet spiritual, is giving heed to him. But she immediately came down from her camel because she turned away from the vices in which she had been placed so loftily in her pride, and carefully covered herself with a veil because, when she had seen the Lord, she blushed at having behaved in such a sick way, and she who had earlier been freely carried by the camel came down, covered in shame. And so it is said through the voice of the Apostle to the same church, converted from her earlier pride, as if to Rebecca, coming down from the camel and drawing a veil over herself, *For what fruit did you have then in those things of which you are now ashamed?* [Rom. 6:21].

39 By oxen sometimes the madness of those who live in a loose fashion, sometimes the bravery of preachers as they work hard, and sometimes the humility of the Israelites is expressed. Solomon indicates

that the word ox designates the madness of those who live loosely by making a comparison when, having mentioned the wantonness of a woman persuading someone to do wrong, he added: *He immediately follows her, like an ox led to the slaughter* [Prov. 7:22]. Again, that the hard work of a preacher is expressed by the word ox is shown by the words of the law, which says: *Do not muzzle the ox treading out the grain* [Deut. 25:4, cf. 1 Cor. 9:9, 1 Tim. 5:18]. As if it were to say openly: Do not prevent a preacher of the word from receiving his stipends. Again, the prophet declares that the Israelite people is represented figuratively by the word ox by making the coming of the Redeemer known in these words: *The ox has known its owner and the ass its master's crib* [Isa. 1:3], indicating clearly by the ox the Israelite people, tamed by the yoke of the law, and by the ass the gentile people, given over to pleasures and irrational to a higher degree.

40   Sometimes the word asses, or she-asses, describes the wantonness of those who live loosely, sometimes the mildness of people without guile, but sometimes, as we have already said, the foolishness of the gentiles. That the wantonness of those who live loosely is expressed by the word asses is declared openly by means of a comparison when it is said through the prophet: *Their flesh is as the flesh of asses* [Ezek. 23:20]. Again, because the life of people without guile is represented by the word she-asses, it is related that our Redeemer came to Jerusalem seated on a she-ass. Why, then, does it indicate that the Lord directs a she-ass towards Jerusalem by sitting on it, if it is not that, when he possesses guileless minds by presiding over them, by his sacred direction he conducts them to the vision of peace?[8] Again, it is shown by the prophet that the foolishness of the gentiles is designated by the word asses, when he says: *Blessed are you who sow beside all waters, sending forth the foot of the ox and ass* [Isa. 32:20]. Now to sow beside all waters is to preach the fruitful words of life to all peoples. But to send forth the foot of the ox and ass is to restrain the ways of the Israelite and gentile peoples with the chains of heavenly precepts.

41   And so, having preserved the literal truth written in the name of blessed Job, we are able to believe that the peoples of the holy church are fittingly designated by all these animals, in as much as all those things which are written by the direction of the Holy Spirit, who orders all things wonderfully, both tell us of things which have happened and predict those which are going to happen. Let us therefore recognize in the sheep the faithful and innocent peoples from Judaea who were formerly satisfied by the pastures of the law. Let us recognize in the camels simple people coming to the faith from among the gentiles whose past practice of sacrilegious things, as though it were

some deformity of their limbs, showed that they were really dirty, clearly because of the filth of vices. And because, as we have said already, sacred speech is careful to repeat what it affirms, the Israelites can also be understood by the oxen, tired out as it were by the yoke of the law. But the gentile peoples, as has been said, are designated by the asses, bowed down in the worship of stones, not hesitating to serve all kinds of idols with animal-like feelings, their backs, as it were, bent over. Therefore the holy church which, oppressed with countless trials in its beginnings, lost both the Israelite people and many of the gentiles, that is those it could not make its own, receives twofold at the end, because there springs up within her a larger number of faithful out of each nation. Preachers can also be understood through the yoked oxen. And so, when the Lord sent them to proclaim, as the gospel bears witness, it is said that he sent them in pairs [cf Mark 6:7, Luke 10:1], so that, whether because there are two precepts of charity, or because there can be no community where there are fewer than two people, the holy preachers would know, from the very manner in which they were sent forth, how they should love harmony within the community. Through the she-asses the minds of people without guile can be designated, as we have said above. But the holy church receives both oxen and she-asses, because both the holy preachers who, struck with dread, had formerly been silent in their time of trial, and the minds of the simple who, overcome by terrors, were afraid to confess her truth, now put forth their voices to confess the truth with a robustness equal to the weakness they experienced when they were afraid.

42   We have said these few things about the way the church is signified, and we recall having said at greater length at the beginning of this work how these things relate to the head of the same holy church. And so anyone who seeks to be more fully satisfied concerning these matters should find it worth his while to read the second book of this work. But if we go on to enquire concerning the numbers of the animals, why they are reckoned as a thousand yoke of oxen, or a thousand she-asses, and six thousand camels and fourteen thousand sheep, we can say briefly that in secular learning the number one thousand is considered perfect, for this reason: it renders the square of the number ten three-dimensional. Now ten times ten make a hundred, which is already a square figure, but it has two dimensions. And for it to be increased and have three dimensions, a hundred is again multiplied by ten, which makes a thousand. Furthermore the number six is perfect, because it is the first in the sequence of numbers to be made up of its parts, that is a sixth, a third and a half, which are one, two and three; added together, these make six. No number lower than six is made up

of the sum of its constituent parts. But because we transcend all these things as we make progress in the depth of sacred scripture, we find in various places why it is that six, seven, ten, and a thousand are perfect. Now the number six is perfect in sacred scripture, because at the beginning of the world the Lord completed on the sixth day the works which he had begun on the first day. Seven is perfect, because every good work is done through the Spirit by means of seven virtues,[9] so that faith and works may be brought to perfection at the same time. The number ten is perfect in scripture, because the law is summed up in the ten commandments, every sin being held in check by no more than ten expressions, and, as the Truth says, the workers at the vineyard are paid with a denarius.[10] Now three and seven added together make the number ten. But a human being, who is formed of soul and body, is made up of seven qualities, living as he does with three qualities which are spiritual and four which are bodily. For he is aroused to the love of God by three spiritual qualities, when it is said to him through the law: *You shall love the Lord your God with all your mind and with all your soul and with all your strength* [Deut. 6:6; Matt. 22:37; Mark 12.30]. But bodily he is made up of four qualities, because he is formed of matter which is hot and cold, moist and dry. A human being who is made up of seven qualities is therefore said to have been paid with a denarius, because in perceiving the country above our seven are joined to the eternal three, so that a human may receive contemplation of the Trinity and, as his work is rewarded, live as if he had been made perfect by a denarius. Or: it is clear that there are seven virtues which form the substance of our toil in this life, and when contemplation of the Trinity is given as a reward for them, the life of those who toil is repaid with a denarius. But whoever is perfect receives a denarius even in this life, when he joins hope, faith and love to these seven virtues. In sacred speech the number one thousand can also be taken as perfect, because the whole people together is designated by this word. And so it is written: *The word which he commanded to a thousand generations* (Ps. 105:8). For since it is impossible to believe that the world will last for a hundred generations, what does a thousand generations mean but the whole number of generations? And so blessed Job received fourteen thousand sheep. For because the perfection of virtues is made available to both sexes in the holy church, the number seven is doubled within her. And there were six thousand camels, because those who in times past perished in the filth of their vices away from her receive the fullness of their work within her. He also received a thousand yoke of oxen and a thousand she-asses, because after her disastrous trials she brings Israelites and gentiles, the learned and the simple, to the point of perfection. He also received seven sons and three daughters, because she adds hope, faith and love to the minds of those whom she generates with seven virtues, so that they may be fully perfect and that, considering that her faithful ones are lacking in no virtue, she might rejoice more truly in her offspring. But, having run through these things succinctly, let us now turn our attention to the names of the daughters as well.

There follows:

17.43 *And he called the name of the first Day, and the name of the second Cinnamon Tree, and the name of the third Cornustibii* [Job 42:14]. Because these names are derived from virtues, the translator has seen fit not to render them as they are found in the Arabic language but, appropriately, to disclose their meanings more openly in Latin speech. For who does not know that Day and Cinnamon Tree are Latin words? But truly, in the case of Cornustibii – although the word is not cornus, but cornu, and the pipe of singers is not called tibium, but tibia – nevertheless I believe he preferred to express the reality, paying little attention to gender in the Latin tongue, and to maintain the property of the language which was being translated.[11] Or, because he formed one word out of two, cornu and tibia, he was free to call by whatever gender he wished the two words which were translated into the Latin language by one part of speech. Why, therefore, does it say that the first daughter of blessed Job was called Day, the second Cinnamon Tree, and the third Cornustibii, if it is not because the whole human race, which was chosen by the kindness of its Creator and the mercy of its same Redeemer, is designated by these names? For the human shone like the day when he was created, because the Creator scattered upon him the brightness of an inborn innocence. But, having fallen by his own free will into the gloominess of sin, having withdrawn from the light of truth, he hid himself as it were in a night of error, because he is said elsewhere to have followed a shadow [cf. Eccles. 34:2]. But because our Creator did not lack wide-ranging goodness, even when confronted with the darkness of our wickedness he went on to summon back from error the one whom he had earlier created for justice with his power, by redeeming him with a power that was greater. Because he lacked the original strength with which he had been created after his fall, he shone upon him, giving him multiple virtues to deploy against the inner wars of rebellious corruption. It is clear that the virtues of people making progress emit a fragrance, coming to the notice of other people as though through sweet scents. For this is what

is said through Paul: *We are a sweet scent of Christ to God* [2 Cor. 2:15].
So it is that the holy church, emitting the scent of a sweet fragrance in
her elect, speaks in the Song of Songs, saying: *While the king reclines at
his table, my nard exhales its scent* [S. of S. 1:12]. As if it were saying
openly: for as long as the king hides himself from my glances, reposing
in his heavenly seclusion, the elect go about their lives with the wonderful scents of virtues, to the end that, while she does not see the
one whom she seeks, she may burn more ardently with desire. Yes,
while the king is reclining at table, the nard exhales scent; when the
Lord is resting in his blessedness, the virtue of the saints in the church
delights us with its great sweetness. And so, because the human race
shone brightly when it was created with the light of innocence,
and later, when redeemed, spread abroad a sweet scent by the practice
of good works, the first daughter is rightly named Day, and the second,
not unsuitably, Cinnamon Tree; she who is diffused through such
a strong scent of a sublime life is well named Cinnamon Tree. Yes, in
that original state of being righteous in which the human was created,
he did not lack those virtues of which he now stands in need, because
if he had wished to stand firm, just as he had been created, he would
have been able to defeat an enemy who was placed outside himself
without any difficulty. But after the enemy once broke into his inner
parts, with the assent of the human, the one who even now would
effortlessly have been driven away when he made his attacks, has
become a conqueror who is cast out with hard work.

44 For we now have to display many qualities which were
unnecessary in Paradise. Yes, now we need the virtue of patience, the
wearisome learning of doctrine, castigation of the body, perseverance
in prayer, confession of faults and overflowing tears, all of which the
newly created person certainly did not need, because from the very
circumstance of his creation he received the good of salvation. Yes, a
cup held out to a sick person so that a disease may be taken away and
he may be restored to a healthy condition is bitter, while there is no
need to tell a healthy person what to take to get better, but what to keep
away from in case he becomes ill. And so now we undertake greater
endeavours, not to maintain our present health but seeking to regain
that which was taken away. And because all these ways in which we
strive to be renewed are held in esteem by authoritative voices within
the holy church, the name of the second daughter deservedly gives
off a smell like a cinnamon tree, so that, whereas the first daughter
appeared as day because of the dignity of her creation, the second would
be a cinnamon tree through the fragrance of her bravery by the grace
of redemption. Whence it is said to the same Redeemer as he comes,

through the prophet: *Myrrh, resin and cinnamon come from your clothes, from steps of ivory; by these the daughters of kings delighted you in your honour* [Ps. 44:9 Vulg.]. What is indicated by the nouns myrrh, resin and cinnamon but the sweetness of virtues? What is expressed by ivory steps but the ascent, gleaming with their great bravery, of people making progress? Therefore, when the Redeemer comes, myrrh, resin and cinnamon are used in his clothing, because from his elect, with whom in his mercy he clothes himself, he spreads about the scent of the virtue of myrrh. Among them the same scent comes up on steps of ivory, because their reputation for virtues is produced not by false show, but by the ascent of work which is true and solid. But it is well added: *by these the daughters of kings delighted you in your honour*. For the holy souls which the ancient fathers brought forth so that they knew the lofty truth delighted their Redeemer in his honour, because they claim for themselves no praise on the basis of that which they do well. But because the human race in its third state, having been made new by the resurrection of the flesh, is taken up in that harmony of eternal praise, the third daughter is called Cornustibii. For what is expressed by Cornustibii but the joy of song? For then it is truly fulfilled what is now said through the prophet: *Sing unto the Lord a new song* [Ps. 149:1]. Then it is truly fulfilled, when a song to the praise of God is now sung not in faith but in the contemplation of that which is seen. Then our Creator, who made day in creating the human race, a cinnamon tree in redeeming it, and 'the horn of a pipe' in taking it up,[12] receives from us songs which praise him in truth. For when created we were light, and having been redeemed we are now a cinnamon tree, and at some time we shall be 'the horn of a pipe', taken up in the exultation of eternal praise. But before the bride arrives at the wedding chamber, she casts off from herself all uncleanness of life, and, getting ready for the love of the groom, adjusts her appearance by means of the ornaments of virtues. Yes, she is keen to please the judgment of the Judge within and, being lifted up by her intimate desires, to transcend the unclean ways of human behaviour.

Whence it fittingly continues concerning the same daughters of blessed Job:

18.45 *There were not found women as attractive as the daughters of Job in the whole land* [Job 42:15]. Yes, the souls of the elect transcend the whole human race which dwells in the land in the way humans do by the grace of their beauty, and the more they despise themselves on the outside with affliction, the more truly they arrange their appearance within. For on this account it is said through the psalmist to the holy church, adorned by the beauty of the elect: *The king greatly desired your beauty* [Ps. 45:11]. It adds concerning her a little while later: *All the glory of the king's daughter is within her* [Ps. 45:13]. For if she had sought glory on the outside, she would not have had that beauty within which the king greatly desired. Indeed, although there are many who shine with this grace of virtues and exceed the merits of others in the perfection of their lives, nevertheless there are not a few, lacking the capacity to attain to higher things and aware of their lack of strength, who are held tightly in her kindly bosom. These are the people who avoid evils as much as they can, although they do not attain to the higher goods as much as they would like to. Nevertheless the Lord receives them in a kindly way, and admits them to himself, rewarding them to a degree that is appropriate.

Whence there follows:

19.46 *And their father gave them an inheritance among their brothers* [Job 42:15]. They are, therefore, because of the merit of those who are perfect, said to have been beautiful, and they too, from being a type of the imperfect, as if they were weak, receive an inheritance among their brothers. For the custom of the old law did not provide for females to share an inheritance with males, because the severity of the law, in choosing things which were strong and placing little value on those which were weak, aimed at strictness rather than mildness in what it enacted. But when our kindly Redeemer came, no-one conscious of his own weakness could despair of being allotted a share in the inheritance which is above. For our Father gave a right of succession to females as well among the males, because he admits the weak and humble together with the strong and perfect to a share in the inheritance above. And so Truth himself says in the gospel: *In the house of my Father are many mansions* [John 14:2]. Yes, the Father's house has many mansions, because in that life of equal blessedness everyone, according to their differing merits, receives a different place. But this inequality is not experienced as deprivation, because whatever they receive is enough for them. Therefore the sisters come to an inheritance with their brothers, because the weak are admitted to that place with the strong, since someone who, because of imperfection, is not the highest, will nevertheless not miss out on a share in the inheritance because of lowliness. Paul indicates that these mansions are allocated according to merits well, when he says: *The brightness of the sun is one thing, and the brightness of the moon another, and the brightness of the stars another. For star differs from star in brightness* [1 Cor. 15:41].

153

There follows:

20.47   *But after these things Job lived for a hundred and forty years; and he saw his children and his children's children until the fourth generation; and he died in old age, full of days* [Job 42:16].

Sacred scripture usually does not mention someone as being full of days, unless it is someone whose life is praised by the same scripture. Indeed, someone is empty of days who, even though he has a long life, fritters away the periods of his life in emptiness. On the other hand, a person is called full of days whose days do not pass away and come to nothing, but obtain a daily reward for his good deeds and are kept with the just Judge after they have passed away.

48   But because there may be some who desire to have these things interpreted as signifying the holy church as well, people whose wishes should be obeyed to the extent that their spiritual understanding is to be rejoiced in, if we multiply fourteen by ten, we come to a hundred and forty. And the life of the holy church is rightly reckoned as ten multiplied by four because, observing as she does both testaments and living in accordance with the law of the ten commandments and the four books of the gospel, she arrives at the very summit of perfection. And so, although the apostle Paul wrote fifteen letters, yet the holy church receives no more than fourteen, to show by the number of letters that the outstanding teacher of the law had also thoroughly examined the secrets of the gospel.[13] It is also well said that blessed Job lived after he was scourged, because the holy church is first struck by the whip of discipline, and then strengthened in the perfection of life. She too looks upon her children and her children's children until the fourth generation, because in this age with its four annual seasons she observes offspring being born to her each day through the mouths of preachers, until the end of the world. And what we have said concerning times being indicated by generations is not inconsistent with the truth. For what is any lineage, but a kind of branch of the race? When the butler of the king of Egypt saw in a dream three shoots coming forth, Joseph, who was skilled in interpreting dreams, declared that the three branches indicated three days.[14] Therefore, if a period of three days is indicated by three branches, why should the four seasons of the year not be represented by four generations? The holy church, therefore, sees her children when she looks upon the first offspring of the faithful. She sees the children's children when she acknowledges others as well, born to faith by the same faithful. She too dies old and full of days because, when light follows as a reward for her daily works, she lays aside the burden of corruption and is changed to the incorruptibility

of the country of the spirit. And so she dies full of days, she for whom the years do not slip away as they pass but are made strong by the reward of her deeds which stand firm. She dies full of days, she who is occupied through these passing times with that which does not pass away. And so it is said to the apostles: *Do not occupy yourselves with food which perishes, but that which endures unto everlasting life* [John 6:27]. Therefore the holy church does not lose her days, even when she departs from this present life, because among her elect she finds lights in ways which are more diverse, the greater the caution and care with which she protects them from every temptation. The church does not lose her days, because in this life she is careful to inspect herself vigilantly every day, and no slovenliness impedes her from doing everything that she properly can. For it is on this account that it is said of her through Solomon: *She considers the paths of her household, she does not eat the bread of idleness* [Prov. 31:27]. Indeed, she considers the paths of her household, because she keeps a careful watch over the deliberations of her conscience. And she does not eat the bread of idleness, because she shows, making it manifest in works before the eyes of the eternal Judge, what she came to know from her understanding of holy scripture. But she is said to die, because when the contemplation of eternity absorbs her it puts a complete end to the changing circumstances of her mutability, so that nothing of any kind which would impede the sharpness of her innermost vision now lives within her. The more fully she dies to exterior things, the more truly she looks upon interior things. Therefore let us both believe that this death, this fullness of days, has occurred in the case of blessed Job, that is one member of the church, and hope that it will occur in the whole church at once; in this way the factual truth may be held in such a way that the prophecy of what is going to happen is not made empty. For the good things which we know of the lives of holy people are nothing if they are not true, and worth very little if they do not contain a mystery. Therefore, the lives of these good people which the Holy Spirit describes should illuminate us with their spiritual meaning, and yet the way in which we understand them should not be at variance from historical truth, so that the mind will remain firm in its understanding, as hope ties it firmly to the future and faith to the past, while it remains standing, so to speak, in a central position of some kind.

20.49 And so, having brought this work to its completion, I see that I must return to myself. Indeed, our mind, even when it tries hard to speak rightly, is scattered widely outside itself. For when words are reflected on with a view to how they should be uttered, they diminish the wholeness of the mind, because they take it outside itself.

It is therefore necessary for me to return from the place of public speech to the senate house of the heart, so that I may summon the thoughts of my mind as if to a consultative council of self-examination, to see there whether I have unthinkingly said bad things, or good things in a bad way. For something good is spoken as it should be when the speaker seeks to please through it only the one from whom he received what he speaks. And indeed, even if I do not find that I have said any bad things, nevertheless I do not maintain that I have not said any. But if I have spoken good things which I have received from God, I confess that I have said them less well because of my own sin. For as I return to myself inwardly, having laid aside the leaves of words and the branches of sentences, and carefully examine what I desired at its very roots, I certainly recognize that I wished most of all to please God through it; but somehow or other a desire for human praise has furtively, I do not know how, planted itself in the middle of that very desire with which I am so keen to please God. When I discern this it is already quite late, and I find myself doing in one way what I know I started to do in another. For it is often the case that a desire for human praise pursues our desire when it begins in a way that is right in the eyes of God, coming after it in secret and taking hold of it as if it were on a journey, in the same way that we eat food out of need, but, when gluttony furtively enters the scene, a delight in eating becomes mixed with the act of eating. And so it very often happens that we complete the refreshment of the body, which we began for the sake of health, for the sake of pleasure. It must therefore be said that our right desire, which seeks to please God alone, is indeed sometimes accompanied in a stealthy way by a less upright desire which seeks to please men through the gifts of God. But if God evaluates us concerning these matters with strictness, what place of safety remains among them, when our evil deeds are purely evil and the good deeds which we believe are ours are unable to be purely good? But I believe that it is worth my while to reveal without hesitation to the ears of my brothers something which I privately rebuke within myself. For because I have not concealed what I felt in my exposition, I shall not hide what I suffer in my confession. In expounding I have made known my gifts; in confessing I expose my wounds. And because among this vast human race there are not lacking small ones who may be instructed by what I have said, nor are there lacking great ones who may have pity on my weakness when it is made known to them, through these two circumstances I bestow on some brothers as much care as I am able, while from others I hope. I have spoken to the former in explaining how they should act; I disclose to the latter in confessing what they should refrain from. I have not withdrawn from the former the medicines of words; I have not concealed from the latter the laceration of my wounds. Therefore I ask whoever reads these things to grant me the support of his prayer before the strict Judge and wash away with tears every unclean thing which he discovers in me. And when the powers of prayer and exposition are compared, my reader's reward will be greater than mine, if, when he receives words through me, he returns tears for me.

NOTES

1 INTRODUCTION

1 *Dial.* 4.36.7. See Giuntella 2000: 181f., and the brilliant discussion of P. Brown 2003: 198f. Evidence for the following account of Gregory's family is provided in Martindale 1992: 549ff (s.v. 'Gregorius 5'). See too Pietri and Pietri 1999: 945 ff (s.v. 'Gregorius 9').

2 The rare name Gordianus may be a further sign of involvement in the Roman church, for it was also the name of a priest who was killed during the Laurentian schism in about 500. This Gordianus had been priest at the church of SS John and Paul, next to which Gregory established what he referred to as 'my monastery' (*Hev.* 19.7, 38.16). Pope Agapetus was son of Gordianus, priest, and known to have been associated as a clergyman with the church of SS John and Paul.

3 While Gregory presumably came to know the odd phrases which any long-term resident in a land where a different language is spoken picks up, and some liturgical Greek, there is no need to query his explicit statements that he did not know this language: *Reg.* 7.29, 11.55.

4 Gregory of Tours, *Libri historiarum* 10.1. No such letter occurs in what survives of Gregory's correspondence, although it need not have.

5 T. Brown 1984.

6 'Nefandissimus': *Reg.* 5.38 to the empress Constantina, 7.23 to the emperor's sister Theoctista.

7 Paul the deacon, *Historia Langobardorum* 2.10.

8 Paul the deacon, *Hist. Langob.* 4.5 mentions the sending of a copy of the *Dialogues* to Theodelinda. It has occurred to me to wonder to what extent their author was responsible for the widespread early circulation of Gregory's books.

9 Lançon 2000 gives a good feeling of the material conditions of the city in this period; specifically on Gregory and Rome, see Jenal 1988.

10 Three of these phrases occur in almost identical form in part of a letter written a few years later to the emperor Maurice (*Reg.* 5.37, quoted above), and a very similar list occurs in *Hez.* 1.9.9. They also have biblical echoes; cf. Lev. 26:31, Isa. 13:9. It will be worth bearing in mind Gregory's

tendency to reuse expressions, and the influence of the Bible on his language in ways he may not always have been conscious of.

11 *Hez.* 2.6.22f.; similar *Hev.*17.17, 28.3; cf. the gloomy prophecy in *Dial.* 2.15.3.

12 Bede, *Historia Ecclesiastica* 2.1.

13 John the deacon, *Vita Gregorii* 2.30 (= *Patrologia Latina* (PL) 75: 98.)

14 Markus 1997: 108ff. on the appointment of bishops; 112ff., together with Recchia 1987, on Gregory as a landlord.

15 De Dreuille 2000; Gameson 1999.

16 *Reg.* 8.29; Gregory puns on the words for 'English' and 'corner' (gens Anglorum in mundi angulo posita). That a letter sent to Egypt is a source for developments in England gives a sense of the breadth of Gregory's world.

17 The following paragraph is based on *Reg.* 1.33, 6.42, 9.232, 11.18 (to Venantius); 3.57 (to Italica); 6.43, 11.25 (to bishop John of Syracuse); 11.23, 59 (to Barbara and Antonina).

18 On Gregory as a teacher, see Cavallero 1990, although he is more confident than I that the *Moralia* can be assigned to the genre *collatio – quaestiones*.

19 That churchmen from Rome and Spain became friends after they met in Constantinople is a sign of the centrality of the imperial city in Latin letters for much of the sixth century.

20 *Reg.* 5.53; copies of the third and fourth parts had been given to monasteries. If a reference to the Britons singing Alleluia (*Mor.* 27.11.21) alludes to the conversion of the English, Gregory was continuing to add material as late as *c.* 597. One inevitably places this beside a famous story in Bede which has Gregory observing that it would be right for Alleluia to be sung among the English (Bede, *Historia Ecclesiastica* 2.1).

21 That the titles of three of the books mention the concerns of pastors, rulers and preachers raise questions of terminology we shall not address here.

22 A vigorous case has been mounted against the authenticity of this work by Francis Clark 1987, but arguments made by Meyvaert 1988 and de Vogüé 1988 are cogent against it; a summary of the debate begun by Clark's study is tucked away in Jenal 1995: 192f. (n. 263). There are some reflections in Moorhead 2003. On its being directed towards an elite public I concur with de Vogüé (intro to *SC* edn, 31ff) against Banniard 1993: 116ff. Miracles are discussed by Boesch Gajano 1979, Boglioni 1974 and McCready 1989.

23 *Hev.* 34.15. Compare the similar conclusion to a long analysis of the power of binding and loosing, *Hev.* 26.6 fin.

24 Columbanus *ep.* 1.

25 *Reg.* 2.22. Norberg 1980 makes this clear. On the other hand, as we have seen, a letter to the emperor bears a clear sign of having been written by the pope himself: see note 10.

26 The *Decretum* of the twelfth-century scholar Gratian contains 260 texts gathered from Gregory's letters: Giordano 1997: 23 n. 29.

27 De Vogüé 1996.

28 Sicut in libris expositionum suarum, quibus sit virtutibus insudandum,
    edocuit, ita etiam descriptis sanctorum miraculis quae virtutum
    earumdem sit claritas ostenderet: Bede, *Historia Ecclesiastica* 2.1.

29 Reproduced in Bede, *Historia Ecclesiastica* 2.1.

30 Leclercq 1963.

31 Hadot 1995: 72f. See further Stansbury 1999: 50ff.

32 P. Brown 2003: 236f.

33 Colish 1990: 252–66, esp. 257ff.

34 *In CC* 44, on S. of S. 1:7 Vulg.; the phrase does not occur in English
    translations. See Courcelle 1974: 204ff.

35 Gregory's expression of contempt for the grammatical rules of Donatus
    (*ep ad Leand*. 5) and strongly worded rebuke of a bishop for teaching
    grammar (*Reg*. 11.34) are judiciously discussed by Jenal 1995: 668–72;
    Markus 1997: 36–40; Riché 1976: 152–7. Note as well the argument
    that Gregory's condemnation of Donatus involved a subtle condemnation
    of Cassiodorus: L. Holtz, in Fontaine *et al*. 1986: 531 ff (an argument
    which offers further evidence for Gregory's looseness in reproducing the
    language of his sources).

36 Markus 1990: 225.

37 *Reg*. 5.46, a sentiment the stronger for its being directed to a layperson,
    the emperor's doctor. On Gregory and the Bible, see Schambeck 1999:
    206ff.; de Lubac 1959 remains a classic treatment.

38 *Mor*. praef. 1f., yet Gregory immediately proceeds to credit Job himself
    with writing the book.

39 Luke 10:24; on all this, *Hez*. 2.4.12. When Gregory refers to Truth
    speaking, he thinks of Jesus, who is the truth (cf. John 14:6).

40 *Hez*. 1.7.16; Gregory's position was similar to that of Ambrose, according
    to whom the Word becomes either smaller or larger, depending on your
    ability: in *Expositio evangelii secundum Lucam* 7.12. The sounds of Gregory's
    Latin connect 'constant' with 'standing' (con*sta*ntia . . . *sta*t), and in both
    cases where the word 'vitam' occurs it is preceded by an adjective ending
    with 'tivam'. Such correspondences often emphasize the structure of
    Gregory's thinking.

41 *Gp ad Leand*. 4. This memorable image gains in force because Gregory
    again uses sounds, in this case a sequence of vowels, to emphasise the
    point: agnus ambulet et elephas natet. This expression occurs in a letter
    to a distant friend, rather than in a work originally delivered orally, sug-
    gesting that Gregory expected even his written words to be apprehended
    aurally.

42 *Mor*. 30.27.81. The principle that a text could be interpreted in more
    than one way is frequently asserted, as at e.g. *Mor*. 15.10.11, 15.19, 51.27.

43 *Mor*. 11.16.25, where Gregory develops St Paul's famous dictum at 2 Cor.
    3:6. Markus 1997: 76–80 examines Gregory on Christians and Jews,
    emphasizing his adherence to Roman law.

44 Boesch Gajano 1979, esp. 39f.

45 *Hev.* 31.1; cf. e.g. *Hev.* 17.1, 18.4, 25.6 Christ enacting his teaching at *Mor.* 1.13.31.

46 *Dial.* 2.2.1f. Gregory goes on to make the point that the legislation of Moses gave different responsibilities to the Levites when they turned 50 (Num. 8:23–5), which he takes to mean that the coldness of the bodies of people over 50 liberates them from such fervent feelings: *Dial.* 2.2.3f. For what follows, see as well Courcelle 1967; Doucet 1975.

47 *Mor.* 27.18.37, with reference to Acts 28:8, 1 Tim. 5:23. Gregory concludes that the apostle acted in this way to bring the former to faith by means of a miracle, something which was not necessary in the case of the latter.

48 Scienter nescius et sapienter indoctus (*Dial.* 2 prol.). But Gregory relishes presenting Benedict as a paradoxical figure; in the first sentence we meet him as one who had the heart of an old man from boyhood (*Dial.* 2 prol. 1).

49 *Dial.* 3.37.20; the phrase is also used by Augustine, *ep.* 130.15.28 (= *PL* 33:505), although in a different sense; this may be another case where Gregory borrowed someone else's words, the paradoxical form of which would have pleased him, without their meaning.

50 'In Western Europe the late sixth century marks a real break with the world of antiquity, closed off access to much of its intellectual culture, and even more drastically, to its ways of looking at, understanding and speaking about that world': Markus 1990: 222.

51 Gregory told his side of the story in his *Moralia in Job* (14.56.72–4), but there may have been another way of looking at it; cf. the brief words of Eutychius' biographer, *Vita Eutychii* 9.89 PG 86:2373–76).

52 *Hez.* 1.5.14; cf. Mark 16:20. The following passage can be compared with the rather harsh letter Gregory wrote to Augustine of Canterbury (*Reg.* 11.36).

53 Gregory was energetic in this matter: financial burdens were to be imposed on peasants on church lands in Sardinia who were reluctant to come to God (*Reg.* 4.26), while funds were sent to a bishop in Corsica to buy clothing for people recently baptized (*Reg.* 8.1).

54 Markus 1997: 76ff. emphasizes Gregory's adherence to Roman law in dealing with Jews.

55 Gregory expressed himself differently concerning the status of the Council of Constantinople (553) to different correspondents, but his diplomatic approach failed to heal the schism.

56 *De Catechizandis Rudibus* 25.48, where there is a long treatment of such people; also 27.55.

57 Although there were many who did not believe in God when they suffered adversity, and others who held that he is not concerned with human affairs (*Mor.* 18.2.3).

58 *Hez.* 2.7.7 on Ezek. 40:22, with Isa. 11:2f.; Gregory's treatment of the eight steps leading to the vestibule moves in another direction: *Hez.* 2.8.2ff.

59 Augustine has a system with seven rungs: *De doctrina christiana* 2.7.9–11 (= CCSL 32: 36–8).

60 Oddly enough, *Reg.* 11.2 is addressed to Abbot John of Mt Sinai, but it is likely he was another John.

61 One could climb to an appreciation of higher levels of beauty 'as on the rungs of a ladder' (*Symposium* 211C), cf. Plotinus 1.6.1.

62 *Consolation of Philosophy* 1.1.4. The ascent from practice to theory is not far removed from Gregory's description of someone going up from the rungs of the active life to the peaks of contemplation (*Mor.* 31.51.102). Augustine as well makes use of a sequence of *gradus* in the second book of his *De Doctrina Christiana*.

63 *Mor.* 16.25.30, arguing to an unusual extent from St Paul; the same occurs where grace is discussed at *Hez.* 1.9.2.

64 Columbanus was aware of six books by Jerome on Ezekiel: *ep.* 1; the tradition of exegesis of Ezekiel has been studied by Neuss 1912.

65 Schambeck 1999:125ff.

66 *Vita Augustini* 26 (= *PL* 32:55). Among other parallels which have been adduced between Gregory and Augustine, a passage in the former which begins 'transeat ergo animus et ab ipsis transcendat omne quod creatum est' (*Hez.* 1.8.16) invites comparison with an account Augustine wrote of a mystical experience he and his mother shared: *Confessions* 9.10.23f. V. Paronetto (n.d.) 'Une présence augustinienne chez Grégoire le grand: le *De Catechizandis Rudibus* dans la *Regula Pastoralis*, Fontaine *et al.* 1986, 511–19; V. Recchia (1985) 'La memoria di Agostino nella esegesi biblica di Gregorio Magno', *Augustinianum* 25: 405–34.

67 Gregory's views are placed in a general context by Daubercies 1963.

68 *Ep ad Leand.* 5. Again, Gregory's formulation involves assonance: quid namque est officium corporis nisi organum cordis.

69 Bede, *Historia Ecclesiastica* 1.27, quaest. 6.

70 Wallace-Hadrill 1983:116.

71 *Mor.* 32.20.35; Gregory is thinking of Ezek. 14:14 and Luke 17:34–36, although in the latter case he changes the order of the groups.

72 Praesse . . . prodesse: *Reg. past.* 2.6.

73 Boesch Gajano 1980: 626–8.

74 It may be fruitful to place this general development against the institutional history of the Roman church in the seventh century, during which a monastic tradition was brought under clerical control; possible tensions within the Roman church during Gregory's pontificate could be similarly explained. On all this, see Llewellyn 1974 with Wollasch 2002.

75 Gregory's development of the speculations of earlier Christian thinkers on the possibility of sins being purged after death has led him to be seen as one of the 'founders of Purgatory' (Le Goff 1984: 88–95), to which add the important study of P. Brown 1999. Gregory's receptiveness to the ordination of monks, an area where his views differed from those of St Benedict (Nußbaum 1961: 58–62) is one of a number of signs of the importance of the Eucharist to him; note the intriguing suggestion that

NOTES

for Gregory the mass became a sort of substitute for his lost contemplative life: de Vogüé 1986.

76 E.g. *Mor.* 3.16.29, 12.43.48, 15.15.19, 29.7.15. But Augustine had already envisaged a body of the Devil, that is of wicked people, in apposition to the body of Christ, namely the church (*de Gen. ad litt* 11.34f. (= *PL* 34:441–3)).

77 *Dial.* 2.8.10–12, 9, 13.1–3. Gregory ends his account of the process of temptation in the last case by making effective use of the technical term for the third stage of sin: consentit et comedit.

78 Harnack 1898: 262. While writing as a historian of religion rather than a theologian, P. Brown 2003 is a fine antidote to such views.

79 *Dial.* 4.59.6, 60.1, 62.3; see on this Moorhead 2003. It is worth noting that the passage on the pleading of the Advocate (see p. 31) comes at the end of a long address, just as that on the Eucharist comes at the end of the *Dialogues*; Gregory was a master of the effective conclusion. It may not be accidental that what is probably the most powerful of his homilies to the people, that which he preached on Lazarus and the rich man, was placed at the end of the collection.

80 *Hev.* 27.4, with an attractive play on words (amicus quasi animi custos), apparently invented by Gregory: Bartelink 1984.

81 *Mor.* 27.15.30; cf. *Mor.* 8.32.54, which also recalls Pascal.

82 Aubin 1974; Dagens 1977.

83 Gastaldelli 1965.

84 *Mor.* 22.15.30; at *Mor.* 4.27.49, the making of a bold defence is given as a fourth stage in the process of sin.

85 *Mor.* 12.39.44; cf. Boglioni 1974: 38.

86 *Reg. past.* 3.16.33ff.

87 '[P]ride and lust manifest the same contumacious authority, one internally, the other externally': Straw 1988: 117.

88 While Gregory does not use the title as often as some modern accounts would suggest, it sometimes occupies prominent places, as in the dedicatory letters to the *Moralia*, the *Homilies on Ezekiel* and the *Homilies on the Gospels*, all sent to bishops. Note too a formula in the *Pastoral Rule*: 'cognoscant se conservos esse servorum' (3.5).

89 *Historia Ecclesiastica* 2.1. Some of the issues in Bede's evaluation of Gregory have been seen by Navarra 1998.

90 Leclercq 1973: 486. But this study remains speculative, and it is hard to see how it could be more than this. One wonders whether author's comments about the 'psychological masochism' of another writer (479) could also apply in some measure to Gregory.

91 'Der Platz des Dazwischens': Schambeck 1999: 7, with 104ff. on dichotomies. See as well Moorhead 2003: 203f.

92 Districtus iudex Iesus: *Hev.* 32.8. Gregory persistently sees the Judge as 'districtus', as at *Mor.* 2.52.83, 3.11.18, 4.6.11, 4.11.19.

93 Paulinus, *Vita Ambrosii* 27, where the Lord is again Jesus.

94 The most obvious translation of 'desiderium' is 'desire', but the

connotations of the English word could be misleading. Its sense is well caught by a word used by German scholars, *Sehnsucht*. The definition is that of Burnaby 1938: 96. Doctor of desire: Leclercq 1974. See further Schambeck 1999: 71ff.

95 That is, Peter; there would be material here for an enquiry into Gregory's concept of episcopal, and specifically papal office. In matters of practice, Gregory was concerned to maintain the standing of the papacy vis-à-vis the church of Constantinople, and asserted that he was prepared to die rather than for the church of blessed Peter to fall away in his days [*Reg.* 5.6]. Yet he does not appear to have sought to widen the influence of the see of Rome, unlike some other popes: Jenal 1988: 143f.

96 1 Pet. 1:12, reading 'in quem' against the Vulgate 'in quae'.

97 Leclercq 1974: 34.

2 THE BIBLE

1 Gregory frequently applies to Job an adjective such as 'blessed'. The reason for this is not theological; rather, because the noun 'Job' cannot be declined in Latin, by adding an adjective Gregory was able to show its grammatical case.

2 Implied here is St Paul's phrase 'that rock was Christ' (1 Cor. 10:4). The biblical phrase here translated 'the faith of Christ' (in Christi fide, Rom. 3:22, Gal. 2:16) has been taken as 'faith in Christ' by Luther.

3 Gregory assumes a moral reading of the Bible, but one which offers in this case not a guide to doing good but a reminder of having done evil.

4 He relies on the etymologies in the *Liber Interpretationis Hebraicorum Nominum* (*CCSL* 72:130f.) rather than those in *In Ezechielem* (*CCSL* 75:5–7), but the understanding of Chaldeans as 'captivantes' is not in Jerome.

5 Ps. 1:3, elegantly quoted, for the subject of this sentence of the psalm, the blessed man of verse 1, is understood by the Fathers to be Christ.

6 'Movement': 'lapsus', perhaps used with a hint of a secondary meaning, that of moral failings.

7 A division familiar in the New Testament; see Acts 28:23 (cf. 26:22), Rom. 3:21; elsewhere a third part, called writings or psalms, is envisaged (e.g. Luke 24:44).

8 Ps. 96:10. The words 'from the tree' were not part of the original text, but added by Christians at a very early date.

9 Jer. 11:19 Vulg.; the phrase immediately following contains the words 'the land of the living', quoted by Gregory in another context shortly before.

10 Cf. Gen. 2:21f. Gregory's language emphasizes the parallel between Adam and Christ, the one sleeping (dormiente) and the other dying (moriente).

11 Rom. 3:25. The Latin word for the place of atonement, propitiatorium, is close to that for propitiation, propitiatio.

12 As it often does, Gregory's mind is operating at more than one level: the mercy seat which represents the mediator is placed in an intermediate place between the Cherubim.

13 At the back of Gregory's mind is 2 Cor. 3:6.

14 The Old Testament speaks an 'eternal covenant' at 2 Sam. 23; Isa. 55:3; Ezek. 37:26.

15 Gregory is thinking of a month of 28 days, 28 being a perfect number, that is a number equal to the sum of its factors.

16 In the background is the formation of Adam from the dust: Gen. 2:7.

17 Job 19:25. Modern translations, however, read 'he shall rise'.

18 The way in which the argument attributed to Eutychius is expressed is suspiciously Gregorian, for the pope often thinks of biblical events as having occurred for a reason, as the rising of the bodies of many saints at the time of the resurrection of Jesus, above p. 61.

3   SERMONS TO THE PEOPLE

1 Despite his enthusiasm for allegory, Gregory was a close reader of the biblical text, and he begins his sermon clearing up an apparent difficulty.

2 Note that Gregory sees Christ's flesh as having been resurrected.

3 An ambiguity in the word Gregory used for 'bad', sinister, which also means 'left', made it highly appropriate in this context.

4 Gregory addresses his congregation by an abstract noun (charity) indicating a quality applicable to them; the practice survives in such modern English expressions as 'Your Majesty' and 'Your Honour'.

5 The reference is to Peter's words reported in the Acts of the Apostles, his letters or epistles in the New Testament, and the miracles which continued in Gregory's time to be worked through his relics in Rome.

6 Isa. 11:2f., reading 'replebit' for 'replevit'.

7 Jas 5:16, again with the additional sense of being saved.

8 Gregory plays on the similarity of sounds: 'ereptionem iuuant . . . correptionem curant'. His pleasure in the rhyme may account for his using the very rare word 'ereptio'.

9 Yet the text which Gregory quotes elsewhere in this homily describes Lazarus as a beggar (mendicus), not a destitute person (egenus).

10 Luke 16:22f. In a period when texts were not as clearly punctuated as now, Gregory takes 'in hell' as part of this sentence; in modern Bibles it belongs to the following sentence.

11 The following four paragraphs occur in a very similar form in *Dial*. 4.16.

12 This town, the modern Palestrina, lies some 40 km to the east of Rome.

13 In classical Latin this word means 'provision for a journey'; Christian authors use it of the Eucharist given to a dying person.

4 HUMAN TYPES

1 *Hez.* 1.4.8; for a fuller discussion, see *Mor.* 25.7.13.
2 The last phrase is emphatically alliterated: protinus a pristina praeparatione dissipater.
3 An interesting observation in the light of Gregory's own priorities.
4 1 Cor. 1:26; Gregory omits the verb, 'are called'.
5 Isa. 54:4f. Both these quotations are directed towards women.
6 Rom. 16:19. The word for 'innocent', simplex, is the word translated elsewhere in this chapter as 'guileless'.
7 Ps. 140:9. Gregory follows the text of the Vulgate, which begins 'labor labiorum'.
8 Gregory uses the same word, duplex, for 'two' and 'duplicitous'.
9 The Latin word salus means both health and salvation.
10 That Gregory suffered from a bad stomach (see e.g. *Hev.* 21.1) may be relevant here.
11 According to Augustine, *City of God* 21.4.
12 Again, Gregory plays on the ambiguity of the word salus.

5 MORALS ON JOB

1 Some of the fittingness arises from the similarity between the Latin words for concerns (curae) and skin (cutis).
2 Again, Gregory takes his information on the meanings of Hebrew names from Jerome.
3 'Contemplatione' is echoed by 'operatione'.
4 Typically, Gregory plays on the similarity between the words for blood relationship (cognationem) and knowledge (cognitionem).
5 Ps. 69:20; English versions give 'looked for' instead of Gregory's 'upheld', which gives better sense.
6 Gregory goes on to make a connection between earring (inauris), listening (auditus) and obedience (oboedientia). Compare the language of the opening sentence of the Rule of Benedict: obsculta . . . aurem . . . per oboedientiae laborem . . . per inoboedientiae desidiam. Gregory sustains the point in the following quotation from 1 Sam., with its references to obedience and hearing.
7 Gregory's words 'aspera et dura' echo a famous phrase in the Rule of Benedict, dura et aspera (*Regula Benedicti* 58.8).
8 Gregory cleverly plays on Christ's being seated and presiding (sedendo . . . praesidendo), and his directing and conducting (ducit . . . perducit). Jerusalem was widely believed to mean 'vision of peace'.
9 Gregory has in mind the seven gifts of the Holy Spirit, listed in Isa. 11:2f. (Vulgate).
10 The denarius (literally 'containing ten') was a coin equal in value to ten smaller coins; the reference is to a parable of Jesus; Matt. 20:9f.
11 Gregory holds that the name Cornustibii was formed from Latin words

meaning 'horn of a pipe', but as he acknowledges, its form would be incorrect.

12 I.e. Cornustibii.

13 Accepting that Paul wrote the epistle to the Hebrews, as Gregory did (see p. 59f.), would credit him with fourteen epistles in the New Testament.

14 Cf. Gen. 40:9–12. The biblical word for shoot, propago, has the basic meaning 'offspring', so it is appropriate for Gregory to take it in apposition to 'generations'.

BIBLIOGRAPHY

Works by Gregory

Dialogorum libri iv SC 251, 260, 265 (transl. O. J. Zimmerman (1959) *Dialogues*, New York: University of America Catholic = *Fathers of the Church* 39).

Homiliae xl in Evangelia CCSL (*Corpus Christianorum Series Latina*) 141 (transl. David Hirst (1990) *Forty Gospel Homilies*, Kalamazoo, MI: Cistercian = *Cistercian Studies Series* 123).

Homiliae in Hiezechielem CCSL 142.

Exposition in Canticum Canticorum CCSL 144 (transl. Denys Turner (1995) *Eros and Allegory: Medieval Exegesis of the Song of Songs*, Kalamazoo, MI: Cistercian, pp. 215–55).

Moralia sive Expositio in Iob CCSL 143 (3 vols) (transl. James Bliss (1844–50) *Morals on the Book of Job*, Oxford: J. H. Parker).

Registrum epistolarum CCSL 140 (2 vols); also ed. *Monumenta Germaniae Historica Epistolae* (*MGH Ep.*) 1. All references are to the former edition; in the second the letters are sometimes numbered differently (transl. John R. C. Martin (2004) *The Letters of Gregory the Great*, Toronto: Pontifical Institute of Medieval Studies).

Regula pastoralis SC 381f. (transl. Henry Davis (1950) *Pastoral Care*, Westminster, MD: Newman Press = *Ancient Christian Writers* 11).

Modern works

Readers should be aware that the following list is the merest skeleton.

Aubin, P. (1974) 'Intériorité et exteriorité dans le Moralia in Job de saint Grégoire le Grand', *Recherches de science religieuse* 62: 117–66.

Banniard, M. (1993) *Viva Voce Communication écrite et communication orale du IVe au IXe siècle en occident latin* Paris: Institut des Études Augustiniennes.

Bartelink, G. J. M. (1984) 'Etymologisierung bei Gregor dem Grossen', *Glotta* 72: 91–105.

Boesch Gajano, Sofia (1979) 'Per una storia degli Ebrei in Occidente tra antichità a medioevo La testimonianza di Gregorio Magno', *Quaderni medievali* 8: 12–43.

——(1980) 'La proposta agiografica dei "Dialogi" di Gregorio Magno', *Studi medievali* 21: 623–64.

Boglioni, Pierre (1974) 'Miracle et nature chez Grégoire le grand', in *Cahiers d'études médiévales*, vol. 1, *Epopées, legendes et miracles*, Montreal/Paris: Bellarmin.

Brown, Peter (1999) 'Gloriosus obitus: the end of the other ancient world', in W. Klingshirn and M. Vessey (eds) *The Limits of Ancient Christianity: Essays on late antique thought and culture in honor of R. A. Markus*, Ann Arbor, MI: University of Michigan Press.

——(2003) *The Rise of Western Christendom* 2nd edn, Malden, MA and Oxford: Blackwell.

Brown, T. S. (1984) *Gentlemen and Officers: Imperial administration and aristocratic power in Byzantine Italy, 554–800*, Rome: British School at Rome.

Burnaby, John (1938) *Amor Dei: A study of the religion of St Augustine*, London: Hodder & Stoughton.

Cavallero, José Pablo (1990) 'La técnica didáctica de San Gregorio Magno en los Moralia in Iob', *Helmantica* 41: 129–88.

Clark, F. (1987) *The Pseudo-Gregorian Dialogues*, 2 vols, Leiden: Brill.

Colish, Marcia L. (1990) *The Stoic Tradition: From antiquity to the early middle ages*, vol. 2, Leiden: Brill.

Courcelle, Pierre (1967) 'Saint Benoît, le merle et le buisson d'épines', *Journal des savants*, 154–61.

—— (1974) *Connais-toi toi-même de Socrate à Saint Bernard*, Paris: Etudes augustiniennes.

Dagens, Claude (1977) *Saint Grégoire le grand: Culture et expérience chrétiennes*, Paris: Etudes augustiniennes.

Daubercies, P. (1963) 'La théologie de la condition charnelle chez les maitres du haut moyen âge', *Recherches de théologie ancienne et medieval* 30: 5–54.

de Dreuille, Chr. (ed.) (2000) *L'Eglise et la mission au VIe siècle: La mission d'Augustin de Cantorbéry et les Eglises de Gaul sous l'impulsion de Grégoire le Grand*, Paris: Cerf.

de Lubac, Henri (1959) *Exégèse médiévale*, vol. 1, Paris: Aubier.

de Vogüé, A. (1986) 'Euchariste et vie monastique', *Collectanea cisterciensa* 48: 120–30.

—— (1988) 'Grégoire le Grand et ses "Dialogues" d'après deuz ouvrages récents', *Revue d'histoire ecclésiastique* 83: 281–348.

—— (1996) 'L'Auteur du Commentaire des Rois attribué à saint Grégoire le Grand: un moine de Cava?', *Revue benedictine* 106: 319–31.

Doucet, M. (1975) 'La tentation de Saint Benoît: Relation ou création par saint Grégoire le grand?', *Collectanea cisterciana* 27: 63–71.

Dudden, F. Homes (1905) *Gregory the Great: His place in history and thought* 2 vols, London: Longmans Green.

Evans, G. (1986) *The Thought of Gregory the Great*, Cambridge: Cambridge University Press.

Fontaine, J., Gillet, R. and Pellistrandi, S. (eds) (1986) *Grégoire le Grand*, Paris: Editions du Centre national de la recherche scientifique.

Friedowicz, M. (1995) *Das Kirchenverständnis Gregors des Grossen Eine Untersuchung seiner Exegetischen und Homiletischen Werke*, Rome/Freiburg: Herder.

Gameson, Richard (1999) (ed.) *Saint Augustine and the Conversion of England*, Stroud: Sutton.

Gastaldelli, F. (1965) 'Il mechanismo psicologico del peccati nei Moralia in Job di San Gregorio Magno', *Salesianum* 27: 563–605.

Gillet, R. 'Grégoire Iᵉʳ le grand', *Dictionnaire d'Histoire et de Géographie Ecclésiastiques* 21: 1387–1420.

Giordano, Lisiana (1995) *Saggi di ermeneutica gregoriana*, Catania: CUECM.

—— (1997) *Giustizia e potere giudiziario ecclesiastico nell'epistolario di Gregorio magno*, Bari: Edipuglia.

Girard, René (1987) *Job, the Victim of his People*, English transl., London: Athlone Press.

Giuntella, Anna Maria (2000) 'Lo spazio monastico e dell'assistenza I Monasteri', in L. Pani Ermini (ed.) *Christiana Loca Lo spazio cristiano nella Roma del primo millennio*, Rome: Palombi.

Godding, R. (1990) *Bibliografia di Gregorio Magno (1890–1989)*, Rome: Città nuova editrice, is very useful for the period it covers; subsequent bibliography is provided annually in *L'Année philologique*.

Gregorio Magno e il suo tempo (1991) 2 vols, Rome.

Hadot, Pierre (1995) *Philosophy as a Way of life: Spiritual exercises from Socrates to Foucault* English transl., Oxford: Blackwell.

Harnack, A. (1898) *History of Dogma*, English transl. Williams and Norgate, London.

Jenal, Georg (1988) 'Gregor der Große und die Stadt Rom (590–604)', in F. Prinz (ed.) *Herrschaft und Kirche*, Stuttgart: Hiersemann (=*Monographien zur Geschichte des Mittelalters* 33).

—— (1995) *Italia ascetica atque monastica Das Asketen- und Mönchtum in Italien von den Anfängen bis zur Zeit der Langobarden (ca. 150/250 – 604)* 2 vols, Stuttgart: Hiersemann.

Lançon, B. (2000) *Rome in Late Antiquity*, English transl., Edinburgh: Edinburgh University Press.

Leclercq, Jean (1963) *Otia monastica: Etudes sur le vocabulaire de la contemplation au moyen âge*, Rome (= *Studia anselmiana* 51).

—— (1973) 'Modern Psychology and the interpretation of medieval texts', *Speculum* 48: 476–90.

—— (1974) *The Love of Learning and the Desire for God* English transl., New York: Fordham University Press.

Le Goff, Jacques (1984) *The Birth of Purgatory*, English transl., Chicago: University of Chicago Press.

Leyser, C. (2002) *Authority and Asceticism from Augustine to Gregory the Great*, Oxford: Clarendon Press.

Llewellyn, P. (1974) 'The Roman Church in the seventh century: the legacy of Gregory I', *Journal of Ecclesiastical History* 25: 363–80.

McGinn, B. (1991) *The Presence of God: A history of western mysticism*, vol. 1, *The Foundations of Mysticism*, London: SCM.

McCready, W. H. (1989) *Signs of Sanctity Miracles in the Thought of Gregory the Great* Toronto: Pontifical Institute of Mediaeval Studies.

Markus, R. A. (1981) 'Gregory the Great's Europe', *Transactions of the Royal Historical Society* 5th series, 31: 12–36.

—— (1990) *The End of Ancient Christianity*, Cambridge: Cambridge University Press.

—— (1997) *Gregory the Great and his World*, Cambridge: Cambridge University Press.

Martindale, J. R. (1992) *The Prosopography of the Later Roman Empire 3, A.D. 527–641*, Cambridge: Cambridge University Press.

Meyvaert, P. (1977) *Benedict, Gregory, Bede and Others*, London: Variorum.

—— (1988) 'The Enigma of Gregory the Great's Dialogues: a response to Francis Clark', *Journal of Ecclesiastical History* 39: 335–81.

Moorhead, John (2003) 'Taking Gregory the Great's Dialogues seriously', *Downside Review* 424: 197–210.

Navarra, L. (1998) 'Il rimpianto per la vita monastica: un tema caro a Gregorio Magno in Beda, *HE*, II, 1, 24–59', *Studi e materiali di storia delle religioni* 22: 51–6.

Nuess, W. (1912) *Das Buch Ezechiel in Theologie und Kunst bis zum Ende des XII Jahrhunderts*, Münster: Aschendorff.

Norberg, D. (1980) 'Qui a composé les letters de saint Grégoire le Grand?', *Studi Medievali* 21: 1–17.

Nußbaum, O. (1961) *Kloster, Priestermönch und Privatmesse*, Bonn: Hanstein.

Pietri, ch. and Pietri, L. (1999) *Prosopographie chrétienne du bas-empire 2 Prosopographie de l'Italie chrétienne (313–604)* Paris: Éditions du centre national de la recherche scientifique.

Recchia, Vincenzo (1987) *Gregorio Magno e il società agricola*, Rome: Edizioni Studium (= *Verba seniorum* new series 8).

Richards, Jeffrey (1980) *Consul of God: The Life and times of Gregory the Great*, London: Routledge and Kegan Paul.

Riché, Pierre (1976) *Education and Culture in the Barbarian West*, English transl., Columbia, SC: University of South Carolina Press.

Schambeck, Mirjam (1999) *Contemplatio als Missio: Zu einem Schlüsselphänomen bei Gregor dem Großen*, Würzburg: Echter.

Stansbury, M. (1999) 'Early Medieval Biblical Commentaries, their writers and readers' *Frühmittelalterliche Studien* 33: 49–82.

Straw, Carole (1988) *Gregory the Great: Perfection in Imperfection*, Berkeley, CA: University of California Press.

—— (1996) *Gregory the Great*, Aldershot: Variorum.

Wallace-Hadrill, J. M. (1983) *The Frankish Church*, Oxford: Clarendon Press.

Wollasch, J. (2002) 'Frühe Bildzeugnisse für das Nachleben Papst Gregors des Großen in Rom?' *Frühmittelalterliche Studien* 36: 159–70.

INDEX